PEACE ABRAHAM

From Dust to Diamonds

Copyright © 2025 by peace abraham

All rights reserved. No part of this publication may be reproduced, stored or transmitted in any form or by any means, electronic, mechanical, photocopying, recording, scanning, or otherwise without written permission from the publisher. It is illegal to copy this book, post it to a website, or distribute it by any other means without permission.

First edition

This book was professionally typeset on Reedsy.
Find out more at reedsy.com

Contents

1	The Beggar in the Alley	1
2	A Kind Stranger	7
3	A Mysterious Coin	13
4	Shadows of a Past	19
5	The Stranger's Secrets	25
6	The Anonymous Protector	32
7	Whispers in the Dark	39
8	A Touch of Refinement	45
9	The First Clue	52
10	A Daring Invitation	59
11	An Unlikely Transformation	67
12	The Threat Within	75
13	A Bond of Trust	83
14	Hidden Intentions	90
15	Clashing Worlds	97
16	A Mysterious Encounter	104
17	Unveiled Suspicion	112
18	The Hidden Vault	120
19	The Rooftop Revelation	128
20	A Sudden Disappearance	136
21	A Warning from the Past	144
22	A Warning from the Past	152
23	The Power Broker	159
24	Chased Through the Streets	167

25	A Heartfelt Confession	175
26	Secrets in the Mansion	183
27	The Newspaper Clipping	191
28	A Nighttime Rescue	199
29	The Code of Betrayal	207
30	The Accidental Kiss	214
31	Emily's Doubts	221
32	A Race Against Time	229
33	The Family Heirloom	237
34	A Spy Among Us	244
35	A Life Saved	252
36	The Hidden Diary	259
37	A Growing Threat	267
38	The Conflicted Choice	275
39	The Safehouse Encounter	283
40	The Undercover Billionaire	290
41	Emily's Shock	298
42	The Hidden Conspiracy	305
43	The Vault Opens	312
44	The Return of an Enemy	320
45	The Ticking Clock	327
46	A Betrayal Confirmed	334
47	A Broken Heart	341
48	The Confrontation	348
49	A Desperate Plea	355
50	The Final Showdown	363
51	A Sacrifice Made	370
52	The Explosion	378
53	The Ultimate Betrayal	387
54	Love Confessed	395
55	The Escape Plan	403

56	The Public Revelation	411
57	A Dangerous Backlash	419
58	The Rescue Mission	426
59	The Legal Victory	434
60	A New Beginning	441
61	The Café Revival	448
62	A Charitable Gesture	456
63	Rebuilding Trust	463
64	The Final Threat	470
65	A Test of Faith	477
66	The Letter of Closure	485
67	The Return of an Heir	491
68	A Proposal Under the Stars	498
69	The Wedding Sabotage	505
70	The Last Obstacle	512
71	Chapter 71	520
72	Chapter 72	528
73	Chapter 73	535
74	Chapter 74	542
75	Chapter 75	550
76	Chapter 76	558
77	Chapter 77	566
78	Chapter 78	573
79	A Life of Purpose	581
80	The Diamond's Shine	589
81	The Promise of Forever	595

One

The Beggar in the Alley

The rain poured relentlessly, turning the cobblestone streets into slick rivers of grime and mud. The bustling noise of the city dimmed under the weight of the downpour as shopkeepers hastily pulled down shutters and pedestrians hurried to find shelter. A dim streetlamp flickered above an alleyway that seemed forgotten by time, its shadows deeper and darker than the rest of the city.

Daniel slouched against a damp brick wall, his tattered coat offering little protection from the elements. He adjusted the worn hat that shielded his face, tugging it lower to obscure his features. His eyes, sharp and calculating despite their dull façade, scanned the street. He didn't move much, not even when the water began seeping through his boots, pooling around his feet. Movement attracted attention, and attention was a luxury he couldn't afford.

A sharp bark of laughter echoed from a nearby pub, followed by the clinking of glasses. The sound grated against Daniel's ears. He longed for the warmth and the noise, for the freedom to walk into a place like that and lose himself in a crowd. But the past had stripped him of such liberties. Instead, he remained rooted in his corner of the alley, invisible to everyone who passed by—just as he preferred.

The scent of freshly baked bread wafted through the air, mingling cruelly with the damp stench of the alley. His stomach growled in protest, but he ignored it, his focus trained on the bakery across the street. He watched as the baker—a burly man with a thick mustache—handed over a steaming loaf to a young boy. The boy's face lit up with gratitude as he darted off into the rain. For a brief moment, Daniel allowed himself to wonder what it might feel like to inspire such joy in another person, but the thought vanished as quickly as it came.

A woman's voice broke through the steady hum of rain. "Sir? Are you okay?"

Daniel's muscles tensed. He hadn't heard her approach—a rare lapse in his vigilance. Slowly, he turned his head, the brim of his hat casting a shadow over his face. She stood a few feet away, her umbrella tilted to shield both herself and the small paper bag she held close to her chest. Her face, though partially obscured by the rain, radiated a warmth that felt out of place in the dreary alley.

"I'm fine," Daniel replied gruffly, his voice hoarse from disuse. He shifted slightly, hoping she would take the hint and leave.

But she didn't. Instead, she crouched down, her eyes level with his. "You don't look fine," she said, her tone firm but kind. "Have you eaten today?"

Daniel hesitated. Something about her gaze unsettled him. It wasn't pity—he was used to that, and it usually came with averted eyes and hasty footsteps. No, her gaze held something deeper. Concern? Curiosity? He couldn't tell.

"I don't need charity," he said finally, his voice edged with defensiveness.

She smiled faintly, unperturbed by his tone. "Good, because this isn't charity. Consider it… a neighborly gesture." She extended the paper bag toward him. The scent of warm bread and roasted chicken filled the air, making his stomach clench painfully.

He stared at the bag for a moment, torn between pride and hunger. Pride had kept him alive all these years, but hunger had a way of eroding even the strongest defenses. Reluctantly, he reached out, his fingers brushing against hers as he took the bag. Her touch was brief but startlingly warm, a sharp contrast to the cold that had settled in his bones.

"Thank you," he muttered, barely audible.

She stood, adjusting her umbrella. "You're welcome." She glanced up at the rain, then back at him. "My name's Emily, by the way. I work at the café down the street. If you ever need anything, just come by."

Daniel said nothing, his gaze fixed on the bag in his hands. When he finally looked up, she was already walking away, her figure gradually disappearing into the rain. For a moment, he considered calling out to her, asking why she had bothered with him, but the words caught in his throat. Instead, he watched her go, the faintest flicker of something unfamiliar stirring in his chest.

He opened the bag carefully, as though it might disappear if he moved too quickly. Inside was a neatly wrapped sandwich, still warm despite the rain. The sight of it brought a lump to his throat that had nothing to do with hunger. He took a bite, the flavors bursting on his tongue, and for the first time in a long while, he felt something close to gratitude.

But the moment was fleeting. A sudden movement at the edge of his vision snapped him back to reality. He turned his head sharply, his hand instinctively reaching for the small blade concealed beneath his coat. A figure lingered at the mouth of the alley, half-hidden by the shadows. Daniel couldn't make out their features, but their posture—rigid and watchful—set his nerves on edge.

The figure didn't approach, nor did they retreat. They simply stood there, a silent sentinel in the rain. Daniel's mind raced. Had they been following him? Had Emily's kindness inadvertently drawn attention to him? He cursed under his breath, his grip tightening on the blade. He was no stranger to danger, but this was different. This felt... personal.

Minutes passed, each one stretching into an eternity. Finally, the figure turned and walked away, their silhouette swallowed by the storm. But the unease lingered, coiling in Daniel's gut like a serpent. He knew better than to ignore it. Danger had a way of finding him, no matter how carefully he hid.

He finished the sandwich quickly, his appetite dulled by the encounter. Standing, he adjusted his hat and pulled his coat tighter around him. The rain continued to fall, washing away the faint trace of warmth that Emily's gesture had left behind.

As he stepped out of the alley and into the night, his mind churned with questions. Who was the figure watching him? Why had Emily approached him? And most importantly, how much longer could he keep his secrets buried beneath the rags?

The city loomed around him, its lights flickering like distant stars. Somewhere in the distance, a church bell tolled midnight. Daniel disappeared into the labyrinth of streets, his figure blending seamlessly with the shadows. But in the back of his mind, a single thought refused to be silenced: No secret stays hidden forever.

Two

A Kind Stranger

The morning sun filtered weakly through the blanket of clouds, its golden rays struggling to pierce the gloom of the city. The rain had ceased overnight, leaving behind slick pavements and puddles that reflected the gray sky above. The alley where Daniel had spent the night was already bustling with life, vendors setting up their carts, and shopkeepers wiping rainwater from their windows. Daniel, as always, remained a silent observer of the world that moved past him.

He stood at the edge of the alley, his hat pulled low over his eyes, his coat buttoned to the top. The events of the previous night lingered in his mind, especially the mysterious figure who had watched him from the shadows. He had replayed the moment over and over, searching for some clue about their identity or intent. And then there was Emily—the woman who had given him the sandwich. Her face was imprinted in his memory, her kindness an anomaly in the cold, indifferent city.

His gaze shifted to the café down the street, its bright red sign a cheerful contrast to the drab surroundings. Through the window, he could see her bustling behind the counter, her movements quick and efficient. She wore her hair tied back today, a few loose strands framing her face. She smiled warmly at a customer, and for a moment, Daniel felt an unfamiliar pang in his chest.

He tore his eyes away, cursing himself for his weakness. He didn't have the luxury of attachments, not in this life. He had spent years perfecting the art of invisibility, blending into the background, ensuring that no one got close enough to see past the rags and the dirt. Emily's unexpected kindness threatened to unravel everything he had worked so hard to build.

Still, he found himself lingering near the café, his feet rooted to the spot as though drawn by some invisible force. The scent of freshly brewed coffee wafted through the air, mingling with the sweet aroma of pastries. His stomach growled, but he ignored it. He wasn't here for food. He wasn't even sure why he was here at all.

"Good morning."

The voice startled him, and he turned sharply to find Emily standing in the doorway, her apron dusted with flour. She held a steaming cup of coffee in one hand and a small paper bag in the other. Her smile was as radiant as it had been the night before, and it disarmed him completely.

"I thought you might be hungry," she said, holding out the bag.

Daniel hesitated, his pride warring with his hunger. "You don't have to do this," he said gruffly.

"I know," she replied simply. "But I want to."

Her sincerity was unsettling. People didn't just do things out of the goodness of their hearts—not in this city. There was always an angle, an ulterior motive. He studied her face, searching for any hint of deception, but found none. She was either an incredible liar or genuinely kind, and he wasn't sure which possibility scared him more.

Reluctantly, he accepted the bag and the coffee. "Thank you," he muttered, avoiding her gaze.

"You're welcome." She leaned against the doorframe, her eyes studying him with quiet curiosity. "What's your name?"

The question caught him off guard. He hadn't used his real name in years, and the fake ones he gave were always chosen on the fly. "Daniel," he said after a brief pause.

"Daniel," she repeated, as though testing how it sounded. "It suits you."

He took a sip of the coffee, letting its warmth seep into his frozen limbs. It had been a long time since anyone had spoken his name aloud, and hearing it now felt oddly intimate. He shifted uncomfortably under her gaze. "Why are you doing this?" he asked.

Emily tilted her head, considering the question. "Because you looked like you needed help."

"It's not that simple."

"Maybe not," she admitted. "But sometimes the simplest things make the biggest difference."

Her words hung in the air between them, heavy with meaning. Daniel wanted to argue, to tell her that life was far more complicated than she seemed to realize. But the way she looked at him, with such unwavering conviction, made him doubt his own beliefs.

A shout from inside the café broke the moment. "Emily! We need you back here!"

She sighed and turned to leave. "I have to go. But if you ever need anything, don't hesitate to ask."

He watched her disappear into the café, her presence leaving an unexpected void. For a moment, he considered walking away, disappearing into the labyrinth of streets as he always did. But something rooted him to the spot, a nagging feeling that he couldn't shake.

A Kind Stranger

Daniel stepped away from the café, finding a quiet corner to open the bag. Inside was a warm croissant, its golden crust glistening with butter. He took a bite, the flaky pastry melting on his tongue. It was a small thing, but it felt monumental. For the first time in years, he allowed himself to savor something without guilt or fear.

His moment of peace was short-lived. As he turned to leave, he noticed a man leaning against a lamppost across the street, his eyes fixed on the café. He wore a tailored suit and polished shoes, his appearance a stark contrast to the grimy streets. But it wasn't his attire that set Daniel on edge—it was the cold, calculating look in his eyes.

Daniel's instincts kicked in, and he melted into the shadows, watching the man from a distance. The man didn't move, his gaze never wavering from the café. Daniel's mind raced. Was he watching Emily? Or was he here for Daniel?

The memory of the figure from the night before flashed in his mind. Could this be the same person? Or was it just a coincidence? He didn't believe in coincidences, not anymore.

The man checked his watch, then pulled out a phone. He spoke briefly, his voice too low for Daniel to hear, before slipping the phone back into his pocket. Then he turned and walked away, disappearing into the crowd.

Daniel's pulse quickened. He didn't know who the man was or what he wanted, but one thing was clear: his presence wasn't random. And if Emily was in danger because of him…

He shook his head, trying to dispel the thought. Emily was just a stranger—a kind one, yes, but a stranger nonetheless. He had no right to involve himself in her life. But as he walked away, his steps heavy with uncertainty, he couldn't shake the feeling that he had just crossed a line he could never uncross.

Three

A Mysterious Coin

The clang of the café's bell signaled another morning rush, with customers piling in, chatting loudly, and placing their orders. Emily moved through the small space behind the counter with practiced ease, her smile bright despite the chaos around her. Daniel watched from his usual spot across the street, shrouded in the shadows of a narrow alley. The sun had broken through the clouds, casting sharp rays across the city, but Daniel still kept to the darker corners, his presence hidden from the casual passerby.

As he leaned against the cool brick wall, his hand brushed against the pocket of his coat. His fingers met the familiar contours of a small coin—its edges rough, its surface smooth save for the faded etching in the center. He pulled it out, turning it over in his hand. The coin was old, its once gleaming surface now tarnished. But the insignia carved into it was unmistakable: a crest of a hawk clutching a dagger, flanked by laurels.

This coin wasn't just any trinket; it was a remnant of his past, a key to a life he had tried to leave behind. He hadn't thought about it in months, but Emily's unexpected kindness had stirred something in him, and now, the weight of the coin seemed heavier than ever. It wasn't valuable in the traditional sense, but its significance was immeasurable. It was a token from a world he had been forced to abandon—a world of privilege, power, and betrayal.

His thoughts were interrupted by the sound of approaching footsteps. Instinctively, Daniel slipped the coin back into his pocket and melted further into the shadows. A group of teenagers passed by, their laughter echoing off the alley walls. He exhaled slowly, his hand brushing against the small blade tucked beneath his coat. The city had a way of keeping him on edge, every sound and movement a potential threat.

His eyes flicked back to the café, where Emily was chatting with a customer—a middle-aged man in a worn suit. Her laugh carried through the glass, warm and genuine. Daniel felt a pang of something he couldn't quite identify. It wasn't jealousy, exactly, but it was close. He shook his head, trying to dismiss the thought. Emily was kind, but she was also curious, and that curiosity could lead to trouble.

Just as he was about to turn away, the door to the café swung open, and Emily stepped outside. She held a tray with a single steaming cup of coffee and a plate of croissants, her gaze scanning the street. Daniel froze, his heart pounding as her eyes locked onto his shadowed corner.

"There you are," she called out, her voice light but insistent.

Daniel hesitated. He considered slipping away, disappearing into the labyrinth of alleys as he had done so many times before. But something about the way she looked at him—determined yet gentle—kept him rooted to the spot.

Reluctantly, he stepped out of the shadows, his hat pulled low over his face. Emily smiled, a genuine expression that made him feel both exposed and oddly comforted.

"I thought you might be hungry," she said, placing the tray on a nearby ledge. "You didn't come by yesterday."

"I was busy," Daniel replied gruffly, though he avoided her gaze.

She leaned against the ledge, studying him with that same unnerving curiosity. "You know, most people would just come inside. It's warmer in there."

"I'm not most people," he muttered.

She laughed softly. "That much is clear."

For a moment, silence settled between them, broken only

by the distant hum of the city. Daniel reached for the croissant, his movements slow and deliberate. Emily didn't say anything, but he could feel her watching him, her gaze sharp and probing.

"You dropped something the other night," she said suddenly, pulling a small object from her pocket. She held it up, the sunlight catching its metallic surface.

Daniel's blood ran cold. It was the coin.

His mind raced, every instinct screaming at him to snatch it from her and disappear. But he forced himself to remain calm, his expression unreadable.

"Where did you find that?" he asked, his voice carefully neutral.

"By the alley where I saw you last," she replied. "I figured it might be yours. It's... unusual."

Daniel took the coin from her hand, his fingers brushing against hers for the briefest of moments. He turned it over, confirming that it was indeed the same coin he had carried for years. The insignia glinted faintly in the sunlight, a stark reminder of everything he had lost.

"It's just a trinket," he said, slipping it back into his pocket.

Emily raised an eyebrow. "That doesn't look like 'just a trinket.' The design is intricate, and it looks old. Family heirloom?"

"No," Daniel said quickly, too quickly.

She tilted her head, her curiosity clearly piqued. "You don't have to tell me if you don't want to. I was just trying to return it."

"I appreciate that," he said, his tone softer now. "But it's nothing important."

Emily didn't press further, but her eyes lingered on him, as though trying to decipher the puzzle he presented. Daniel shifted uncomfortably under her gaze, his fingers brushing against the coin in his pocket. He knew he couldn't afford to let her get too close, not with the secrets he carried.

"I should go," he said abruptly, stepping back.

Emily's expression faltered for a moment, but she recovered quickly. "Alright. But if you ever need anything, you know where to find me."

Daniel nodded, tipping his hat slightly before turning and walking away. He could feel her eyes on his back as he disappeared into the crowd, his mind racing with questions. How had he dropped the coin? And more importantly, how much had Emily seen?

As he rounded a corner, he slipped into a narrow alley and leaned against the wall, his breath coming in shallow gasps.

He pulled the coin from his pocket, studying it intently. The insignia seemed to mock him, a symbol of a life he could never return to.

The sound of footsteps reached his ears, and he tensed, his grip tightening on the coin. A man appeared at the far end of the alley, his face obscured by the brim of his hat. He paused, his gaze fixed on Daniel.

For a moment, neither of them moved. Then, the man tipped his hat and turned, disappearing into the shadows.

Daniel's heart pounded in his chest. He knew that gesture. It was a warning.

The coin felt heavier than ever in his hand.

Four

Shadows of a Past

The world felt quieter in the hours just before dawn, when the city's perpetual hum softened to a distant whisper. Daniel moved through the empty streets like a ghost, his boots treading soundlessly on the damp pavement. The chill of the night seeped through his worn coat, but he didn't feel it. His mind was too consumed by the events of the past days—the coin, Emily, and the mysterious man who had been watching him.

He ducked into a narrow alley, pausing beneath the flickering glow of a streetlamp. His hand slipped into his pocket, pulling out the coin that had resurfaced like an unwelcome specter. The insignia glinted faintly in the dim light, its intricate design a cruel reminder of the life he had left behind.

Daniel flipped the coin between his fingers, the motion practiced and soothing. The crest of the hawk and dagger was as familiar to him as his own name, etched into his memory as deeply as it was into the metal. It was the emblem of the Laurent family—a dynasty built on wealth, power, and influence. A dynasty that had once been his.

He turned the coin over, revealing the initials engraved on the reverse: R.L. Raphael Laurent. His brother.

The name sent a chill down his spine. Raphael had always been the golden child, the one groomed to inherit their father's empire. Daniel, the younger son, had been relegated to the shadows, expected to follow orders without question. But Raphael's ambition had been boundless, and it was that ambition that had destroyed everything.

Daniel's grip tightened on the coin, his mind flashing back to the night it had all fallen apart. The opulent ballroom of the Laurent estate, filled with laughter and clinking glasses. The sharp smell of brandy and cigar smoke hanging in the air. And then the revelation—a betrayal so deep it had shattered his world.

He could still see Raphael's face, calm and composed as he delivered the news. Their father was dead, poisoned by a rival. But the truth, Daniel had discovered, was far more sinister. Raphael had orchestrated the entire plot, eliminating their father to seize control of the family fortune. When Daniel confronted him, Raphael hadn't even bothered to deny it.

"What did you expect?" Raphael had said, his tone devoid of remorse. "Father was weak. His way of doing things was outdated. I'm building something greater."

"You murdered him," Daniel had hissed, his fists clenched. "You destroyed our family."

"Our family?" Raphael had laughed, a cold, hollow sound. "You were never part of this family, Daniel. You were a liability. And now you're nothing."

The memory made Daniel's chest tighten with rage, but he forced himself to take a deep breath. That was years ago. He had left that world behind, disappearing into the city's underbelly where no one could find him. He had traded his name for anonymity, his wealth for survival. But now, with the coin back in his possession, the shadows of his past were closing in.

A distant noise broke his reverie—the faint scrape of a shoe against concrete. Daniel froze, every muscle tensing. He slid the coin back into his pocket and reached for the blade concealed beneath his coat. His eyes scanned the alley, searching for the source of the sound.

Nothing.

Still, the sense of unease lingered. He knew better than to dismiss it. Danger had a way of sneaking up on you when you least expected it. He moved deeper into the alley, his steps deliberate and quiet, his ears straining for any sign of pursuit.

As he turned a corner, he spotted a figure leaning against the wall at the far end of the alley. The man's face was obscured by the brim of his hat, but his posture was casual, almost nonchalant. Daniel's grip on the blade tightened.

"Daniel," the man called out, his voice low and even. "It's been a long time."

Daniel didn't respond. He took a step closer, his free hand brushing against the edge of the coin in his pocket. "Who are you?" he asked, his tone cold.

The man chuckled. "Come now. Don't tell me you've forgotten me."

He stepped into the light, and Daniel's breath caught. The man's face was older, lined with the passage of time, but there was no mistaking the sharp blue eyes and the scar that ran down the side of his jaw. It was Victor Hayes, Raphael's most trusted enforcer.

"Victor," Daniel said, his voice laced with disdain. "I thought you'd be dead by now."

Victor smirked. "Disappointed to see me alive?"

"Depends on why you're here."

Victor took a step closer, his hands tucked casually into the pockets of his tailored coat. "I'm here to deliver a message. Raphael knows where you are."

Daniel's blood ran cold. He had spent years staying off the radar, erasing every trace of his existence. The thought that Raphael had found him sent a wave of dread crashing over him.

"What does he want?" Daniel asked, his voice steady despite the turmoil inside him.

Victor's smirk widened. "He wants what he's always wanted—control. He knows you've been keeping secrets, Daniel. He wants the rest of the family's fortune. And he's willing to do whatever it takes to get it."

Daniel's jaw clenched. He had suspected as much, but hearing it confirmed was another matter entirely. The coin in his pocket seemed to burn against his skin, a tangible reminder of the leverage Raphael sought.

"Tell Raphael he'll get nothing from me," Daniel said, his tone hard.

Victor's expression darkened. "You know it's not that simple. He's not asking, Daniel. He's demanding. And if you don't comply…" He trailed off, letting the threat hang in the air.

Daniel took a step forward, the blade in his hand glinting faintly in the light. "Tell Raphael if he wants something from me, he can come and get it himself."

Victor's eyes flicked to the blade, but he didn't flinch. "I'll deliver the message," he said evenly. "But don't say I didn't warn you. Raphael doesn't like to be crossed."

With that, Victor turned and walked away, his footsteps echoing against the walls of the alley. Daniel watched him go, his mind racing. He knew this was only the beginning. Raphael wouldn't stop until he had what he wanted, and Daniel was running out of places to hide.

As the first rays of sunlight crept over the city, Daniel slipped the coin from his pocket and stared at it. It was more than just a piece of metal—it was a key to his past, and now, it was a link to the danger that loomed ahead. He clenched it tightly in his fist, his resolve hardening.

If Raphael wanted a fight, Daniel would give him one. But he wouldn't be fighting for himself. He would be fighting to protect the fragile sense of humanity he had found in the unlikeliest of places—in the kindness of a stranger named Emily.

Five

The Stranger's Secrets

The rain returned in the evening, casting the city in a veil of shimmering mist. Emily leaned against the counter of her café, absently wiping a clean glass as her thoughts wandered. Business was slow, the usual chatter and bustle replaced by the soft patter of rain against the window. She glanced outside, her eyes instinctively searching for a familiar figure among the scattered pedestrians.

He wasn't there. Daniel rarely came inside, but she had grown used to catching glimpses of him in the shadows across the street or lingering near the edge of her vision. His absence tonight left an uneasy void, a gnawing feeling she couldn't explain. There was something about him—something enigmatic and heavy, like he carried the weight of a thousand unspoken stories.

Her curiosity had only deepened after she found the coin. Its intricate design haunted her thoughts, the hawk clutching the dagger, the initials etched on the back. She had tried to search for its origin online but found nothing definitive. It wasn't an ordinary trinket, and she couldn't shake the feeling that it was tied to a larger story. To Daniel's story.

A loud crash startled her from her thoughts. She turned to see one of the cooks fumbling with a stack of pans in the kitchen. Emily offered a reassuring smile, waving off his apology. "It's fine," she said, her voice steady despite the unease bubbling beneath her surface.

The bell above the door jingled, and her heart leapt before she could stop herself. But it wasn't Daniel. A middle-aged man with a heavy coat and a weary expression stepped in, shaking water from his umbrella. Emily greeted him with a practiced smile and took his order, though her mind remained elsewhere.

As the man settled into a corner booth, the door jingled again. This time, it was Daniel.

Emily froze, her heart racing for reasons she couldn't quite place. He looked different tonight—tense, more guarded than usual. His coat was soaked through, droplets of rain clinging to his hair and beard. He didn't linger in the doorway as he usually did, blending into the shadows. Instead, he stepped inside, his movements purposeful.

"Daniel," she said, her voice filled with surprise and something close to relief. "You're finally coming in?"

He didn't answer immediately, his sharp eyes scanning the room. Satisfied, he stepped closer to the counter, his presence commanding even in his disheveled state. "Can we talk?" he asked, his tone low.

Emily nodded, her curiosity overtaking her surprise. "Of course."

She gestured to a quiet corner of the café, away from the other customers. Daniel followed her, his steps measured. She noticed the way he kept his back to the wall, his eyes darting to every exit and window as though anticipating a threat. When they reached the corner, he sat with his hands folded on the table, his gaze fixed on her.

"You found something the other night," he said without preamble. "The coin."

Emily hesitated, caught off guard by his directness. "Yes," she admitted. "I gave it back to you. Is something wrong?"

Daniel's jaw tightened, and he exhaled slowly, as though weighing his words. "That coin... it's not just a keepsake. It's a piece of something much bigger."

Emily leaned forward, her curiosity burning brighter. "What do you mean?"

He hesitated, his fingers tracing an invisible pattern on the table. "The less you know, the safer you'll be."

Her brow furrowed. "That's not much of an answer, Daniel. If it's dangerous, why are you carrying it? Why not get rid of it?"

"Because I can't," he said simply. His voice was calm, but there was an edge to it—a simmering intensity that made her stomach twist. "It's tied to my past, to people who would do anything to get it back. If they knew you'd touched it…" He trailed off, his expression darkening.

Emily's heart skipped a beat. "Are you saying I'm in danger?"

"You could be," he admitted. "That's why I need you to be careful. Don't tell anyone about the coin. Don't mention me to anyone."

Her mind raced with questions, but she forced herself to focus. "Who are these people, Daniel? Why are they after you?"

For a moment, he looked as though he might shut her out completely, his walls rising once more. But then something in her expression softened his resolve. "My family," he said finally. "Or what's left of them."

Emily blinked, taken aback. "Your family?"

He nodded, his eyes distant. "The coin is a symbol of their power, their legacy. It's a reminder of everything they've built—and destroyed. They don't care about me. All they care about is maintaining their control, and if I stand in the way..."

His voice trailed off, but the implication was clear. Emily felt a chill run down her spine. "Why would you stand in their way? Aren't they your family?"

"They stopped being my family the day they betrayed everything we stood for," Daniel said, his voice hard. "They're dangerous, Emily. They'll stop at nothing to protect their secrets, and anyone who gets in their way..." He didn't need to finish the sentence.

Emily sat back, her mind reeling. She had sensed there was more to Daniel than met the eye, but she hadn't expected this. His words painted a picture of a man caught in a web of power and corruption, a world she could barely comprehend.

"Why are you telling me this?" she asked quietly.

"Because you deserve to know," he said. "You've been kind to me, and I didn't want you to think I was just some vagrant wandering the streets. But you need to understand, Emily— being near me puts you at risk."

Her heart ached at the vulnerability in his voice, the weight of his confession. "Daniel, I don't care about the risk," she said. "You've been through so much. I just want to help."

He shook his head, a wry smile tugging at his lips. "You don't know what you're saying. My world isn't something you can just step into, Emily. It's dark, and it's dangerous. I've seen what it does to people."

"Then let me in," she said, her voice firm. "You don't have to do this alone."

Daniel's gaze softened, and for a moment, the hard edges of his demeanor seemed to crumble. "You're stubborn," he muttered, though there was no malice in his tone.

She smiled faintly. "So I've been told."

The sound of the door opening drew both their attention. A man in a dark coat stepped inside, his face obscured by a wide-brimmed hat. Daniel stiffened immediately, his hand moving to his side. The man scanned the room, his eyes lingering on Daniel for a fraction too long before moving on.

"Stay here," Daniel said, his voice low but urgent. He rose from his seat, his movements fluid and deliberate.

"Daniel—"

"Stay here," he repeated, his tone leaving no room for argument.

Emily watched helplessly as he approached the man, her chest tight with fear. The two exchanged words she couldn't hear, their postures tense. The man gestured toward the door, and Daniel nodded curtly before following him outside.

She sat frozen in her seat, her mind racing. Who was the man? What did he want with Daniel? The moments stretched into an eternity, and when Daniel didn't return, a knot of dread formed in her stomach.

She had wanted to uncover his secrets, but now that she had, she couldn't help but wonder if she had stepped into something far more dangerous than she could handle.

Six

The Anonymous Protector

The night was restless. A storm raged above the city, lightning illuminating the darkened streets and thunder echoing like a warning from the heavens. Rain cascaded down in relentless sheets, soaking the sidewalks and drumming against windows. Emily sat at the counter of her café, the last customer having left hours ago. She should have gone home by now, but unease rooted her to the spot.

Her thoughts were a whirlwind of unanswered questions and lingering fear. Daniel's warnings about his past had unsettled her, but it was his absence that gnawed at her the most. Since the night he followed the man in the dark coat, she hadn't seen or heard from him. The silence was suffocating, leaving her to imagine the worst.

The Anonymous Protector

She glanced at her phone for the tenth time in an hour, willing it to ring. Outside, the rain showed no sign of letting up. The glow of the streetlights reflected off the wet pavement, casting eerie shadows that danced like specters.

A loud knock shattered the quiet, causing Emily to jump. She turned toward the door, her heart pounding. A figure stood outside, their features obscured by a drenched hood. Lightning flashed, and for a split second, she thought it might be Daniel. But the frame was wrong—too broad, too rigid.

The figure knocked again, more insistently this time. Emily hesitated, every instinct screaming at her to lock the door and stay hidden. But curiosity and a strange sense of courage compelled her forward. She approached cautiously, her hand trembling as she unlocked the door and opened it just enough to peer out.

"Miss Emily Turner?" the man asked, his voice deep and unfamiliar.

Her grip tightened on the door. "Who's asking?"

The man pulled back his hood, revealing a sharp-featured face with piercing blue eyes. "I was sent to deliver a message."

Her stomach churned. "By who?"

He didn't answer immediately, his gaze flicking behind her

as if checking for eavesdroppers. Finally, he said, "Someone who doesn't want to see you hurt."

The cryptic response only heightened her anxiety. "What kind of message?"

The man reached into his coat, and Emily's pulse spiked. Her mind flashed to every worst-case scenario, her breath catching in her throat. But instead of a weapon, he withdrew a small envelope and held it out to her.

She hesitated, her eyes darting between him and the envelope. "What is this?"

"Instructions," he said. "Follow them, and you'll be safe."

Emily stared at him, her heart racing. "Safe from what?"

The man's expression darkened. "From the people who've been watching you."

The air seemed to leave her lungs. "Watching me? What do you mean?"

"You've been noticed," he said bluntly. "You're asking questions, getting involved in things that don't concern you. That makes you a target."

Emily's mind raced. Had Daniel's enemies already caught on to her connection to him? Was she in danger simply because she had cared?

Before she could respond, the man stepped back, pulling his hood up once more. "Read the letter," he said. "And stay out of sight."

Without another word, he turned and disappeared into the storm, his figure swallowed by the rain. Emily stood frozen in the doorway, the envelope clutched tightly in her hand. The street was empty again, as if he had never been there.

Her fingers trembled as she locked the door and turned the deadbolt. She leaned against the cool glass, her breath coming in shallow gasps. The envelope felt heavy in her grasp, its weight far greater than the paper it contained.

She moved to the counter, the sound of the rain now a distant hum against the roaring in her ears. Carefully, she opened the envelope, revealing a single sheet of paper folded neatly inside. The handwriting was bold and precise, the words sending a chill down her spine.

—-

Emily,

Leave the café tonight. Do not go home. Pack a bag and stay somewhere crowded—a hotel, a shelter, anywhere but your usual places. Avoid being alone. If you see someone following you, do not confront them. You've been marked, and they won't hesitate to use you to get to him.

Trust no one.

—A Friend

—-

Her hands shook as she read the note again, her mind struggling to process the warning. "Marked." The word echoed in her head like a curse. Marked by who? And why? She thought of Daniel, of his cryptic warnings and the dangerous world he had described. Was this what he had meant?

The café suddenly felt too quiet, too exposed. Every shadow seemed to loom larger, every creak of the building amplified. She grabbed her phone and dialed Daniel's number, her heart pounding as it rang. And rang. And rang.

No answer.

She tried again, each unanswered call deepening her dread. Where was he? Was he even alive?

The sharp sound of glass shattering jolted her out of her thoughts. She whipped around, her eyes scanning the café. A window near the back was broken, rain dripping through the jagged opening. Panic surged through her as she realized someone had thrown a small object through the glass.

Her feet moved before her mind could catch up, rushing to the source. On the floor lay a brick, wrapped in a piece of paper. She knelt to pick it up, her fingers trembling as she unwrapped it. The message was hastily scrawled, the ink smudged by the rain.

—-

You can't protect him. Stay out of this, or you'll regret it.

—-

A cold shiver ran down her spine. The note was unsigned, but the threat was clear. Whoever had thrown it knew about her connection to Daniel, and they wanted her to back off. But how did they know? How long had they been watching her?

The sound of footsteps outside made her heart lurch. She dropped the note and brick, rushing to the front window. Through the rain, she saw a figure standing across the street, partially obscured by the shadows. They didn't move, their presence deliberate and menacing.

Emily's breath hitched. The phone in her hand felt like her only lifeline. She dialed again, praying for Daniel to answer. This time, the call connected.

"Emily." His voice was low, urgent.

"Daniel, thank God," she whispered, her voice shaking. "Someone just—"

"I know," he interrupted. "I'm close. Stay where you are.

Lock the doors. Don't let anyone in."

"How do you know—"

"I'll explain later," he said. "Just do as I say."

The line went dead before she could respond. Emily clutched the phone to her chest, her heart pounding. She moved quickly to lock the café's back entrance, her every nerve on edge. The figure outside was gone when she returned, but the sense of being watched lingered like a shadow.

Minutes passed, each one stretching into an eternity. Then the bell above the door jingled softly, and she spun around, her heart leaping into her throat.

It was Daniel. Soaked from the rain, his face etched with tension, he closed the door behind him and flipped the lock. His eyes swept the room, lingering on the broken window and the brick on the floor.

"They're watching you," he said, his voice grim. "We need to get you out of here."

Emily's mind was a blur of fear and questions, but she nodded. For now, she would trust him—her anonymous protector.

Seven

Whispers in the Dark

The wind howled through the narrow streets, carrying with it an eerie silence that seemed to suffocate the city. Daniel and Emily moved through the maze of alleys, their footsteps muffled by the rain-slicked cobblestones. The storm above showed no signs of relenting, lightning casting fleeting glimpses of their surroundings in stark relief. Daniel's pace was brisk, his posture rigid, as though he expected danger to spring from every shadow.

"Where are we going?" Emily whispered, struggling to keep up. Her breath fogged in the cold night air, but the adrenaline coursing through her veins kept her moving.

"Somewhere safe," Daniel replied curtly, his eyes darting to every corner, every window. He held her arm firmly, guiding her as though she might disappear if he let go.

"Safe from who?" she pressed, her voice trembling. "Who's after me?"

Daniel hesitated, glancing over his shoulder before answering. "The people I warned you about. They've been watching you, Emily. The moment you got involved with me, they saw you as leverage."

The words hit her like a blow, her stomach twisting with fear. "Leverage? For what?"

"To draw me out," he said simply, his tone laced with frustration. "They know I care about you."

Emily faltered at his admission, but there was no time to dwell on it. A sudden noise—a sharp clatter of metal—echoed through the alley, freezing them both in place. Daniel's grip tightened, his body coiled like a spring ready to snap.

"Stay behind me," he whispered, his voice low and steady. He reached beneath his coat, pulling out the small blade he always carried. The cold steel gleamed faintly in the dim light.

Emily's heart pounded as she pressed herself against the wall, her eyes scanning the shadows. The noise came again, this time closer—a deliberate sound, not the random chaos of the city. Someone was following them.

Daniel stepped forward cautiously, his every movement calculated. "Show yourself," he called out, his voice echoing through the narrow passage.

For a moment, there was silence, broken only by the distant rumble of thunder. Then, from the darkness, a figure emerged. The man was tall and lean, his face partially obscured by a hood. He stopped a few feet away, his posture relaxed but his presence menacing.

"Daniel," the man said, his tone mocking. "Always the hero, aren't you?"

Daniel's jaw tightened. "What do you want?"

The man tilted his head, as if considering the question. "It's not about what I want. It's about what Raphael wants. And you know what that is."

Emily felt the blood drain from her face. Raphael. Daniel's brother. She had heard the name before, but this was the first time it had been spoken aloud with such weight, such malice.

"Tell Raphael he's wasting his time," Daniel said coldly. "He's not getting what he wants."

The man chuckled, the sound low and menacing. "That's not how this works, Daniel. He doesn't take no for an answer. And now..." His gaze shifted to Emily, his smile widening. "He has a new bargaining chip."

Emily shrank back, her fear palpable. Daniel stepped in front of her, his blade held steady. "If you so much as touch her—"

"You'll what?" the man interrupted, his tone dripping with disdain. "Fight me? Kill me? We both know you're not that kind of man."

Daniel didn't respond, but the tension in the air was suffocating. The man took a step closer, his movements slow and deliberate. "You should've stayed gone, Daniel. You could've disappeared forever, let Raphael win. But no—you had to play the martyr."

"I'm not playing anything," Daniel said sharply. "I'm protecting what matters."

The man's smile faded, replaced by a cold, calculating expression. "Then you know how this ends. Give Raphael what he wants, or he'll take everything from you. Starting with her."

Before Daniel could respond, the man turned and vanished into the shadows, his departure as sudden as his arrival. The silence that followed was deafening, broken only by the sound of Emily's ragged breathing.

"Who was that?" she whispered, her voice trembling.

"One of Raphael's men," Daniel said, his tone bitter. "A reminder that he's always watching."

Emily's knees threatened to give way, but she steadied herself against the wall. "Why me, Daniel? Why did you let me get involved?"

"I didn't mean to," he said, his voice softening. "I tried to keep my distance, to keep you safe. But you didn't make it easy."

Despite the fear coursing through her, Emily felt a flicker of warmth at his words. "What does Raphael want so badly that he's willing to do this?"

Daniel hesitated, the weight of the answer heavy in his silence. Finally, he said, "He wants the rest of our family's fortune. What's left of it. But he knows I won't give it to him. Not after what he's done."

Emily stared at him, her mind racing. "And the coin? Is that part of it?"

"It's more than that," Daniel admitted. "It's a key. A symbol of everything Raphael wants to control. And as long as I have it, I'm a threat to him."

The pieces began to fall into place, but the picture they formed was darker than Emily had imagined. "Then why not destroy it? Get rid of it and disappear?"

"Because it's not just about the coin," Daniel said. "It's about stopping him. If Raphael gets what he wants, he'll hurt more people than just me."

Emily swallowed hard, the gravity of his words sinking in. "So what do we do now?"

Daniel's gaze softened as he looked at her, his expression conflicted. "We run. For now. But this isn't over."

She nodded, her fear replaced by a fierce determination. "Then let's go."

They moved quickly, their steps silent as they disappeared deeper into the city. The storm raged on, the rain masking their presence as they slipped through the darkness. But even as they ran, the whispers of danger followed them, a constant reminder that the shadows of the past were never far behind.

Eight

A Touch of Refinement

The hotel was far from luxurious, but it was clean and quiet—a rare sanctuary amid the chaos that seemed to follow Daniel and Emily. Its modest lobby smelled faintly of old wood polish, and the dimly lit corridors offered an unsettling sense of privacy. It wasn't the kind of place one would choose for a vacation, but for those looking to disappear, it was perfect.

Daniel led Emily down the hallway, his steps soundless on the threadbare carpet. His sharp gaze swept over every detail—the creak of a door hinge, the faint hum of an air vent, the flickering bulb at the end of the corridor. He pushed open the door to their room, stepping aside to let Emily enter first.

The room was sparse but functional: a single bed, a desk

From Dust to Diamonds

with a wobbly chair, and a small window overlooking the back alley. Emily set her bag down on the bed, her fingers brushing against the frayed quilt as she took in their temporary refuge. The tension in her chest hadn't eased since the encounter with Raphael's man, and the silence between her and Daniel only added to her unease.

"You should get some rest," Daniel said, closing the door behind him and locking it with a decisive click.

Emily turned to face him, her arms crossed. "Rest? After everything that's happened tonight? You can't be serious."

His expression softened, but the weariness in his eyes was unmistakable. "You need it, Emily. I'll keep watch."

She shook her head, the events of the night replaying in her mind. "I can't just… sleep, Daniel. Not with everything going on."

He exhaled, running a hand through his hair. "I understand, but you need to be ready for whatever comes next. Exhaustion isn't going to help you."

Emily hesitated, torn between her instinct to push for answers and the nagging realization that he was right. She sat down on the edge of the bed, her hands clasped tightly in her lap. "Then tell me something. Anything. I'm drowning in questions, and you're the only one who can answer them."

Daniel remained by the door, his silhouette sharp against

the faint light filtering through the window. He seemed to wrestle with her request, the weight of his secrets pressing down on him. Finally, he stepped forward, pulling a chair from the desk and sitting across from her.

"What do you want to know?" he asked, his voice low.

She studied him, her gaze searching for cracks in the armor he so carefully wore. "Start with the coin. You said it's a key. A key to what?"

He leaned back in the chair, his fingers tracing the edge of the armrest. "To a vault," he said after a moment. "One that holds the last remnants of my family's fortune. It's not just money—it's documents, records, things that could destroy Raphael if they ever came to light."

Emily's breath caught. "And Raphael knows you have it?"

"He doesn't know where it is," Daniel clarified. "That's why he's been chasing me. He thinks I'll lead him to it."

Her mind raced as she pieced together the implications. "Why not use what's in the vault against him? Expose him for who he really is?"

Daniel's jaw tightened. "It's not that simple. Raphael's reach is vast. He has allies in powerful places, people who would protect him even if the truth came out. If I make a move against him, I have to be sure it counts."

Emily absorbed his words, the gravity of his situation sinking in. "And me?" she asked softly. "What do I have to do with any of this?"

His gaze met hers, the intensity in his eyes making her heart skip a beat. "You were never supposed to be involved. I stayed away because I didn't want you caught in the crossfire. But when I saw what they were doing—targeting you—I couldn't stay silent."

She frowned, her emotions a whirlwind of gratitude and frustration. "But why, Daniel? Why risk yourself for me?"

For a moment, his expression wavered, and she thought he might shut down again. But instead, he leaned forward, his voice dropping to a near whisper. "Because you're the first person in years who's looked at me and seen more than what I've become. You reminded me of the man I used to be."

The confession hung in the air, raw and unguarded. Emily felt her throat tighten, her heart aching at the vulnerability in his voice. She reached out instinctively, her hand brushing against his. "You're still that man, Daniel," she said firmly. "You just need to believe it."

He didn't pull away, but the flicker of emotion in his eyes was quickly replaced by a steely resolve. "Believing it doesn't matter if I can't protect you," he said. "Raphael won't stop until he has what he wants. And if he thinks hurting you will get him closer to it..."

His voice trailed off, but Emily didn't need him to finish the thought. The danger was all too real, and the stakes were higher than she had ever imagined. She tightened her grip on his hand, her resolve hardening. "Then we'll face him together."

Daniel shook his head, a faint smile tugging at his lips. "You're stubborn, you know that?"

"I've been told," she said, her smile mirroring his.

The moment was brief but grounding, a flicker of warmth amid the chaos. But the reprieve didn't last long. A sharp knock at the door shattered the quiet, sending a jolt of adrenaline through Emily's veins.

Daniel was on his feet in an instant, his blade in hand. He motioned for Emily to stay back, his movements silent as he approached the door. The knock came again, louder this time, followed by a voice.

"Room service."

Emily's heart raced. "We didn't order anything," she whispered.

Daniel nodded, his body tense. He pressed his ear to the door, listening intently. When the knock came a third time, he spoke, his voice cold. "Wrong room."

The silence that followed was deafening. Then, without

warning, the doorknob jiggled violently, as though someone was trying to force it open. Daniel reacted instantly, shoving the desk against the door to barricade it.

"Emily, window," he said urgently.

She hesitated for only a second before rushing to the window. The rain had slowed, but the alley below was still slick and treacherous. She pushed the window open, the cool air rushing in as she looked down.

"It's a drop," she said, her voice trembling.

"I'll go first," Daniel said, already at her side. He climbed onto the sill, his movements quick and practiced. "I'll catch you."

She nodded, her fear overridden by the urgency in his voice. Daniel dropped to the ground below, landing with a soft thud. He looked up, his arms outstretched. "Jump!"

Emily climbed onto the windowsill, the height making her stomach lurch. She didn't hesitate for long, pushing off and letting gravity take her. Daniel caught her easily, his arms steady despite the impact.

"Move," he said, grabbing her hand and leading her down the alley. Behind them, the sound of the door breaking open echoed through the night.

As they disappeared into the shadows, Emily's mind raced

with questions, but one thought stood out above the rest: She was no longer a bystander in Daniel's fight. She was part of it now, for better or worse. And there was no turning back.

Nine

The First Clue

The night air was thick with tension as Daniel and Emily emerged from the shadows of the alley, the faint glow of distant streetlights barely illuminating their path. The rain had eased, leaving the city damp and glistening under the faint moonlight. They moved quickly, their breaths visible in the cool air, every sound around them magnified by the quiet.

Daniel kept Emily close, his grip firm but not forceful. His sharp eyes scanned their surroundings, cataloging every detail—the glint of a puddle, the faint rustle of a trash bag in the wind, the echo of their footsteps. He trusted no corner, no shadow, and Emily could feel the weight of his vigilance pressing on her like an invisible burden.

They reached an abandoned warehouse near the edge of the

city, its once grand facade now crumbling and overgrown with ivy. Daniel paused, pulling Emily back into the shelter of a doorway. "We'll hide here for now," he said, his voice low and controlled. "It's off the grid."

Emily looked at the derelict structure, her heart still racing from the events of the night. "This is your idea of safe?"

"It's not about comfort," Daniel replied, his gaze fixed on the warehouse. "It's about staying invisible."

He guided her inside, the rusted door groaning in protest as he pushed it open. The interior was cold and cavernous, the faint smell of oil and damp metal clinging to the air. Broken machinery and scattered debris littered the floor, but Daniel navigated it with ease, leading Emily to a corner where an old desk sat half-buried beneath a tarp.

"Sit," he instructed, pulling the tarp aside to reveal a battered toolbox and a few other supplies. Emily obeyed, sinking into a rickety chair as Daniel crouched by the desk, rummaging through the contents of the box.

"What are you looking for?" she asked, her voice breaking the oppressive silence.

"Something to give us an edge," he said without looking up. "Raphael's men are relentless. If we're going to stay ahead of them, we need information."

Emily watched as he pulled out a small device that looked

like a radio. He adjusted the dials, his expression focused. The machine crackled to life, emitting faint static before settling into a low hum. Daniel set it on the desk, his fingers deftly twisting knobs and flipping switches.

"What is that?" Emily asked, leaning forward.

"A frequency scanner," Daniel explained. "If Raphael's men are communicating nearby, we might pick it up."

Emily felt a shiver run down her spine. The thought of Raphael's people being close enough to monitor sent a surge of fear through her. "And if they are?"

"Then we'll know what they're planning," Daniel said, his tone grim. "Or at least where they're going."

The scanner crackled again, and Daniel leaned in, his expression sharpening. A faint voice broke through the static, distorted but audible.

"—sighted near the warehouse district. Keep a perimeter. No mistakes this time."

Emily's heart skipped a beat. "They're talking about us, aren't they?"

"Most likely," Daniel said, his jaw tightening. He adjusted the scanner, trying to refine the signal. Another voice came through, clearer this time.

The First Clue

"Unit three, check the southern blocks. The others will hold positions until confirmation."

Daniel cursed under his breath. "They're closing in."

Emily's pulse quickened, the weight of their situation pressing down on her. "What do we do?"

Daniel straightened, his mind already working through a plan. "We can't stay here. If they've locked down the area, it's only a matter of time before they find us. But this"—he gestured to the scanner—"might give us a clue about their next move."

He turned back to the desk, pulling out a small notebook and flipping through its pages. Emily watched as he scribbled down fragments of the intercepted conversation, his movements quick and precise.

As he worked, a faint glint caught Emily's eye. She looked closer, noticing a small metallic object partially buried beneath a pile of old papers. Curiosity piqued, she reached for it, brushing aside the debris to reveal a tarnished key. It was heavy and ornate, its bow shaped like a hawk in flight.

"Daniel," she said, holding it up. "What's this?"

He glanced over, his eyes narrowing as he took the key from her. His expression darkened, a mix of recognition and dread. "Where did you find this?"

"Right there," she said, pointing to the spot on the desk. "What is it?"

Daniel turned the key over in his hand, his thumb tracing the intricate design. "It's part of the vault," he said quietly. "One of the keys to open it."

Emily's eyes widened. "What's it doing here?"

"That's the question," Daniel muttered, his mind racing. He turned to the scanner, the voices still crackling faintly. His grip on the key tightened. "This changes everything."

Before Emily could ask what he meant, a sharp noise echoed from outside—a car door slamming, followed by the crunch of gravel underfoot. Daniel's head snapped up, his instincts kicking in. He grabbed the scanner and shoved it into his bag, motioning for Emily to follow him.

"Move. Now," he said, his voice low but urgent.

They slipped out through a side door, the night air biting against their skin. Daniel led the way, the key still clutched in his hand. Emily followed close behind, her heart pounding with every step. The warehouse loomed behind them, its dark silhouette fading as they moved deeper into the shadows.

Daniel paused at the corner of a building, peering around the edge. In the distance, the faint glow of flashlights cut through the darkness, accompanied by muffled voices.

The First Clue

"They're sweeping the area," he said, his tone grim. "We need to get out of here."

Emily's gaze flicked to the key in his hand. "What does it mean, Daniel? Why was it there?"

"It means Raphael's reach is deeper than I thought," he said. "And it means someone else might be pulling strings."

Her stomach churned at the implication. "You mean someone inside the family?"

"Or someone who knows too much," Daniel said. "Either way, we have to find out who."

They slipped through the alleyways, their movements quick and silent. The streets around them seemed to close in, every shadow a potential threat. Emily's mind raced with questions, but there was no time to ask them.

As they rounded a corner, Daniel suddenly stopped, pulling her back into the shadows. She followed his gaze and saw a black SUV idling at the far end of the street, its engine rumbling softly. A man stood by the driver's side, speaking into a radio.

"We can't go that way," Daniel murmured. He scanned their surroundings, his eyes landing on a fire escape above them. "Up there."

Emily followed his lead, climbing the metal ladder as quietly as she could. The fire escape groaned under their weight, but they reached the rooftop without incident. From their vantage point, they could see the SUV more clearly, the faint glow of a laptop visible through the windshield.

Daniel crouched low, pulling Emily down beside him. "They're coordinating from there," he said. "If we can get close enough…"

Emily's breath caught. "You're not seriously thinking about going back, are you?"

"If we don't, we'll never know what they're planning," Daniel said. "And we'll never stay ahead of them."

The key in his hand gleamed faintly in the moonlight, a silent reminder of the mystery they had just uncovered. Emily's fear warred with her determination, but as she looked at Daniel, she saw the same resolve she had come to rely on.

"Okay," she said, her voice steady despite the fear coursing through her. "Let's do it."

Daniel nodded, his expression grim but resolute. Together, they prepared to take the first step into the unknown, the weight of the key and the secrets it held guiding their every move.

Ten

A Daring Invitation

The rain had ceased for a few hours, but the thick, oppressive humidity clung to the air like an invisible shroud. Daniel and Emily moved through the streets, keeping to the shadows, the weight of the key still heavy in Daniel's pocket. Each corner they turned seemed to bring them closer to something—something they couldn't yet see, but felt in their bones, like an inevitable storm. The silence between them was thick, filled with the unspoken tension of the situation they found themselves in.

"Where are we going?" Emily asked, breaking the silence, her voice barely above a whisper. She hadn't asked that question in hours, but now it felt like the right time. Every step they took seemed to echo, each footfall a reminder of the danger that trailed behind them.

"To the city center," Daniel replied, his voice strained with fatigue but firm with purpose. He never took his eyes off their surroundings, his gaze scanning every passerby, every shadow, every flicker of movement that might indicate they were being followed.

Emily, still clutching the small bag she had packed earlier, cast a glance at him. She was about to ask why when he spoke again, his words a slight reassurance that gave her a little comfort.

"There's someone I need to meet. Someone who might have answers."

"Answers?" Emily repeated. She wasn't sure what answers she was looking for anymore—answers about Daniel's past, answers about the people chasing them, answers about the mysterious coin. She had thought they were in control, but now she felt like she was riding along a wave that had long ago broken, and there was no stopping the crash.

"Answers about what's going on. About the people behind this, the ones who are pulling Raphael's strings," Daniel said, his voice growing quieter as they walked. "I don't trust them, but I trust this contact. They might be able to help us."

Emily couldn't help but feel the anxiety building within her. "Who is this person?"

Daniel hesitated. "I'll tell you when we get there."

A Daring Invitation

It was an answer that should have made her feel better, but in truth, it did the opposite. The words echoed with the same cryptic unease that had colored everything about Daniel's world since she'd met him. He had secrets—too many, maybe—but they had kept her safe, kept her alive thus far.

The city center loomed ahead, with its towering glass structures and brightly lit streets, a stark contrast to the shadowy alleyways and dark corners they had been hiding in. As they drew closer, Daniel slowed his pace, pulling her into an alley and out of view of the main roads. They crouched low, the sudden quietness between them more pronounced now.

"We wait here," Daniel said, scanning the area one more time.

Emily didn't argue, though she couldn't suppress the rising feeling of unease that washed over her. She had no idea who they were waiting for, or what kind of meeting this was going to be, but she couldn't shake the thought that something wasn't right. This whole situation felt wrong on every level—like a carefully laid trap that only revealed itself in pieces.

Minutes stretched into what felt like hours as they waited. The faint murmur of traffic echoed from the main street, but their alley remained disturbingly silent. Emily's pulse quickened. She hadn't realized until now how vulnerable they were—how exposed.

Just as the anxiety was starting to overwhelm her, a figure appeared at the far end of the alley. She didn't hear the footsteps until they were almost on top of them, and her heart lurched in her chest as she tensed. The figure was cloaked in a long coat, a wide-brimmed hat shadowing their face.

"Stay close," Daniel muttered, standing to his full height. His hand rested lightly on the blade tucked beneath his coat. Emily did the same, instinctively clutching the strap of her bag, but she didn't move. She trusted Daniel. She trusted that he knew what he was doing, even though the situation screamed danger.

The figure stopped a few paces away, their hands hidden inside the coat. For a moment, there was only silence, and then the figure spoke.

"Daniel," the voice was low, almost a whisper, but unmistakably familiar. It sent a chill racing down Emily's spine.

"Good to see you again, Elias," Daniel replied, his tone neutral but carrying an undercurrent of something else. Something guarded.

Elias stepped forward, his face finally visible beneath the brim of his hat. He was older than Daniel, his features sharp and weathered. His eyes were dark and calculating, scanning the alley with the same level of caution that Daniel had shown. His gaze lingered on Emily for a moment, his expression unreadable, before turning back to Daniel.

A Daring Invitation

"This is the one?" Elias asked, his voice betraying a hint of skepticism.

Daniel's jaw tightened, but he didn't falter. "Yes."

Elias nodded slowly, his eyes narrowing. "She's involved, then."

"Everything's changed," Daniel said sharply, his patience thinning. "I wouldn't be here if I didn't need answers. If you want to help, now's the time."

Elias held up his hands, a gesture that seemed to balance between caution and curiosity. "Alright. But don't expect me to make this easy on you. We're not just talking about Raphael anymore. There's more at play here than you realize."

"Then tell me," Daniel demanded. "What's going on?"

Elias's expression softened just a fraction, as if weighing his words carefully. "You've been walking a dangerous line, Daniel. And now, they know you're alive. Not just Raphael, but others who have their own interests in this game."

"What game?" Emily asked, her voice sharp, her curiosity finally outweighing her fear. "What are you talking about?"

Elias shifted his weight, considering her for a moment. "There are things you don't know, things that can't be explained in a few words. You've been dragged into something much larger than Raphael's family feud."

Emily felt a cold shiver sweep through her, the implications of his words hanging heavily in the air. She turned to Daniel, her voice shaking. "What is he talking about?"

Daniel hesitated, his gaze flicking to Elias. "It's not just about the family or the coin. There are people—organizations—that want control of everything."

"Everything?" Emily echoed, her heart sinking with the weight of his words. "What does that mean?"

Elias cut in before Daniel could respond. "It means you're a pawn in a much bigger game, miss. A game that could determine the future of this entire city."

Emily swallowed hard, the realization hitting her with a gut-wrenching force. She had been thrust into a battle she didn't fully understand, surrounded by enemies with motives far beyond what she had imagined. She looked back at Daniel, searching his face for answers.

"We need to move," Elias said, snapping her out of her thoughts. "The clock's ticking. We've been compromised, and the longer we stay here, the more danger you're in."

Daniel nodded, his expression tight. "Lead the way."

Elias turned on his heel and began walking, his pace swift and purposeful. Daniel followed immediately, and Emily, though shaken, didn't hesitate to follow behind. The alleyways became a blur as they navigated the labyrinth of streets, keeping to the shadows, avoiding the main roads. Emily's mind raced with the information they had just been given. She had known this was bigger than just Raphael's obsession with the coin, but she hadn't realized how far-reaching it truly was.

After what seemed like hours, they arrived at a nondescript building nestled between two much larger, more modern structures. Elias led them inside, and the door clicked shut behind them, sealing them off from the outside world.

The room was small, dimly lit, and smelled faintly of dust and stale air. A single table sat in the center, covered with maps, documents, and files. The walls were lined with bookshelves, most of them empty except for a few old, tattered books. Elias motioned for them to sit, and Daniel immediately pulled out a chair, his face set in a mask of concentration.

"I'm assuming you didn't come all the way here just for small talk," Elias said, dropping a stack of papers onto the table. "So let's get to it."

Emily sat down cautiously, her nerves fraying as Elias flipped open one of the files. "This is the first clue," he said, pushing it toward Daniel.

Daniel didn't waste any time. He flipped through the papers, his eyes scanning the contents rapidly. His fingers stopped on a document, and Emily leaned forward, her eyes following his gaze.

The document was a list of names, some crossed out, others circled in red ink. Each name was associated with a location—an address, a company, a date. But it wasn't just the names that caught her attention. It was the final name at the bottom of the list.

"Raphael Laurent," she whispered, pointing to the name.

Elias leaned over, his eyes narrowing. "That's what we need to figure out. This isn't just about a family legacy. There's something deeper, and we need to find it before they do."

Eleven

An Unlikely Transformation

The city felt different now, like a vast labyrinth, its twisting alleyways and towering skyscrapers closing in with each passing day. The steady pulse of the night—distant chatter, the hum of traffic—was no longer reassuring. It was a constant reminder of how far they had fallen into the web, how deeply entangled they were in a game that had no rules.

Daniel walked with a newfound urgency, the weight of the folder in his hands heavier than any blade could be. He wasn't the same man he had been just a few weeks ago, when all he had cared about was staying hidden, staying safe. But that man was gone, replaced by someone who had nothing left to lose.

Emily kept pace beside him, her footsteps quick but hesitant, as if unsure of the path ahead. Her eyes were wide, scanning the surroundings, but there was something different about her too. It wasn't just fear anymore—it was determination. She had stepped into this world, into Daniel's world, and the transformation was evident in the set of her jaw, the way her posture had changed, even the way she looked at him now. She wasn't the innocent bystander she had been. She was in this just as much as he was.

They had spent the last few hours sifting through the documents Elias had given them, piecing together the mystery of Raphael and the strange organization pulling his strings. The more they uncovered, the more it seemed like an impossible puzzle, but there was one thing they both knew for certain—time was running out.

Daniel stopped abruptly, his head jerking up at the sound of a distant engine. He reached out, grabbing Emily by the arm, his grip firm but not hurting. She froze, meeting his eyes. There was a quiet intensity there that both unsettled and reassured her at the same time.

"We're being followed," he whispered.

Emily's pulse quickened, but she didn't ask how he knew. She didn't need to. Daniel had a way of sensing things that seemed beyond reason. He was always alert, always watching, always one step ahead. But this time, he wasn't just acting out of instinct. He was leading them somewhere, and every part of him was focused on making sure they got there in one piece.

Without a word, he turned on his heel, pulling her into a side alley. They moved quickly, ducking into the shadows and pressing themselves against the cold stone wall of a nearby building. The sound of the engine grew louder, and Emily felt her breath catch in her throat. The headlights of a black SUV cut through the mist, the vehicle cruising past them, its tires whispering against the wet pavement.

It didn't stop. It didn't even slow.

Daniel exhaled in a quiet, relieved breath. "Not them," he muttered, glancing at Emily. But he didn't allow himself to relax. Not yet.

They continued moving, this time with more urgency, weaving through the side streets and alleyways until they reached a small, rundown building tucked between two much larger structures. The place looked abandoned, a relic of a past that no longer had a purpose in the ever-growing city. But Daniel seemed to recognize it, and when he reached the door, he didn't hesitate. He knocked three times in quick succession, then paused.

A soft click came from inside, and the door creaked open just a few inches. A face appeared in the narrow gap, eyes sharp and calculating. The man's expression softened slightly when he saw Daniel.

"You made it," the man said, his voice low. His gaze flicked to Emily, lingering for a fraction of a second before he stepped back, allowing them entry.

The room inside was dimly lit, with only a few scattered lamps providing light. The walls were bare, save for a couple of old maps pinned to the corners. A table sat in the center of the room, cluttered with papers, electronics, and a few half-empty mugs. It looked like the kind of place where information came to die—a place of quiet urgency, not unlike the one Daniel had once lived in.

"You sure this is the best place?" Emily asked, looking around nervously. "I thought we were trying to stay off the radar."

"We are," Daniel replied, his voice tight. "But we need answers. And I know who can give us some."

The man who had opened the door nodded, motioning them inside. "Sit," he said, his voice gruff. "You're going to need all your wits about you for what's coming."

They sat at the table, the man joining them after a moment. He looked at Emily, his expression unreadable, before turning his attention to Daniel.

"Talk," he said.

Daniel pulled out the folder he had been holding and laid it on the table. "We've been digging through everything we could find. Documents from Raphael's men, intercepted messages, everything. There's something bigger going on here, something that Raphael isn't even aware of."

The man's gaze flickered over the papers, his eyes narrowing as he scanned the contents. "Bigger than Raphael?" he murmured. "You've got to be kidding me."

"I'm not," Daniel said, his voice steady. "Whoever is pulling Raphael's strings is playing a game on a much larger scale. This isn't just about family money or power—it's about control. Control of everything."

The man leaned back in his chair, the weight of Daniel's words settling in the air between them. "You're telling me there's an organization out there that wants control of everything?"

Daniel nodded, his fingers brushing the edge of the folder. "That's exactly what I'm saying. And the key to all of it…" He reached into his pocket, pulling out the tarnished coin. It glinted in the dim light, its worn surface now a symbol of everything they were fighting for—and against.

The man's eyes widened slightly, and he leaned forward. "Where did you get that?"

Daniel didn't answer immediately. Instead, he let the silence stretch, letting the weight of the question sink in. "From someone who tried to bury it. Someone who wants everything gone—every connection severed, every piece of evidence erased."

Emily glanced at Daniel, sensing the shift in the air. This wasn't just about the coin. It wasn't even about the family anymore. It was about something much darker. And they were closer to uncovering it than they realized.

The man looked at the coin with something akin to awe. "So this is the key? This is what it's all about?"

Daniel nodded again. "Yes. This coin unlocks everything. But it's not just about a vault. It's about revealing the truth."

Emily leaned in, her curiosity piqued. "The truth about what?"

Daniel hesitated, as if weighing how much to reveal. "The truth about the people who've been controlling everything behind the scenes. The ones who have been pulling Raphael's strings and using him to further their own agenda."

"And what happens when you expose them?" the man asked, his voice steady but with a hint of fear buried beneath the surface.

Daniel's expression hardened. "They'll do everything they can to stop us."

The room was silent for a moment, the gravity of his words hanging in the air. Emily's mind raced, trying to connect the dots, trying to make sense of the fragmented pieces that had been handed to her. But it was like trying to put together a puzzle where half the pieces were missing.

"You have a plan, right?" the man asked, breaking the silence. "Because if you're expecting me to just sit back and let you take on an entire organization, I need to know what you're thinking."

Daniel looked at him, his gaze steady. "I've been planning this for a long time," he said quietly. "But now, we need to move fast. The longer we wait, the more time they have to cover their tracks."

The man nodded slowly. "Then what's next?"

"We need to find the missing piece," Daniel said. "The one that ties everything together. The person who's been orchestrating all of this."

For the first time, Emily felt a ripple of doubt slip into her thoughts. "And how do we do that? How do we even know who they are?"

Daniel met her gaze, his expression serious but resolute. "We start by using the coin. It's not just a symbol of power—it's a map."

She blinked, confusion clouding her mind. "A map?"

"It's all connected," Daniel said, his voice growing quieter. "This coin—it's been passed down for generations. Every keyholder knew their role in this, but they kept it hidden. If we trace the origins of the coin, we'll find the person who's been pulling the strings all along."

Emily looked down at the coin again, the weight of it suddenly feeling more oppressive than ever. She felt as though she were standing at the edge of a cliff, the drop too steep to see the bottom, but with no other choice but to jump.

But as much as she feared what lay ahead, she knew one thing: there was no going back now.

Twelve

The Threat Within

The room was silent, save for the occasional hiss of static from the old radio on the desk. The city outside seemed to throb in rhythm with the pulse of the night, distant sirens and the occasional honk of a car breaking through the otherwise still air. Inside, the dim glow from a single overhead bulb cast shadows that danced on the walls, making the small space feel even more claustrophobic than it already was.

Daniel stood by the window, peering out into the dark streets below. His face was a mask of concentration, but underneath the composed exterior, his mind was racing. The documents they had uncovered earlier—maps, old correspondence, and a list of names—had only brought more questions than answers. He felt the weight of the situation pressing on him more than ever. The more they discovered, the more tangled the web seemed to become.

Emily sat at the desk, flipping through the file Elias had given them. The pages were filled with scrawled notes and highlighted sections, but her eyes kept drifting back to the same spot—the name that had stood out like a flashing neon sign. The name that made her pulse race every time she read it.

Raphael Laurent.

It had started with the coin, the mysterious key to something far larger than either of them had anticipated. But now, it wasn't just about Raphael and his family's fortune. It wasn't even about the strange organization that seemed to be pulling the strings behind the scenes. No, it had become clear: there was a betrayal, a betrayal from within. And it was a betrayal they hadn't seen coming.

"What's the next move?" Emily asked, her voice breaking the silence. Her fingers paused over the file as she glanced up at Daniel.

He didn't respond immediately. His eyes were still on the street, scanning for movement, for anything that seemed out of place. There was something in the air tonight—something heavy, like the calm before a storm.

"The next move..." Daniel muttered, his voice low, almost as if he were speaking to himself. "We need to find the source of the leak. There's a mole in the operation—someone who's been feeding information to Raphael and his people. And I think we know who it is."

Emily felt her breath catch in her throat. The realization had come to her, too, though she hadn't dared voice it until now. "You're not saying…" she began, her voice trailing off.

He turned sharply, his gaze meeting hers with an intensity that sent a shiver down her spine. "I'm saying exactly what you think I'm saying. Someone from within—someone close to me—has been working against us. And if we don't act fast, they'll bring everything crashing down."

Her heart hammered in her chest. She didn't need to ask who he meant. She already knew. She could see it now, the way he was talking, the way his eyes were haunted by the weight of it all. It was someone he trusted. Someone who had been by his side for years, someone he had thought was loyal. But loyalty had become a rare commodity in this world.

"Who?" she asked, her voice barely a whisper.

Daniel hesitated, his jaw clenching. "Elias."

The name hit her like a punch to the gut. Elias. The man who had helped them, the man who had given them the information they needed to move forward. He had been their ally. Or so she had thought. But now, everything was different. The pieces of the puzzle had fallen into place, and the image that emerged was one of betrayal—a betrayal that cut deeper than anything she had anticipated.

"You're sure?" Emily asked, her mind struggling to grasp the full scope of what Daniel was saying. "Elias? How can you be sure?"

Daniel's face darkened, his fists clenching at his sides. "I've been watching him. I've been watching everyone. And there's too much at stake for this to be a coincidence. Every time we make progress, every time we uncover something important, it's like he's one step ahead. He's been leaking information to Raphael's people. I don't know how, but I can feel it. And now, I have no choice but to confront him."

Emily swallowed hard, trying to steady her breathing. She had always known the risks, but this... this felt different. Elias had been a constant in their journey, a steady presence in the chaos. To think that he had been working against them all this time—feeding Raphael and his people the very information they had been working to uncover—it was a bitter pill to swallow.

But she couldn't ignore what Daniel was saying. The pieces were starting to fit together, no matter how much she wanted to deny it.

"Are we going to confront him?" Emily asked, her voice steady despite the storm raging inside her.

Daniel nodded. "We have no choice. We need to know how deep this goes. We need to find out who else is involved and how they're planning to use the information they've been getting."

Emily felt a cold sense of dread settle over her. She wasn't sure she was ready for what was coming next. But she couldn't back down. Not now. She had already chosen her side, and there was no turning back. Not when lives were on the line.

"We'll need proof," Emily said, her mind working through the next steps. "If we're going to confront him, we need evidence. We can't just go in and accuse him without anything solid to back it up."

"I know," Daniel replied. "And that's why we're going to pay him a visit."

—-

The night was thick with tension as Daniel and Emily made their way through the city's labyrinthine streets. The shadows seemed to stretch longer than usual, the faint glow of streetlights casting distorted shapes on the wet pavement. Every corner they turned, every alley they passed, seemed to lead them deeper into a trap they couldn't see.

When they arrived at Elias's hideout—a small, inconspicuous apartment above a closed bookstore—Daniel didn't hesitate. He knocked three times, just like Elias had done before. The sound echoed in the quiet, but this time it wasn't a welcoming gesture. It was a call to confrontation.

There was no answer.

Daniel knocked again, this time more forcefully. The tension in the air was palpable. Emily stood just behind him, her hand resting lightly on the edge of her bag. She knew what they were walking into, but there was no turning back now. They had to face the truth, no matter how much it hurt.

Finally, the door creaked open, but it wasn't Elias who greeted them. It was a woman—a stranger with a hard expression and eyes that immediately put Emily on edge.

"Can I help you?" the woman asked, her voice flat and professional.

Daniel didn't hesitate. "Where's Elias?" he asked, his tone demanding.

The woman's gaze flickered briefly to Emily before returning to Daniel. "He's not here."

Daniel's jaw tightened. "We know he's here. We need to speak with him. Now."

The woman didn't move. Her stance was firm, unwavering. "He's not available," she repeated, her voice growing colder. "And I suggest you leave."

Before Emily could react, Daniel stepped forward, his eyes narrowing. "You don't understand," he said, his voice low but filled with a dangerous calm. "I don't think you're in a position to give me orders."

A tense silence followed, thick with unspoken threats. Then, without warning, the woman stepped aside, opening the door fully. "Come in," she said, her tone now laced with something that almost sounded like a warning.

Daniel didn't flinch. He stepped past her, moving into the apartment with Emily at his heels. The moment they crossed the threshold, the door slammed shut behind them, and the air seemed to grow colder.

The apartment was sparse, with little in the way of decoration or warmth. A few chairs, a small table, and a stack of papers were scattered about, but nothing seemed to suggest this was Elias's home. The woman led them to a back room, where the faint glow of a single lamp illuminated a desk piled high with paperwork.

Elias's absence was palpable, but it didn't make the situation any less real. If he wasn't here, it meant he was already one step ahead—just like Daniel had feared.

"Where is he?" Daniel asked again, his voice hard.

The woman's lips curled into a faint smile. "He's not coming back. You've been played, Daniel. The game is over."

At those words, Emily's stomach dropped. The threat was clear now. They weren't just dealing with a betrayal.

They were dealing with something far more dangerous—something that had been right under their noses all along.

Suddenly, the room seemed much too small. The walls closed in as the woman reached for something on the desk, her hand brushing against a small envelope. She slid it toward Daniel, her eyes never leaving his.

"Take it," she said, her voice icy. "And leave."

Daniel hesitated for a moment, then grabbed the envelope, tearing it open. Inside was a single photograph. It was black and white, grainy but unmistakable. It was a picture of him—of Daniel—standing next to Elias. But it wasn't just any photo. There were other figures in the background, shadows that Daniel couldn't quite make out.

And in the foreground, there was a face he knew all too well.

Raphael Laurent.

Daniel's hand shook as he looked at the photo. The pieces were finally falling into place, and the realization hit him like a tidal wave.

The threat within wasn't just Elias. It was much closer. It was someone he had trusted, someone who had been pulling the strings from the start.

This was far from over.

Thirteen

A Bond of Trust

The silence in the small, dimly lit room was deafening. The photograph Daniel had found in the envelope seemed to burn a hole in his hand, its edges curling slightly as he stared at it. Raphael's face—clear, unmistakable—looked back at him from the photograph, a grim reminder of how deeply his brother's reach extended, how tangled the web of betrayal truly was.

Emily stood beside him, her breath shallow, as her eyes flicked between the photograph and Daniel's clenched fist. There was no mistaking the shock on her face, but she said nothing. She didn't need to. The weight of the moment, the realization that someone they trusted had been working against them all along, hung between them like a thick fog.

"Daniel…" Emily's voice was barely above a whisper. She

reached out to touch his arm, but stopped, as though afraid he might flinch away.

Daniel didn't flinch. His muscles were tense, his body locked in place, but he didn't withdraw. His jaw tightened, his gaze still fixed on the photograph in his hand. "This… this is it," he murmured. "This is the proof I needed."

Emily stood still, trying to read him. It wasn't just about the photograph. It wasn't just about Elias anymore. It was about the final, crushing realization that his brother—Raphael, the man Daniel had once called family—was the puppet master behind the entire operation. This was personal. This was deeper than anything they had prepared for.

"How do we stop this?" Emily asked, her voice laced with urgency. She wasn't asking just for herself anymore. She was asking for him—asking for them both. The stakes had risen higher than either of them could have imagined, and in that moment, everything else felt irrelevant. Their survival, their future—those were the things that mattered now.

Daniel exhaled slowly, lifting his gaze from the photograph. His eyes, darkened with frustration, met hers. "We go after Raphael. We don't have a choice anymore."

"Daniel, are you sure? This is your brother, your family," Emily said, the words leaving her lips with a sense of disbelief, even as she knew the truth. "This is beyond just a family feud. You know that, right?"

He nodded, his eyes never leaving hers. "I know. I know better than anyone. But what Raphael is doing—what he's willing to sacrifice for power, for control—it's not just about family anymore. It's about everything."

"Everything?" Emily echoed. She couldn't quite grasp the magnitude of what he was saying, but she could see the fire in his eyes—the same fire that had been present when he first told her about the key, the coin, the secrets that had shaped his life. "What are you saying?"

He paused, his hand tightening around the photograph before he set it down on the desk between them. "I'm saying that Raphael has set things in motion. This isn't just about power within the family—it's about controlling everything. The city. The economy. The networks of influence. He's already too deep in the game. And the people backing him—" He stopped himself, shaking his head, as if to rid himself of the words. "If we don't stop him now, if we don't take him down before he gets what he's after, everything will be lost. And I'm not willing to let that happen."

Emily's heart pounded in her chest as she absorbed the weight of his words. He wasn't just talking about revenge anymore. He wasn't even talking about his brother. He was talking about the fate of everything—the city, the lives of people who had no idea they were being manipulated, dragged into a fight they didn't even know existed.

And somehow, she had become a part of it.

She swallowed hard, her mind racing. She had known from the moment she met Daniel that this wasn't going to be easy. But she hadn't expected the truth to hurt this much. She hadn't expected the man standing before her—this man who had opened up, let her in, trusted her—to be carrying the weight of an empire on his shoulders.

But as much as it frightened her, something else stirred within her—a quiet resolve. She had never been one to sit idly by, to let someone else make all the decisions. She had seen too much to simply walk away now. And if Daniel was going to face this, if he was going to take the fight to Raphael, then she would be with him every step of the way.

"I'm with you," Emily said quietly, her voice steady as she met his gaze. "Whatever it takes. We do this together."

For a moment, Daniel didn't speak. He just looked at her, his expression unreadable. But then, the briefest flicker of something crossed his face—something almost like relief. He nodded, though the weight of the situation still hung heavily between them.

"Together," he echoed.

There was a long pause as the two of them stood there, processing what had been said. The air around them seemed to grow heavier, as though the very walls of the room were closing in with the gravity of their decision. But this was it. This was the turning point. There was no turning back now.

A Bond of Trust

Daniel's hand moved to the desk, and he grabbed the map Elias had provided them. The lines were still fresh in his mind, the locations marked with precision, the roads and connections laid out like a roadmap to destruction. He traced a finger along the lines, his gaze hardening as he considered the next move.

"We need to find Raphael's headquarters," Daniel said, his voice calm but resolute. "That's where this ends."

"Where is it?" Emily asked, stepping closer, peering over his shoulder.

Daniel traced the map once more, his finger coming to a stop at a spot near the edge of the city. "Here. The old industrial complex by the docks. It's been abandoned for years, but I know the place. I've been there before."

Emily's mind raced as she processed the information. "How do you know it's where Raphael is hiding?"

Daniel didn't look up. "Because that's where he would be. It's remote enough to be hidden but close enough to keep an eye on the city. It's the perfect location for someone like him—someone who wants control but can't afford to be seen."

Emily nodded, absorbing the cold logic in Daniel's words. She could see the determination in his eyes, but there was something else there too. Something dark. The pain of what he was about to do.

"Then we go," Emily said, her voice steady. She was still trying to wrap her mind around it all, but she couldn't afford to question him now. They were running out of time, and they needed to act fast.

Daniel looked at her, his eyes softening for just a moment. "Are you sure? You don't have to—"

She cut him off. "Yes, I'm sure. I've been sure ever since I found that coin, Daniel. I'm not running away from this. We do this together. No more running."

A flicker of something—gratitude, or maybe a hint of admiration—passed across Daniel's face, and he nodded. "Alright. We'll need to move quickly. It won't be easy."

"I don't care how hard it is," Emily replied, her voice unwavering. "We finish this."

Daniel gave her a look that said more than words ever could. In that moment, she understood. She understood that, in spite of everything, in spite of the betrayal, the lies, the danger—they were in this together. And that bond of trust, fragile as it was, had the power to turn the tide in their favor.

They spent the next hour preparing—gathering supplies, checking their weapons, and planning the route. Daniel was meticulous, making sure every detail was accounted for. Emily followed his lead, her mind focused on the task at hand. There was no room for hesitation, no room for second-guessing. They had made their choice, and now there was nothing left but to see it through.

As they left the apartment, the weight of the decision settled over them both, but there was a flicker of something else now—a quiet sense of unity, of shared purpose. They moved through the streets with a new determination, side by side, ready to face whatever came next.

They were no longer just two people caught in a game they didn't understand. They were allies, partners—bound together by something far stronger than fear.

And together, they would take down the threat within.

Fourteen

Hidden Intentions

The night was thick with the tension of what was to come. The city felt alive under the cloak of darkness, each street corner brimming with secrets, each shadow holding its breath. Emily's heart raced in time with her footsteps as she followed Daniel through the narrow, rain-slicked alleyways leading to the old industrial complex near the docks. The path was winding, the surroundings eerily quiet, as though the world around them was holding its breath. There was no turning back now.

Daniel's pace remained steady, his jaw clenched tight in concentration, his eyes flickering between the path ahead and the occasional glance over his shoulder. The further they ventured into the heart of the city's forgotten district, the more the air seemed to thicken, charged with an undeniable sense of foreboding. Every corner they turned seemed to lead them deeper into a place where the past, present, and future all blended into something that felt as unstable as the ground beneath their feet.

Emily stayed close, her eyes darting around, every whisper of wind, every creak of the dilapidated buildings, making her jump. It felt like they were being watched, and she couldn't shake the unsettling feeling that danger was creeping ever closer. She had to admit it—the deeper they got into this mess, the more her initial resolve began to fray at the edges. There were moments when she wasn't sure how much more of this she could take. But then, Daniel's sharp gaze would meet hers, steady, determined, and she would remember why she was here.

The file they had found earlier had been more than a key—it was a map of hidden intentions, a blueprint to something larger and more dangerous than they could have imagined. Every document, every note, every piece of evidence had pointed them here, to this place—a place where truths were buried deep beneath layers of lies and deception. And now they were about to unearth something that could destroy everything.

"Are you ready for this?" Daniel's voice broke the silence, low and controlled, but there was a quiet edge to it, something that told her that even he was nervous.

Emily nodded, her voice tight with apprehension. "I'm ready."

Daniel led the way to a rusted, steel door at the back of the complex. It was nondescript, weathered with time, and hidden from view by a tangled mess of ivy and overgrown weeds. No one had passed through this entrance in years, and that was exactly why they had chosen it. A safe passage through the chaos, a way into the heart of the beast without anyone noticing.

He paused in front of the door, testing the lock. A flick of his wrist, and the door creaked open, the sound loud in the otherwise silent night. They slipped inside, into the darkness of the building, and Daniel immediately moved toward a set of stairs leading up into the unknown.

Emily followed, her footsteps hesitant, but resolute. They ascended in silence, their movements muffled by the thickness of the air and the weight of what lay ahead. The door at the top of the stairs was slightly ajar, and a faint light seeped through the crack, casting long shadows across the walls. Daniel's hand brushed against the door, and he paused, his breath shallow as he listened.

Footsteps echoed from within.

Daniel motioned for Emily to stay back, his body tense with readiness. He moved forward silently, his steps barely audible. He nudged the door open just enough to peer through the gap, his eyes narrowing as he scanned the dimly lit room. What he saw inside made his blood run cold.

Raphael.

The sight of his brother in the dim light, sitting at a desk, surrounded by files and papers, made Daniel's fists clench at his sides. Raphael was speaking to someone, his voice low, smooth, and devoid of warmth.

"We can't move too soon. If Daniel gets his hands on the coin, everything will be lost," Raphael said, his tone laced with venom. "We need to make sure he stays in the dark about what we're really after."

Emily felt a shiver race up her spine at the sound of Raphael's voice. She had only heard about him in passing, but to hear the coldness in his words now—there was no mistaking it. This was a man who was willing to destroy anything and anyone to achieve his goals.

Daniel's face hardened, the recognition settling deep in his gut. He hadn't been prepared to confront his brother like this, not now, not when the stakes were so high. But the truth was clear: Raphael wasn't just after the family's fortune. He wasn't even after the control of the city. He had his eyes set on something much darker, something far more dangerous.

Daniel's mind raced. He had always known Raphael had ambitions, had always suspected his brother's darker desires. But this—this was something else entirely. His brother wasn't just pulling strings. He was orchestrating an empire of shadows, one where every move was calculated, every player a pawn.

Daniel took a deep breath, his mind snapping back to the present. They couldn't stay hidden here. They couldn't afford to wait any longer.

"We need to get closer," Daniel whispered to Emily. She gave a quick nod, her face set in determination. They had come too far to stop now.

They slipped further into the building, inching closer to the room where Raphael was speaking, listening intently to the conversation that would change everything.

Raphael's voice came again, sharp, like a whip cutting through the air. "We need to find the coin before Daniel figures out what it truly unlocks. The vault—everything—depends on it. You're telling me that my brother's been running around the city like an idiot, and we're letting him get away with it?"

"Relax, Raphael," a deep voice responded. "He's being watched. He won't get far. But we have to make sure he doesn't find out who's really in charge."

The mention of "who's really in charge" made Daniel's blood run cold. They weren't talking about Raphael anymore. They were talking about the people pulling his strings—the true masterminds behind the scenes.

Daniel's grip on the railing tightened as the weight of the situation settled over him. He had suspected there were others involved, but now it was confirmed. And from the way Raphael spoke, he wasn't just working with a few underlings. He was working with an entire network—an underground empire built on secrecy, power, and manipulation.

"Where do we stand on the operation?" Raphael's voice again, this time edged with impatience.

"It's moving forward," the deep voice responded. "The pieces are in place. We just need to make sure Daniel stays out of the picture. If we move too soon, we risk blowing it."

The conversation felt like it was dragging Daniel deeper into a web, and the more he heard, the more the urgency to stop it all became crystal clear. He had to stop Raphael, had to stop the people behind him, before it was too late.

"Emily, listen carefully," Daniel said, his voice tight with resolve. "We need to get the information we came for. We can't leave here empty-handed. I don't care what it takes—just make sure we get what we need."

Emily nodded, her gaze steely. "I'm with you. Whatever happens next, we do it together."

They moved swiftly, with purpose, their bodies blending into the shadows as they crept closer to the room. They had one chance—one chance to find the truth before it was buried forever.

And as they inched toward the door, Daniel's mind raced

with a new determination. This wasn't just about finding the key to the vault. It was about stopping Raphael, stopping the empire of shadows from swallowing everything whole. There was a threat within, and they were about to face it head-on.

They were getting closer to the truth. But with every step, the danger only grew.

Fifteen

Clashing Worlds

The underground room was colder than it should have been, the air thick with the scent of damp concrete and rust. The dim light from a single bulb flickered overhead, casting long, jagged shadows on the cracked walls. Daniel stood motionless at the threshold, his back pressed against the door, his hand on the handle. He could hear the faint murmur of voices coming from the far side of the room, the only sign that anyone was inside.

His muscles were coiled tight, every fiber of his being ready to spring into action at a moment's notice. He didn't need to look at Emily to know that she was right behind him, the silence between them thick with shared tension. He had grown used to the idea that danger was always just one step away, but tonight felt different. They weren't just walking into a confrontation—they were walking into the heart of the storm itself.

This was Raphael's domain. This was where everything would culminate—the final battle for control. And as much as Daniel wanted to turn back, as much as he wanted to walk away from this family, from the blood that bound him to this nightmare, he knew that he couldn't. They had crossed a line. There was no turning back now.

"Are you ready?" Emily whispered, her voice barely audible.

He exhaled, the weight of her question settling into his chest. "As ready as I'll ever be."

They both knew the stakes. What they were about to face was beyond anything they had imagined, a war that had been waged in the shadows for years. Raphael's empire was built on lies and manipulation, a structure so carefully crafted that no one had been able to see its true form until now. But Daniel had seen it. He had seen the cracks. He had seen the truth beneath the surface.

And he wasn't about to let it destroy everything.

He opened the door with a soft creak, stepping into the room with Emily close behind. The air inside was warmer, filled with the heavy scent of cigar smoke and the buzz of low conversation. The room was large, with a long table in the center surrounded by leather chairs. In the corner, a bar was stocked with expensive bottles of liquor, and a few members of Raphael's inner circle were gathered around it, talking in hushed tones.

At the far end of the room, Raphael sat behind a massive oak desk, his silhouette illuminated by the dim light of a lamp. His back was to them, his posture relaxed, but Daniel knew that the moment he stepped into this room, every muscle in Raphael's body would tense. The man had always been quick to react, and this time, he would be no different.

Daniel stepped forward, his movements slow, deliberate. He could feel Emily's presence at his side, her footsteps matching his, her breath steady, though he could sense the nervous energy radiating from her.

Raphael's voice cut through the air like a blade. "I was wondering when you'd show up, Daniel."

Daniel's gaze never wavered. "You should have known it wouldn't be long before I came for you."

Raphael turned slowly in his chair, a smirk playing at the edges of his lips. "I expected as much. You've always been predictable." He gestured to the chairs around the table. "Sit down. We have much to discuss."

Daniel stood his ground, not moving an inch. "I'm not here to talk, Raphael. I'm here to end this."

Raphael's eyes gleamed with amusement. "End it? Daniel, you've been trying to end this for years. You think you're the hero in some grand story, that you can fix everything by confronting me. But you're wrong." He stood, his movements fluid, the confidence in his posture like a wave crashing over the room. "You've never understood the game, Daniel. You never understood what it takes to be in charge."

Daniel's jaw tightened, his hand instinctively resting on the hilt of his knife. "I understand more than you think. I understand that you've been using everyone around you, manipulating them, including me. And I'm done being your pawn."

Raphael laughed, a low, sinister sound that echoed off the walls. "You think you've been a pawn? You were never a pawn, Daniel. You were always the king, the one I chose to keep in the dark. And now, here you are, trying to play the role of the hero. But it's too late for you. Too late for all of you."

Daniel's eyes flicked to the table, where the photograph he had found earlier lay. He had studied it repeatedly, his mind piecing together the fragments of a puzzle that had seemed impossible to solve. But now, with Raphael standing before him, his words barely registering, it became clear. The photograph was more than just a piece of evidence. It was a statement. Raphael had always known. He had always been in control.

"I'm not the one who's lost, Raphael," Daniel said, his voice cold and steady. "You are. You've been lying to everyone, to yourself. And now, it's all coming down."

Raphael's smirk faltered, a flicker of something darker passing through his eyes. "You're wrong, Daniel. I've built this empire, this kingdom, from the ground up. Every decision, every sacrifice—it's all been for this moment. You think you're the one who can stop me?" He took a step forward, his voice dropping to a dangerous whisper. "You're nothing. You always have been."

Daniel didn't flinch. "Maybe I am. But I won't let you win."

There was a tense pause, the weight of Raphael's words hanging in the air like a suffocating fog. Emily's hand brushed against Daniel's, and for a brief moment, he felt the warmth of her presence, the unspoken bond between them. It gave him the strength to keep his ground.

Raphael's eyes flicked to Emily, narrowing with a mixture of curiosity and contempt. "So this is the woman who's been keeping you distracted, Daniel. The one who's dragged you into this mess." His gaze shifted to the men standing around the room, his voice now dripping with venom. "She's just another pawn in your little game."

Emily straightened, her eyes locking with Raphael's. "I'm no pawn, Raphael. And neither is Daniel. You've underestimated him, just like you've underestimated everything else."

Raphael's expression darkened, but before he could respond, one of the men in the corner spoke up. "We've got a problem." His voice was low, filled with urgency. "There's movement at the entrance. They're here."

The room erupted into chaos. Daniel's senses went on high alert as the air shifted, the realization sinking in. The game had changed. They were no longer just dealing with Raphael. They were dealing with an army—a network of people who had been waiting for this moment, ready to strike. And now that moment had come.

Daniel turned to Emily, his eyes hardening. "We need to get out of here. Now."

Before she could respond, the door to the room burst open, and a wave of armed men poured in, their weapons raised, their faces grim. The sound of footsteps echoed throughout the room, and in the distance, Daniel could hear the faint wail of sirens approaching. The entire building was about to explode into a full-scale conflict, and they were right in the middle of it.

Raphael's smirk returned, this time darker, more satisfied. "I told you, Daniel. You can't fight this. You can't fight me."

But Daniel didn't listen. His mind was already working, calculating their next move. He grabbed Emily's arm and yanked her toward the back exit. "Come on!"

They sprinted through the hallway, the sound of footsteps and shouting growing louder behind them. Daniel didn't dare look back, didn't dare slow down. He knew that if they hesitated for even a second, they wouldn't make it out alive.

Clashing Worlds

As they reached the back door, Daniel threw it open, the cold night air rushing in to greet them. They ran into the alley, the distant sound of gunfire ringing in their ears. The fight was no longer about saving themselves. It was about survival—about getting to the truth before it was too late.

But even as they ran, even as the chaos exploded around them, Daniel couldn't shake the feeling that something deeper was at play. They had come here looking for answers, but now, they were running from a storm they hadn't fully understood. And as they disappeared into the night, Daniel knew that the real fight was just beginning.

They had clashed with Raphael, with the world he had built. But now, they were facing something far more dangerous—something that would test everything they had.

And they would have to face it together.

Sixteen

A Mysterious Encounter

The night was suffocating, thick with the weight of unspoken words and silent dread. Daniel's lungs burned with each step, his breath shallow as he and Emily raced through the maze of alleyways. The sharp click of their footsteps echoed off the cracked pavement, but it felt as though the sound was swallowed by the night. There were no sirens now, no pursuit that Daniel could hear—but he knew better than to trust the quiet. His instincts told him the danger wasn't over. It had only just begun.

They turned another corner, the familiar scent of old brick and damp air filling their lungs. The city had never seemed this desolate before, the towering buildings closing in on them like dark sentinels. Daniel felt the eyes of the world pressing against his back, the knowledge that they were running not just from Raphael, but from the secrets that had been uncovered, from the people behind it all who still lurked in the shadows.

"This way," Daniel said, his voice low but urgent. He grabbed Emily's arm and steered her toward a narrow door tucked away between two faded shops. It was a hidden entrance, one that led to an old, abandoned building—one of the few places in the city where they might be safe, at least for a while.

Emily stumbled slightly, her exhaustion evident in the quick, shallow breaths she took. They had been running for what felt like hours, adrenaline keeping them alive, but her body was betraying her. She was scared, tired, and on edge, but she refused to show it. She kept her eyes focused ahead, her mind working through the possibilities, the danger, the next steps.

"What's the plan, Daniel?" she asked, her voice strained, but trying to maintain its usual firmness. "Where do we go from here?"

Daniel didn't answer immediately, his gaze scanning the street behind them one last time before pushing open the door. The hinges creaked loudly, cutting through the stillness, but he didn't pause. Once they were inside, he closed it softly behind them, blocking out the world outside.

Inside, the building was dark and stale. Dust hung in the air, and the smell of mold and decay clung to the walls. But Daniel knew this place. He had been here before—many years ago, before everything had gone wrong, before the world had fallen apart around him. The place was safe. At least, for now.

He led Emily down a set of narrow stairs that creaked beneath their weight. The dim light from a small bulb at the bottom illuminated the narrow hallway. It was silent except for their footsteps, the sound muffled by the thick air. Daniel's pulse was still racing, and his hand rested on the hilt of the knife tucked into his jacket, his fingers itching for any sign of danger.

At the end of the hallway, a door was slightly ajar, and beyond it, the faint glow of a candle flickered in the otherwise dark room. Daniel stepped inside, motioning for Emily to follow. As soon as she crossed the threshold, the door slammed shut behind them, and the room seemed to breathe a little easier.

Inside, the room was sparse, the walls lined with shelves filled with old books and artifacts. A heavy desk sat at the far corner, and a few chairs were scattered around the room. But it wasn't the room itself that caught Emily's attention. It was the man standing in the middle of it.

He was tall, with sharp features and an unsettling calmness to his demeanor. His eyes were hidden beneath the brim of his hat, but there was something in the way he carried himself that made Emily feel both intrigued and unnerved. His posture was perfect, like a predator waiting for his prey to make a move. And in that moment, Emily couldn't shake the feeling that they had just walked into a trap.

Daniel stiffened, his hand tightening around the knife. "You."

The man smiled, a slow, deliberate movement that didn't reach his eyes. "I was wondering when you'd show up, Daniel."

Emily glanced at Daniel, confusion flickering in her gaze. She had never seen this man before, but there was something unsettlingly familiar about him. She felt as though she had stepped into a scene she didn't quite understand, one that had been written long before she had even arrived.

"Who are you?" she asked, her voice sharp, demanding. She wasn't sure who this man was or why Daniel seemed so on edge, but she wasn't going to let him get the better of them.

The man didn't respond immediately. Instead, he glanced between them, taking in the tension that hung in the air. Finally, he spoke, his voice smooth and measured. "You both have questions. But the answers you seek aren't as simple as you think."

Daniel's hand dropped to his side, his fingers still flexing, his eyes fixed on the man with an intensity that made Emily uncomfortable. "I don't have time for riddles. What do you want?"

The man chuckled softly, the sound chilling. "What I want

isn't important. What you want is. You've been looking for answers. I can give you those answers—if you're willing to listen."

Emily's stomach twisted. She wasn't sure if she could trust this man, but she knew one thing for certain—he knew more than he was letting on. And if they were ever going to stop Raphael, they needed every piece of the puzzle.

"I'm listening," Daniel said, his voice cold, almost distant. "But make it quick."

The man nodded, stepping closer to the desk, his movements fluid. He lifted a single envelope from the pile of papers and tossed it toward them. It landed on the table with a soft thud, and for the first time, Emily noticed that his hands were bare. No rings, no gloves—just skin, smooth and devoid of any sign of the life he led.

The man's eyes flicked to Daniel. "You're looking for the key to unlock everything. What you don't realize is that the key is already in your possession."

Daniel's brows furrowed as he took the envelope, opening it with a deliberate motion. Inside, there was a single sheet of paper, its surface covered with symbols and letters that Emily didn't recognize.

"What is this?" she asked, her voice low, her mind racing as she tried to make sense of the strange writing.

A Mysterious Encounter

"It's a map," the man said. "Not a physical one, but a map to your answers. The symbols—" He paused, watching Daniel closely. "They're linked to the very source of power Raphael has been drawing from. The source that's been manipulating all of you."

Daniel's eyes widened slightly as he studied the paper. "This..." His voice trailed off, as if the enormity of what he was holding was only beginning to sink in.

The man's gaze softened. "This is what you need to stop him. Raphael's been using it for years—building his empire, pulling strings, controlling everything from the shadows. But he's not the only one who knows how to use it."

"Who else?" Emily asked, stepping closer to the table. "Who's behind all of this?"

The man didn't immediately respond. Instead, he reached into his coat pocket and withdrew a small, worn book. He placed it beside the envelope, sliding it over to Daniel. The cover was faded, the title in a language that looked ancient and unreadable.

"I can only give you part of the answer," the man said quietly. "The rest, you'll have to find for yourselves."

Daniel's fingers brushed the book, his brow furrowing as he glanced up at the man. "What's in this book?"

"It's a guide," the man replied. "A guide to everything you

need to know. It explains how to decode the symbols, how to break the chains that Raphael has been using to keep control. But it's not something you can read in a few minutes. It requires understanding, patience."

Emily felt a rush of frustration. She wanted answers now, not riddles, not half-answers. But she held her tongue, knowing that the man in front of them wasn't just another obstacle. He had knowledge they needed. Knowledge they could use to bring Raphael down once and for all.

The man took a step back, his posture straightening as he regarded them both with a mixture of respect and something darker—something that felt too much like pity. "There's one more thing you need to know," he said softly. "You're not just fighting Raphael anymore. You're fighting an entire system, an empire built on secrets, manipulation, and lies. The closer you get to the truth, the more dangerous it becomes. So be prepared. Trust no one. Not even each other."

His final words hung in the air like a warning, sharp and biting. And just as quickly as he had appeared, the man turned, moving toward the far corner of the room.

"Remember," he said, his voice fading as he walked away. "Trust is the greatest weapon you have—and the deadliest trap you can fall into."

With that, he disappeared into the shadows, leaving Daniel and Emily alone in the room, their minds racing with the weight of what had just been revealed.

Seventeen

Unveiled Suspicion

The night air felt unusually cold as Daniel and Emily stepped out of the abandoned building, the heavy door creaking shut behind them with a finality that echoed in the silent street. The city seemed almost alien under the cover of darkness, the hum of traffic distant, the world on pause. Every step they took felt deliberate, purposeful, but the heaviness in the air was palpable—something was shifting, and Daniel could feel it in his bones.

The man who had given them the cryptic map and the mysterious book—he hadn't revealed much. His words lingered in Daniel's mind like a fog, thickening the air around them, blurring the lines between truth and deception. Trust no one. Not even each other. The phrase kept ringing in his ears, louder with every passing second.

Emily walked beside him, her face drawn in thought, her hand subtly brushing against her side where the book rested. She hadn't said much since their encounter with the stranger, but he could feel the questions swirling within her, just as they were swirling in his mind. Who was he really? Why had he helped them? And what did he know that they didn't?

Daniel's grip tightened on the envelope they had left behind in the room, the strange symbols printed on the paper still burned into his memory. But the book was a different matter entirely. It was as if it contained the missing pieces of a puzzle they hadn't yet found, a guide to something much larger, much darker. But could they trust it? Could they trust the stranger who had handed it to them?

The alleyway they walked through was silent, save for the distant sound of tires on wet pavement. It was dark, but not completely. Streetlights flickered above, casting a soft, yellow glow that barely illuminated the path ahead. The sound of their footsteps echoed eerily as they neared the corner where the street opened up to a more populated area.

Daniel kept his eyes forward, his thoughts racing as he tried to sort through everything that had happened over the last few days. Elias, the mole who had betrayed them. Raphael, the brother he had once loved, now a figure of corruption and deceit. The mysterious stranger who had given them the map and the book. It was all beginning to fit together, but the pieces didn't make sense. There was something wrong—something that felt like a game, a deadly game, and he didn't know the rules.

Emily stopped walking, her gaze darting to the alley behind them. She was silent for a moment, then spoke, her voice quiet, but laced with an undercurrent of concern. "We're being followed."

Daniel's pulse quickened. He hadn't heard anything, but the way Emily stood, her eyes scanning the darkness, told him she had already sensed it. He immediately felt the familiar rush of adrenaline, his senses sharpening as he scanned the shadows. But he couldn't see anything, not yet. The alley remained eerily still, but he could feel the hairs on the back of his neck rise.

"Are you sure?" he asked, his voice low, controlled.

"I can feel it," Emily replied, her voice tight. "Someone's out there."

Daniel's fingers twitched, itching for the familiar grip of his knife. He took a slow breath, his instincts screaming at him to act. But he couldn't risk drawing attention. They needed to move, to get to safety. They couldn't afford to be cornered again, not after everything they had uncovered.

Without a word, he motioned for Emily to follow him, his hand subtly reaching for the back of his jacket to ensure the blade was still there. He didn't speak, didn't acknowledge the tension between them, but in that moment, they were united in the same sense of urgency. They were being hunted, and they knew it. But who were they running from? Raphael's men? Someone else?

They moved quickly through the alley, their steps synchronized as they neared the end of the path, where the streetlights were brighter and the sounds of the city hummed in the distance. Daniel glanced over his shoulder once more, his eyes narrowing as he thought he saw a flicker of movement behind them. But when he turned to look, the alley was empty again.

"Stay close," Daniel said softly, his voice sharp with caution.

Emily's gaze flickered to the left, and she grabbed his arm, her fingers tightening in warning. "There," she whispered, pointing toward the far corner.

A figure stood in the shadows, just beyond the reach of the streetlight's glow. Daniel's heart skipped a beat. The figure was tall, their features hidden beneath a hood, but they were unmistakably watching them. He could feel the weight of their gaze, even from a distance.

Before Daniel could react, the figure took a step forward, their silhouette moving with fluid precision. It wasn't a gesture of threat, not yet. But it was deliberate. They weren't running. They were waiting.

Emily stepped closer to Daniel, her breath shallow. "What do we do?"

Daniel's eyes stayed locked on the figure. The hairs on the back of his neck stood up as the tension between them seemed to stretch, pulling at the air with a force he could almost feel. His mind raced, trying to calculate the next move. There was no way to know who this person was, or what they wanted. But he knew one thing for sure—they weren't here by accident.

He stepped forward slowly, his voice steady as he spoke. "Who are you?"

The figure didn't answer immediately. Instead, they lifted their hand, pushing the hood back just enough for Daniel to see their face.

Daniel froze.

It wasn't the face he had expected. Not at all. The man standing before them wasn't a stranger. In fact, he was someone Daniel had never expected to see again. Not here. Not now.

"Elias?" Daniel's voice was barely a whisper, a mix of disbelief and anger that only intensified as the man before him stepped closer.

The world seemed to tilt on its axis as Daniel's heart raced. Elias, the man who had once been his ally, the man who had betrayed them all—he stood before him, as calm and composed as ever.

Elias's eyes flickered between Daniel and Emily before he spoke, his voice smooth, as though they hadn't just been on the run from Raphael's people. "I know you have questions," Elias said, his tone neutral. "And I know you're not happy to see me. But there's something you need to understand. Things aren't what you think they are."

Daniel's mind was spinning, his pulse pounding in his ears. "You betrayed us," he spat, his voice rising in anger. "You were supposed to be on our side. And now you're—what? Working for Raphael?"

Elias's face didn't change, but there was something in his eyes that made Daniel pause—a flicker of regret, perhaps. "It's not as simple as you think, Daniel. I didn't betray you. I didn't betray anyone. But I couldn't keep following your lead. You were blind to the bigger picture. You still are."

The words hung in the air like an accusation, heavy with unspoken meaning. Daniel felt a flash of confusion, followed by a growing sense of distrust. He wanted to lash out, to scream at Elias for everything he had done, but the calmness in Elias's voice stopped him. There was something different about him now, something that didn't sit right.

"Then why are you here?" Emily demanded, her voice sharp, her patience clearly running thin. "What do you want from us?"

Elias looked at her, his gaze shifting in a way that made her shiver. "I'm not here to hurt you. I'm here to help."

Daniel shook his head, his disbelief palpable. "Help? How? After everything you've done, you think we'll just believe that?"

"I don't expect you to believe me right now," Elias said, his voice surprisingly calm. "But you need to listen. What's coming… it's bigger than Raphael. It's bigger than all of us. And I'm here to make sure you don't end up being the ones who lose everything."

Daniel took a step forward, his gaze never leaving Elias's face. "You're playing a dangerous game, Elias. And I'm not going to trust you again. Not after everything that's happened."

Elias didn't flinch. "Maybe you shouldn't trust me. But you need to understand the truth, Daniel. Raphael doesn't control everything. There are forces at play you haven't even seen yet. And if you don't act soon, it will all be over."

For a moment, the tension between them was thick enough to slice with a knife. Daniel's mind raced as he tried to process Elias's words. But they didn't make sense. None of it made sense. And yet, something deep inside him couldn't shake the feeling that Elias wasn't lying—at least not completely.

"Why are you telling us this?" Emily asked, her voice low, but her eyes searching.

Elias looked at her, his expression unreadable. "Because I

can't let you make the same mistakes I did. This isn't just about power. It's about survival. And if you're going to beat Raphael, you need to see the whole picture. You need to understand who's really pulling the strings."

Daniel stood still, his mind a whirlwind of conflicting thoughts. He had always thought he understood the world he was fighting against, but Elias's words were shaking the foundations of everything he had believed.

As Elias turned to leave, he spoke one final time, his voice softer now, but still filled with that same weight. "Trust no one, Daniel. Not even me. But you'll know when the time comes."

With those words, he was gone, disappearing into the night like a shadow swallowed by darkness. And as Daniel and Emily stood there, alone once more, the unease that had settled in their hearts deepened. The game was far from over.

But now, more than ever, Daniel knew one thing for certain: the truth had only just begun to reveal itself.

Eighteen

The Hidden Vault

The air in the old warehouse felt dense, thick with dust and the stale scent of forgotten things. The silence seemed to stretch out, pressing in on Daniel and Emily as they moved cautiously through the cavernous space. Every footstep echoed, the only sound between them as they made their way toward the rear of the building, where the map they had discovered earlier pointed them. A map that would, according to the stranger's cryptic words, lead them to the hidden vault—a vault that contained the answers to everything they had been searching for. Answers to the game that Raphael had been playing all along.

Daniel's mind raced, the cold weight of the book and the strange symbols inside it still fresh in his memory. They had followed the clues, the twisting path that had taken them from one secret to the next, each discovery unveiling a deeper layer of deception. But they were here now, at the final destination—at the place where everything would either fall into place, or crumble entirely.

Emily's breath was shallow beside him, her every step measured, her eyes darting to every corner as though she could sense the danger lingering just out of sight. She had grown stronger throughout this journey, her fear masked by a quiet resolve that matched Daniel's own. He could feel the unspoken tension between them, the shared burden of what lay ahead. This was no longer just about survival—it was about understanding the truth, uncovering the long-hidden secrets that had shaped their world.

The warehouse was nothing more than a shell of its former self. The walls were battered and scarred, the windows shattered or covered by old, rotting boards. The floor was littered with debris, broken machinery, and forgotten relics of a time long past. It felt as though they had stepped into a forgotten corner of the world, a place where history had been erased, and only the present remained—a present filled with shadows and secrets.

"Are you sure this is the place?" Emily whispered, her voice barely audible in the heavy silence.

Daniel nodded, his gaze fixed on the far wall of the warehouse, where a series of steel doors were hidden behind a thick layer of grime. The map they had found had led them here—led them to this door, this hidden passageway, where they were supposed to find the vault. But as he stood there, staring at the cold metal, a sense of unease crept into his chest. He had expected this moment for so long, but now that it was here, he wasn't sure he was ready for whatever it would reveal.

"We're close," Daniel said quietly, his fingers brushing against the rough metal of the door. He looked over at Emily, meeting her gaze. "If we're right, the vault should be just behind this."

Emily's eyes searched his face for any sign of doubt. "What if we're wrong?" she asked softly.

Daniel hesitated, his grip tightening on the door as if he were trying to will it open with sheer force. "Then we'll deal with it. But we can't stop now. We've come too far."

She didn't argue, didn't question him further. Instead, she stood beside him, her posture tense, ready for whatever came next. They had both been to the edge of darkness, and there was no turning back now.

With a slow, deliberate motion, Daniel turned the handle and pushed the door open. The hinges groaned in protest, the sound sharp in the stillness. Inside, the space beyond was even darker, but Daniel could make out the faint outline of a staircase leading down. A chill ran down his spine as he stepped inside, the sense of something hidden—something ancient—pressing in around him. This wasn't just a vault. This was a place meant to be kept secret.

"Stay close," he murmured to Emily, his voice low but urgent. He wasn't sure what they would find down there, but every instinct in him told him it wouldn't be easy. He had no idea who else might be in the building—who else might be watching.

They descended the staircase together, the air growing colder with every step. It was as though they were leaving the world behind, stepping into a different dimension, one where time no longer mattered, and the past had been buried too deep to ever resurface.

At the bottom of the stairs, they reached another door, smaller than the first, but just as heavy. The metal was cold to the touch, and as Daniel reached for the handle, he felt a shift in the air, a subtle change that made the hairs on the back of his neck rise.

He hesitated for a moment, then turned the handle. The door swung open with a groan, revealing a small, dimly lit chamber. The walls were lined with shelves and cabinets, some empty, others filled with old documents and objects that had long since lost their purpose. The air was thick with the smell of old paper and forgotten memories, a place where secrets had been stored away, waiting to be unearthed.

In the center of the room stood a large, ornate chest—covered in dust, its surface etched with intricate designs that Daniel had never seen before. It was the vault. The hidden vault. And it was finally within reach.

"Do you see it?" Emily's voice was barely a whisper, her eyes wide with disbelief.

Daniel nodded, his pulse quickening. This was it. He moved toward the chest, his fingers brushing the edges of the carvings as he reached for the lock. His breath caught as the intricate patterns seemed to pulse with a life of their own, as if the chest itself were alive—waiting, breathing, anticipating what was to come.

He paused, his hand hovering over the lock. "The key," he said softly.

Emily stepped forward, the book they had taken from the man at the warehouse now clutched tightly in her hands. She opened it, her fingers moving across the pages with careful precision. Her eyes scanned the symbols, the ancient writing that seemed to match the patterns on the chest. For a moment, there was nothing but silence, the only sound the quiet flipping of pages.

Finally, Emily looked up, her gaze locked on the lock of the chest. "I think I've got it," she said. She stepped forward, positioning the book in her hands, and muttered something under her breath.

The chest seemed to respond, the lock clicking open with a soft, metallic sound. Daniel held his breath as the lid creaked upward, revealing the contents hidden within.

Inside, stacked carefully in rows, were old documents—files, papers, and photographs, all encased in dark, weathered leather. But it wasn't just the papers that drew Daniel's attention. At the bottom of the chest was a small, ornate box. It shimmered faintly in the dim light, its surface etched with intricate symbols that mirrored the designs on the chest.

Daniel's heart skipped a beat as he reached for the box, his fingers brushing against the cold metal. He could feel the weight of it—an object that held the final piece of the puzzle. He opened it slowly, his breath catching in his throat as he revealed what lay inside.

A ring.

But it wasn't just any ring. It was a signet ring, the seal of the Laurent family etched into the surface. The symbol—the hawk and the dagger—was unmistakable. This was the key. This was the object Raphael had been chasing, the one that held the power to unlock the future of their empire.

Daniel's mind raced as he held the ring in his hand. It wasn't just a family heirloom. It was a symbol of power, a symbol of control. And it was now in his possession.

But before he could examine it further, a sharp sound echoed from above. A creak in the floorboards. Then a voice.

"Well, well, what do we have here?"

Daniel froze, the ring still clutched in his hand, his heart racing as he turned toward the entrance. The voice was familiar—too familiar. His stomach dropped as he recognized the figure standing in the doorway.

Raphael.

The figure in the doorway stepped forward, his face lit by the dim light, his eyes gleaming with a mixture of amusement and disdain. "I should have known you'd be here, Daniel. I was wondering when you'd find it."

Daniel's breath caught in his chest as he slowly stood, the weight of the ring still heavy in his hand. This was it. The moment he had been dreading. The moment everything would come crashing down.

"Raphael," Daniel said quietly, his voice tight with anger. "It's over."

But Raphael only smiled, a cold, calculating smile that sent a shiver down Daniel's spine.

"No, Daniel," Raphael replied, his voice soft and dangerous. "It's just beginning."

And in that moment, Daniel realized the true depth of the game he had been caught in—the vault wasn't just a key to the past. It was the beginning of a new war. One where there would be no winners. Only survivors.

And he was about to find out just how far Raphael was willing to go.

Nineteen

The Rooftop Revelation

The world outside the small, dimly lit room felt distant—like a far-off dream. Every muscle in Daniel's body was taut with tension as he stood facing Raphael, the brother he had once loved, now a cold, calculating figure who seemed to revel in the power he wielded over their fractured world. The ring—the symbol of the Laurent family's legacy—still sat heavy in Daniel's palm, its cool weight a constant reminder of what had brought them to this moment.

Raphael's eyes glinted in the dim light, a smug smile curling at the corners of his mouth as he stepped closer, his gaze fixed on the ring in Daniel's hand. "You've always been so predictable, Daniel," Raphael said, his voice low and filled with an eerie calm. "You think this is over, but it's just beginning."

The Rooftop Revelation

Daniel's grip on the ring tightened. His mind raced, trying to process the enormity of what was unfolding before him. This wasn't just about family. It wasn't just about revenge. Raphael was playing a much larger game—one that involved far more than just them. The ring, the vault, the strange symbols—it was all part of a twisted scheme that stretched far beyond the boundaries of the Laurent family's wealth and power.

"I know what you're trying to do," Daniel said, his voice steady despite the storm of emotions swirling inside him. "But you won't win, Raphael. This—" He held the ring up, the glint of the family crest catching the light. "This is over."

Raphael's smile faded, and his eyes narrowed. "You don't get it, do you?" he said quietly. "You never have."

Daniel's pulse quickened. "I get it well enough. You've been playing us all—manipulating everyone around you to get what you want."

Raphael laughed, a hollow, humorless sound that seemed to echo in the room. "You still think you're in control, don't you, Daniel? You're so naive." He paused, his eyes flicking over to Emily, who stood motionless by the doorway, her eyes darting between the two brothers. "And now, you've brought her into this mess."

Emily stepped forward, her gaze hardening. "This isn't just about you anymore, Raphael. This is about stopping the chaos you've created. You've manipulated everyone—the family, the city, and now, you think you're going to control the rest of us too?"

Raphael's smirk returned, but there was something darker behind it now, a flicker of recognition that sent a chill down Daniel's spine. "You're both so misguided," he said softly, his voice filled with an edge of contempt. "You think stopping me will solve anything? The truth is far more complicated than that."

Daniel's throat tightened. "What are you talking about? What's the real plan?"

Raphael's gaze lingered on the ring before he stepped closer, his presence almost suffocating. "The world is changing, Daniel. It's been changing for a long time. And you've been too blinded by your own morals to see it. The vault—the ring—it's the key to a new order, a new world. One where power, control, and influence belong to those who understand what truly matters."

Daniel's heart hammered in his chest. "This isn't about some new order. It's about you holding onto power for yourself. You've been doing this for years, controlling people, destroying lives. But you won't get away with it."

Raphael tilted his head, as though considering his brother's words. "I'm not the one destroying lives, Daniel. You and Emily—you're just pawns in a much larger game." His eyes flicked to the far wall, and for a moment, Daniel thought he saw something like regret pass through his brother's features. But it was gone in an instant, replaced by the cold, calculating demeanor Daniel had come to despise.

Before Daniel could respond, a voice broke through the tense silence.

"Enough."

The voice was calm, but the authority it carried was unmistakable. Daniel's heart skipped a beat as a shadow moved from the far corner of the room. He turned quickly, his breath catching in his throat as the figure stepped into the dim light.

It was the man—the one who had given them the map, the strange book, and the cryptic warnings. His face was partially obscured by a hood, but the sharp glint in his eyes was unmistakable. Daniel felt a jolt of recognition mixed with suspicion. How had he found them? How had he known this moment would come?

"Who are you?" Daniel demanded, his voice rising in anger. "What do you want?"

The man smiled, but it wasn't a reassuring smile. It was the smile of someone who knew far more than he was letting on, someone who had been watching everything unfold from the shadows. "I'm the one who's been trying to help you, Daniel. And I've been trying to warn you all along." His gaze flicked to Raphael, a brief moment of understanding passing between them. "But it's too late for all of you."

Daniel's chest tightened. "What do you mean, 'too late'? What's going on? Who are you really?"

The man stepped further into the light, revealing his full figure. He was tall, with an air of authority about him that made Daniel's instincts scream. This wasn't just some rogue figure lurking in the shadows. He was something more, something dangerous. "You're both caught in a trap," the man said, his voice low and almost sympathetic. "You've been chasing the wrong answers all along."

"Trap?" Emily said, her voice rising. "What do you mean? Who are you to say we're chasing the wrong answers?"

The man's eyes softened, but there was a hardness to his gaze that was impossible to ignore. "Because, Emily," he said gently, "you're both chasing a truth that's been hidden from you. You've both been blinded by what you think you know."

Raphael crossed his arms, his eyes gleaming with something like amusement. "You should listen to him, Daniel. He's been playing his own game, and now he's trying to tell you it's too late. It's all part of the plan."

Daniel's head spun. He couldn't keep up with the flood of information. The pieces didn't fit. "What plan? What are you both talking about?"

The man smiled faintly, a dark humor playing at the edge of his lips. "The plan to change the world," he said softly.

The Rooftop Revelation

"The one that's already in motion. The one that Raphael has been too short-sighted to understand."

Daniel's breath caught. "What do you mean, 'change the world'?" His voice was hoarse now, a mix of disbelief and fear creeping into his chest. "This isn't about changing the world. It's about control. It's always been about control."

Raphael's smirk deepened. "Exactly. Control is everything, Daniel. You've always been too weak to see that."

The man stepped forward again, his voice cutting through the tension. "That's where you're both wrong. You're still playing by the rules they want you to follow. The truth, the real truth, has always been out of reach for both of you."

Daniel's pulse thundered in his ears. "Who are you working for?" he demanded, his grip on the ring tightening.

The man didn't answer immediately. Instead, he looked at Raphael, a flicker of something passing between them. Then, slowly, he turned back to Daniel and Emily, his voice low and controlled. "It doesn't matter who I'm working for. What matters is that you understand what's happening, what's already in motion."

"Enough with the games!" Emily snapped. "Tell us what's really going on!"

The man exhaled, his expression unreadable. "What's happening is that everything you know—the power, the families, the control—it's all going to be torn down. The vault, the ring, the coin—it's all part of the same plan. And you're both caught in the middle of it."

Daniel's mind reeled. It was like he was standing on the edge of a precipice, looking down into a void that stretched out for eternity. Everything he had believed, everything he had fought for, was now in question. "You're saying all of this—the family, the power—is just part of a bigger plan?" He took a step back, his mind struggling to keep up.

The man nodded. "A plan you're both too close to see. But it's already happening. And you've got to make a choice. You can either keep playing along with the old game, or you can join me and see it for what it truly is."

Daniel's head spun, and he could feel the ground beneath him shift. The world he had known—the world he had been fighting for—was collapsing, and he had no idea what was left in its wake.

Raphael's voice broke through the chaos in Daniel's mind. "The choice was always yours, Daniel. But you were too weak to make it. You always were."

Daniel's eyes flicked between Raphael and the man, his mind a whirl of confusion. He didn't know what to believe anymore, didn't know who to trust. The game had changed, and the rules had been rewritten without his knowledge.

But there was one thing he did know. The time for hiding

was over. It was time to face the truth.

And in that moment, everything—the ring, the vault, the truth—became crystal clear.

This wasn't just about Raphael. It wasn't about family. It was about something much larger, something that neither Daniel nor Emily had ever truly understood until now.

The world was changing, and they had to decide where they stood in it.

The question was: would they survive it? Or would they be consumed by it?

Twenty

A Sudden Disappearance

The tension in the room was thick, like the moment before a storm. Daniel stood at the center, his eyes darting between Raphael and the enigmatic figure who had just revealed the magnitude of the situation. The world they thought they knew had shattered. The rules had changed, and now they were in a fight for something far bigger than family—far bigger than any of them had anticipated.

Emily stood beside him, her face pale but her stance resolute. Her eyes were locked on the man who had been at the heart of the web they'd been unraveling, the man whose knowledge and cryptic words had kept them on edge. Now, standing before them in the dim, flickering light of the warehouse, he was the catalyst for everything Daniel had feared. His sudden appearance had shifted the game into a higher gear, one that they couldn't afford to ignore.

"I told you," the man said, his voice smooth but edged with urgency, "this was never about Raphael. It's about the system—the one that has been running everything in the shadows."

Raphael's lips curled into a sly smile, but there was something sharp in his eyes. "And you think you can control it?" he asked, his voice low but carrying a dangerous edge. "You think you can just walk in here and rewrite the rules?"

The man chuckled, a humorless sound that grated on Daniel's nerves. "No, Raphael. I don't need to control it. I just need to expose it for what it really is." He turned his attention to Daniel, his eyes cold and calculating. "And you, Daniel, have a part to play. Whether you like it or not."

Daniel's heart pounded in his chest as the weight of the man's words sank in. His pulse quickened as he stood on the precipice of a truth he hadn't yet been able to fully comprehend. What was this system they were talking about? What game were they all a part of? And what role did he—someone who had once been nothing more than a pawn—play in it?

"I don't need your help," Daniel said, his voice sharper than he intended. "We'll stop Raphael and whatever this is on our own."

The man's smile only grew. "Oh, Daniel. That's where

you're wrong." He took a step closer, his gaze unwavering. "You've already lost. You just don't know it yet."

Before Daniel could respond, the sound of footsteps echoed through the room. A door creaked open, and the distant shuffle of movement signaled that they weren't alone. Daniel tensed, instinctively reaching for the blade hidden beneath his coat, but he knew better than to jump to conclusions. Raphael's men could be anywhere. They had been hunting them for days.

But the man who had been standing in front of them remained unfazed. He gave Daniel a knowing look, his expression unreadable. "You should have left when you had the chance," he said softly. "Now, it's too late."

Suddenly, a figure appeared at the far end of the warehouse—a shadowy figure stepping from the gloom like a ghost. Daniel squinted, his heart sinking as the figure moved into the faint light. His breath caught in his throat.

It was Elias.

The man who had betrayed them, the one who had been working with Raphael all along, stood before them with a grim expression on his face. His eyes met Daniel's for only a moment before he shifted his gaze to the man beside them. There was a brief exchange between them, too subtle for Daniel to catch the words, but the tension was palpable.

"Elias," Daniel said, his voice dripping with disbelief. "I

should have known you were behind this."

Elias didn't respond immediately. He just nodded once, as if acknowledging the truth of Daniel's words. Then, without another word, he turned and moved toward the far side of the room, his footsteps deliberate, steady.

Daniel's eyes followed him, his mind racing. What was going on? Elias, the man who had once been a trusted ally, was now working with the very people who had caused so much destruction in his life. His hands clenched into fists, the weight of betrayal settling heavily in his chest.

But before Daniel could make sense of the scene unfolding before him, the man beside him spoke again, his voice tinged with an unsettling calm.

"You're too late," the man said, his gaze shifting toward the door Elias had just walked through. "The pieces are already in motion. The plan is already set."

Daniel's blood ran cold. The urgency in the man's voice, the finality of his words, made him feel like they were already walking into a trap. He turned to Emily, but her eyes were wide, filled with fear. She could sense it too—the storm was approaching, and they had no way of stopping it.

"What do you mean, 'too late'?" Daniel asked, his voice low, his body coiled in anticipation. "What's happening?"

The man didn't answer immediately. Instead, he reached

into his coat pocket and pulled out a small device—one that looked like a communicator, but far more sophisticated. His fingers danced across the buttons, his expression focused as he waited for a response.

And then, suddenly, the world seemed to tilt.

The device in the man's hand buzzed to life, its screen lighting up with a series of numbers and symbols Daniel couldn't quite understand. His mind raced, trying to make sense of it, but before he could ask, the man spoke.

"It's starting," he said, his voice colder now, filled with a sense of finality. "The countdown has begun."

Daniel's heart skipped a beat. "Countdown? What are you talking about?"

The man's lips curled into a knowing smile. "You'll see soon enough. But don't worry, Daniel. You've already done your part. The rest is out of your hands."

The words felt like a punch to the gut. Daniel's mind spun as he tried to make sense of everything. This wasn't just about Raphael. It wasn't about the vault, the ring, or even the hidden truth anymore. It was something far more insidious, something they hadn't yet even begun to comprehend.

Before Daniel could ask another question, the lights flickered above them, casting the room into darkness for a brief, heart-stopping moment. Then, as quickly as it had happened, the lights returned, only to reveal an empty space where the man had been standing.

Daniel blinked, his mind racing, but the man was gone. Vanished. There was no sign of him—nothing but the eerie silence of the warehouse that seemed to press in around them like a vice.

"Where did he go?" Emily's voice trembled, her eyes scanning the room.

Daniel's eyes darted around, searching for any sign of movement, any clue as to where the man had disappeared to. But there was nothing. No footprints, no sign of struggle—just the oppressive silence of the building that seemed to swallow everything.

"Stay close," Daniel muttered, his voice tight. His senses were on high alert, his eyes narrowing as he scanned every corner of the room. "Something's wrong. This isn't over."

But just as he finished speaking, there was a loud crash from behind them, followed by the unmistakable sound of someone—or something—rushing toward them.

Daniel's heart jumped in his chest. He turned sharply, his eyes wide with alarm, only to be met with a terrifying sight.

Elias stood in the doorway, his hand raised in the air. But it wasn't a gesture of peace. In his grip, he held something—a gun, its barrel pointed directly at Daniel.

"Elias—" Daniel's voice caught in his throat as the weight of the situation pressed down on him. His thoughts scrambled for any way out, but the fear in Elias's eyes was unmistakable. He was no longer the man Daniel had once trusted.

And in that moment, everything seemed to fall apart.

Elias's hand shook as he held the gun, his eyes flicking between Daniel and Emily. "I didn't want it to be like this," he said, his voice barely above a whisper, trembling with something Daniel couldn't place. "But I don't have a choice anymore."

Daniel stepped back slowly, his heart pounding. "What do you mean? What's happening, Elias?"

The gun in Elias's hand wavered slightly as he took a deep breath, trying to steady himself. "It's too late to stop it now," he said, his voice breaking. "You don't understand. The plan is already in motion. And you—" He paused, swallowing hard. "You're all going to disappear."

Daniel's eyes widened in realization as Elias raised the gun higher, his finger tightening on the trigger. But before Daniel could react, before he could think, the lights in the warehouse went out again, plunging them all into darkness.

And then—nothing.

The world went silent.

A Sudden Disappearance

And when the lights returned moments later, Elias was gone.

Daniel blinked in confusion, his body frozen. The gun, the threat, the words—everything had vanished. He was left standing in the same empty warehouse, his heart racing, his mind reeling.

Emily's voice broke the silence, her words trembling with fear. "Where did he go? What happened?"

But Daniel didn't answer. He couldn't. Because somewhere in the darkness, something had shifted. Something had disappeared.

And he knew, deep down, that they were no longer just dealing with betrayal. They were dealing with something far darker—and the truth was slipping further out of their reach.

Twenty-One

A Warning from the Past

The oppressive silence of the warehouse hung in the air like a dense fog, and Daniel's heart continued to race as his eyes scanned the empty space. The sudden disappearance of Elias had left him disoriented, and for a fleeting moment, he felt like he was trapped in a nightmare—one where the lines between reality and illusion blurred beyond recognition. He stood still, his breath shallow, and his mind scrambled to piece together the fragments of what had just happened. Everything that had led them here, everything they had fought for, seemed like it had shifted out of their control in the span of a few heartbeats.

"Where did he go?" Emily's voice broke through the silence, her words tinged with both fear and confusion. She was standing just a few feet away from him, her expression tight

A Warning from the Past

with anxiety. She, too, was trying to process the surreal events unfolding in front of them. The gun. The cryptic words. The sudden vanishing act. It was all too much, too fast.

"I don't know," Daniel said, his voice hoarse. He looked around the room again, as if expecting to see Elias appear from the shadows, but the warehouse remained eerily still. "But we need to get out of here. Now."

Emily nodded without hesitation, the urgency in her eyes matching his own. They had both learned the hard way that waiting, hesitating—those were luxuries they could no longer afford. They had come too far, seen too much, to let themselves be caught in another trap.

Daniel moved quickly, heading for the door they had entered through, but as he reached it, something stopped him. A faint noise, almost imperceptible, came from behind them. It was a whisper, too soft to make out, but enough to send a chill crawling down his spine.

"Did you hear that?" Emily asked, her voice barely above a whisper. Her gaze flicked to the far corner of the room, where the shadows seemed to shift and breathe in ways that were far from natural.

Daniel nodded. He turned slowly, his hand instinctively resting on the hilt of his knife as he stepped toward the darkened corner. "Stay close."

But as he moved toward the sound, it grew louder—more distinct. And then, without warning, the air shifted, and the shadows coalesced into a figure emerging from the darkness.

A figure Daniel knew all too well.

His breath caught in his throat.

"Father?"

The man who stepped into the dim light wasn't the shadow of a ghost, wasn't an illusion crafted by fear or memory. It was real. He could see the familiar features—the sharp jawline, the strong brow, the piercing eyes that had once been filled with both love and authority. But now, those eyes were filled with something else—something that made Daniel's heart race. It was a mix of sorrow, regret, and a deep, unspoken guilt.

The man who stood before them was none other than his father, the patriarch of the Laurent family, the man whose disappearance years ago had set everything in motion—the man who had been thought dead, his body buried, his legacy erased.

But now, here he was.

"Father…" Daniel's voice trembled, though he tried to keep it steady, tried to hold onto whatever control he had left. His mind struggled to process the impossible reality of the situation. "How... how is this possible?"

His father didn't answer immediately. Instead, he stepped forward, his eyes locked on Daniel with an intensity that felt both familiar and foreign. "You've come a long way, my son," he said, his voice quiet, but powerful. "But you should have stayed away."

Daniel's heart pounded in his chest, a mixture of emotions surging through him. Anger, confusion, disbelief. He didn't know what to feel. Everything he thought he knew was unraveling, and now, his father—the man who had disappeared without a trace all those years ago—stood before him, like a specter from the past.

"Why?" Daniel's voice was hoarse, the word coming out before he could stop it. "Why did you leave? Why did you disappear?"

His father's face remained impassive, but there was a flicker of something in his eyes—something that made Daniel feel as if his world was about to implode. "I didn't leave, Daniel. I was... forced to disappear. There are things you don't understand. Things I couldn't protect you from. And you still don't understand them."

Daniel shook his head, his thoughts scattered. "You think I'm supposed to just believe this? After everything? After everything I've seen?"

The man's eyes softened, but only for a moment. "No,

Daniel. You're not supposed to believe it. You're supposed to understand it. You're supposed to see the bigger picture. The truth."

"The truth?" Emily interjected, her voice sharp with suspicion. "What truth? How can we trust you? How can we trust anything you say after what we've been through?"

His father turned toward her, his gaze cold and calculating. "You shouldn't trust me," he said bluntly. "But you will have to, if you want to survive."

Daniel's chest tightened as the weight of his father's words hit him. "Survive what?" he demanded. "What's going on? What are you talking about?"

His father's gaze shifted back to Daniel, his eyes piercing. "The system is collapsing. The empire we built—the empire you think you've been fighting for—it's about to fall. And if you don't understand why, if you don't realize who's behind it all, you'll be consumed by it."

Daniel's mind reeled. "The system?" He repeated the words, trying to grasp their meaning. "What are you saying? Who's behind it?"

His father sighed, a sound filled with the weight of years of secrets. "I tried to protect you from the truth, Daniel. But the truth is always waiting to be uncovered. You've already started to see it, to piece together the puzzle. But you haven't seen the entire picture. You've been chasing shadows, and now the real threat is here."

Daniel took a step back, his thoughts swirling. "No. This doesn't make sense. Everything I've fought for…" He trailed off, his voice breaking as the realization started to settle in. "The vault, the ring, the coin—it's all part of this, isn't it? Part of some bigger plan."

His father's expression darkened. "Yes. And now you're caught in the middle of it."

Emily's hand tightened on Daniel's arm, her voice filled with urgency. "What do we do now?" she asked, her gaze flicking between Daniel and his father. "How do we stop this?"

His father's lips pressed together into a thin line. "There's nothing you can do. The pieces are already in motion, and no one can stop it now. Not even you."

Daniel's stomach twisted with fear and frustration. He had been so sure that everything they had done—every decision, every step they had taken—had been leading them toward victory. But now, with his father standing before him, telling him that it was already too late, that everything was spiraling out of control, he felt like the ground had been ripped out from beneath him.

"No," Daniel said, shaking his head. "I won't accept that. I won't believe that."

"You have no choice," his father said quietly. "The world is changing, Daniel. The people in control—the ones who have always held the reins—they've already made their move. And when the dust settles, they'll control everything. The vault is the key to it all. The ring, the coin, everything—it's all part of a plan that's been in motion for centuries."

Daniel's breath caught. "Centuries?"

His father nodded slowly, his eyes grave. "The Laurent family was never just about wealth. It was about power—control of a system that has been in place long before either of us were born. And now, it's too late to change anything. The system is already shifting, and you're caught in its wake."

Daniel's mind reeled with the weight of his father's words. The system. Power. Control. The Laurent family had never just been a family. It had been the keystone in a much larger game. A game that he had been unknowingly playing his entire life.

"You're saying that we're powerless?" Daniel's voice was barely above a whisper, disbelief mixing with anger. "That we can't fight back? That it's already over?"

His father's gaze softened, just a fraction, but there was no sympathy in it. "You can fight, Daniel. But you'll lose. The game is rigged, and you're already out of moves."

A sudden noise broke through the tension—footsteps, fast

and urgent, echoing from the distance. Daniel's heart skipped a beat as he turned, his hand instinctively reaching for his knife. But before he could react, his father's hand shot out, gripping his arm with surprising strength.

"Don't," he warned. "It's too late for that. They've already found us."

The words were a death sentence. Daniel's heart raced as the door to the room burst open, and a figure stepped inside—a familiar face, one that Daniel never expected to see again.

Elias.

But this time, he wasn't alone.

Behind him, a group of armed men filed into the room, their faces grim, their weapons raised.

Daniel's breath caught in his throat as he realized the true depth of the trap they were in. They weren't just fighting Raphael. They weren't just fighting for survival. They were fighting against a system that had been waiting for them all along.

And in that moment, Daniel knew that the true battle was just beginning.

Twenty-Two

A Warning from the Past

The oppressive silence of the warehouse hung in the air like a dense fog, and Daniel's heart continued to race as his eyes scanned the empty space. The sudden disappearance of Elias had left him disoriented, and for a fleeting moment, he felt like he was trapped in a nightmare—one where the lines between reality and illusion blurred beyond recognition. He stood still, his breath shallow, and his mind scrambled to piece together the fragments of what had just happened. Everything that had led them here, everything they had fought for, seemed like it had shifted out of their control in the span of a few heartbeats.

"Where did he go?" Emily's voice broke through the silence, her words tinged with both fear and confusion. She was standing just a few feet away from him, her expression tight with anxiety. She, too, was trying to process the surreal events unfolding in front of them. The gun. The cryptic words. The sudden vanishing act. It was all too much, too fast.

"I don't know," Daniel said, his voice hoarse. He looked around the room again, as if expecting to see Elias appear from the shadows, but the warehouse remained eerily still. "But we need to get out of here. Now."

Emily nodded without hesitation, the urgency in her eyes matching his own. They had both learned the hard way that waiting, hesitating—those were luxuries they could no longer afford. They had come too far, seen too much, to let themselves be caught in another trap.

Daniel moved quickly, heading for the door they had entered through, but as he reached it, something stopped him. A faint noise, almost imperceptible, came from behind them. It was a whisper, too soft to make out, but enough to send a chill crawling down his spine.

"Did you hear that?" Emily asked, her voice barely above a whisper. Her gaze flicked to the far corner of the room, where the shadows seemed to shift and breathe in ways that were far from natural.

Daniel nodded. He turned slowly, his hand instinctively resting on the hilt of his knife as he stepped toward the darkened corner. "Stay close."

But as he moved toward the sound, it grew louder—more distinct. And then, without warning, the air shifted, and the shadows coalesced into a figure emerging from the darkness.

A figure Daniel knew all too well.

His breath caught in his throat.

"Father?"

The man who stepped into the dim light wasn't the shadow of a ghost, wasn't an illusion crafted by fear or memory. It was real. He could see the familiar features—the sharp jawline, the strong brow, the piercing eyes that had once been filled with both love and authority. But now, those eyes were filled with something else—something that made Daniel's heart race. It was a mix of sorrow, regret, and a deep, unspoken guilt.

The man who stood before them was none other than his father, the patriarch of the Laurent family, the man whose disappearance years ago had set everything in motion—the man who had been thought dead, his body buried, his legacy erased.

But now, here he was.

"Father…" Daniel's voice trembled, though he tried to keep it steady, tried to hold onto whatever control he had left. His mind struggled to process the impossible reality of the situation. "How… how is this possible?"

His father didn't answer immediately. Instead, he stepped forward, his eyes locked on Daniel with an intensity that felt both familiar and foreign. "You've come a long way, my son," he said, his voice quiet, but powerful. "But you should have stayed away."

Daniel's heart pounded in his chest, a mixture of emotions surging through him. Anger, confusion, disbelief. He didn't know what to feel. Everything he thought he knew was unraveling, and now, his father—the man who had disappeared without a trace all those years ago—stood before him, like a specter from the past.

"Why?" Daniel's voice was hoarse, the word coming out before he could stop it. "Why did you leave? Why did you disappear?"

His father's face remained impassive, but there was a flicker of something in his eyes—something that made Daniel feel as if his world was about to implode. "I didn't leave, Daniel. I was... forced to disappear. There are things you don't understand. Things I couldn't protect you from. And you still don't understand them."

Daniel shook his head, his thoughts scattered. "You think I'm supposed to just believe this? After everything? After everything I've seen?"

The man's eyes softened, but only for a moment. "No, Daniel. You're not supposed to believe it. You're supposed to understand it. You're supposed to see the bigger picture. The truth."

"The truth?" Emily interjected, her voice sharp with suspicion. "What truth? How can we trust you? How can we trust anything you say after what we've been through?"

His father turned toward her, his gaze cold and calculating. "You shouldn't trust me," he said bluntly. "But you will have to, if you want to survive."

Daniel's chest tightened as the weight of his father's words hit him. "Survive what?" he demanded. "What's going on? What are you talking about?"

His father's gaze shifted back to Daniel, his eyes piercing. "The system is collapsing. The empire we built—the empire you think you've been fighting for—it's about to fall. And if you don't understand why, if you don't realize who's behind it all, you'll be consumed by it."

Daniel's mind reeled. "The system?" He repeated the words, trying to grasp their meaning. "What are you saying? Who's behind it?"

His father sighed, a sound filled with the weight of years of secrets. "I tried to protect you from the truth, Daniel. But the truth is always waiting to be uncovered. You've already started to see it, to piece together the puzzle. But you haven't seen the entire picture. You've been chasing shadows, and now the real threat is here."

Daniel took a step back, his thoughts swirling. "No. This doesn't make sense. Everything I've fought for..." He trailed off, his voice breaking as the realization started to settle in. "The vault, the ring, the coin—it's all part of this, isn't it? Part of some bigger plan."

His father's expression darkened. "Yes. And now you're caught in the middle of it."

Emily's hand tightened on Daniel's arm, her voice filled with urgency. "What do we do now?" she asked, her gaze flicking between Daniel and his father. "How do we stop this?"

His father's lips pressed together into a thin line. "There's nothing you can do. The pieces are already in motion, and no one can stop it now. Not even you."

Daniel's stomach twisted with fear and frustration. He had been so sure that everything they had done—every decision, every step they had taken—had been leading them toward victory. But now, with his father standing before him, telling him that it was already too late, that everything was spiraling out of control, he felt like the ground had been ripped out from beneath him.

"No," Daniel said, shaking his head. "I won't accept that. I won't believe that."

"You have no choice," his father said quietly. "The world is changing, Daniel. The people in control—the ones who have always held the reins—they've already made their move. And when the dust settles, they'll control everything. The vault is the key to it all. The ring, the coin, everything—it's all part of a plan that's been in motion for centuries."

Daniel's breath caught. "Centuries?"

His father nodded slowly, his eyes grave. "The Laurent family was never just about wealth. It was about power—control of a system that has been in place long before either of us were born. And now, it's too late to change anything. The system is already shifting, and you're caught in its wake."

Daniel's mind reeled with the weight of his father's words. The system. Power. Control. The Laurent family had never just been a family. It had been the keystone in a much larger game. A game that he had been unknowingly playing his entire life.

"You're saying that we're powerless?" Daniel's voice was barely above a whisper, disbelief mixing with anger. "That we can't fight back? That it's already over?"

His father's gaze softened, just a fraction, but there was no sympathy in it. "You can fight, Daniel. But you'll lose. The game is rigged, and you're already out of moves."

A sudden noise broke through the tension—footsteps, fast and urgent, echoing from the distance. Daniel's heart skipped a beat as he turned, his hand instinctively reaching for his knife. But before he could react, his father's hand shot out, gripping his arm with surprising strength.

"Don't," he warned. "It's too late for that. They've already found us."

The words were a death sentence. Daniel's heart raced as the door to the room burst open, and a figure stepped inside—a familiar face, one that Daniel never expected to see again.

Elias.

But this time, he wasn't alone.

Behind him, a group of armed men filed into the room, their faces grim, their weapons raised.

Daniel's breath caught in his throat as he realized the true depth of the trap they were in. They weren't just fighting Raphael. They weren't just fighting for survival. They were fighting against a system that had been waiting for them all along.

And in that moment, Daniel knew that the true battle was just beginning.

Twenty-Three

The Power Broker

The warehouse had once been a place of secrets, a dimly lit relic of an era that seemed to have faded into memory. But now, with every creak of the floorboards and the quiet whispers of the men standing in the shadows, it felt like a ticking bomb waiting to explode. The dim lighting only amplified the tension hanging thick in the air, like a storm on the verge of breaking. And Daniel knew that the calm before the storm was the most dangerous moment of all.

His grip tightened around the cryptic key—the coin—still warm from the handoff earlier. He could feel its cold edges pressing into his palm, as if reminding him that the power contained within this small object was too much for him to fully comprehend. His father's warning echoed in his mind, a constant reminder that once the power was unlocked, there was no turning back. But the real question remained: Could he even trust himself to wield such power? And, more importantly, could he trust the people around him?

The man who had entered the warehouse earlier, his father—Daniel couldn't even begin to fathom the depth of betrayal and lies that had brought them to this point. His world had been upended, turned inside out, and now, faced with the man who had once been his mentor, his guide through the labyrinth of the family's operations, he felt like a stranger in his own life. Every piece of the puzzle had come crashing down, but the image that had emerged was far from the clarity he had once hoped for.

Elias stood off to the side, watching the exchange with an unsettling calm. The loyalty Daniel had once felt for him now seemed like a distant memory, something broken and irreparable. And behind him, the armed men, loyal to Raphael, stood like statues, silent and ready to pounce at a moment's notice. They had always been a threat, but now, the true danger came from within.

"Do you have any idea what you've done?" Daniel's father's voice broke through the silence, his words hanging in the air with the force of an accusation.

Daniel straightened, his eyes narrowing. "I didn't do anything, Father. You're the one who led us here. You're the one who kept secrets."

The older man's expression remained unreadable, but

his eyes flashed with a mixture of regret and something darker—something that unsettled Daniel to his core. "You think you know the full story, don't you?" His father took a step closer, the weight of his words hanging between them like a heavy cloak. "You think you understand what's at stake here, but you don't. You never have."

"I understand more than you think," Daniel shot back, his voice steady despite the turmoil raging inside him. "I know that everything I thought I knew was a lie. You've been pulling the strings all along, haven't you? You and Raphael. You've been playing this game from the beginning."

His father's gaze hardened, and Daniel saw the brief flicker of something—guilt, maybe, or perhaps an attempt at regret—but it vanished quickly, replaced by an impenetrable mask of authority. "You still don't see the bigger picture. You never did. But you will. Soon enough."

Daniel could feel the weight of the coin in his pocket, a constant reminder that the game was far from over. His father's words, however cryptic, held a ring of truth. They were all pawns in a much larger game, and now, with the key to everything in his hand, Daniel had to decide which side he was on. There was no turning back.

The air in the warehouse shifted, thickening with the unspoken tension as Elias stepped forward, his eyes now focused solely on Daniel. There was no mistaking the cool calculation in his expression.

"Do you really believe you have a choice?" Elias asked, his voice low and smooth, like a snake coiling in the grass. "You're already part of this system, Daniel. You've been playing by its rules for far longer than you've realized. You think the coin changes things, but it doesn't. It just exposes what's already been set in motion."

Daniel's heart skipped a beat, the meaning of Elias's words settling over him like a fog. "What do you mean?" he demanded, his voice rising. "You've always acted like you were on my side. What is this system you're talking about?"

Elias gave a small, humorless laugh. "You really don't get it, do you? This isn't about Raphael. It's about the people who truly hold the power. The ones who've been pulling the strings for centuries. They're the ones who created the game. And now, you're standing at the threshold, Daniel. The key is in your hands, but it's not a key to freedom. It's a key to a new world order—a world that you're not prepared to control."

Daniel's mind raced as he processed Elias's words. New world order? He was no longer speaking in riddles. The cryptic references to power, control, and the game they had all been caught in were starting to take on a chilling clarity.

"You want me to join you," Daniel said, his voice tight with disbelief. "You want me to take control, to be part of whatever twisted system you're talking about."

Elias's gaze didn't waver. "Control? It's never been about

control, Daniel. It's about understanding. Understanding that the power brokers, the ones who truly pull the strings, have been using people like you—like me—to further their agenda. And now, it's your turn to either accept your place or be destroyed."

Daniel clenched his fists, his breath shallow as his thoughts spiraled. He could feel the weight of everything bearing down on him, the choice, the betrayal, and the responsibility that now fell to him. It was overwhelming. His father, Elias—they were no longer the figures of authority he had once trusted. They were part of the very system they had taught him to fight against. The system they had controlled. And now, with the coin, the key to unlocking everything, Daniel stood at the center of it all, faced with the terrifying truth that he was part of something far larger than he could comprehend.

"We're not playing this game anymore," Daniel said, his voice firm, though his heart was hammering in his chest. "I won't be a part of this twisted system. I won't be controlled by you, or anyone else. Not after everything that's happened."

Elias's eyes flashed with amusement. "You still don't understand," he said softly. "You never will."

Before Daniel could respond, the sound of footsteps echoed from behind him. The door to the warehouse creaked open, and a figure stepped inside.

Daniel's heart skipped a beat.

The figure was cloaked in shadows, their face obscured by a hood. But there was no mistaking the presence—the aura that surrounded them. It was as if the air itself bent in their direction.

"You should have listened to him, Daniel," the figure said, their voice a low, melodic whisper that seemed to reverberate in the room. "You were always meant to be a part of this world. There is no escaping it."

Daniel's stomach dropped. He knew that voice. It was the man who had helped him—the one who had given him the map, the book, the cryptic warnings. But now, as he stepped into the light, Daniel realized that the man was no ally. He was something far more dangerous.

The figure pulled back the hood, revealing a face that was both familiar and foreign. It was a face Daniel had seen before, but this time it was older, harder—marked by years of unseen battles and decisions made in the dark. The man was none other than the one known as the "Power Broker." The man who had been the architect of the system they had been running from.

"You?" Daniel's voice was barely a whisper, disbelief and anger rising in him like a tidal wave. "You've been the one pulling the strings all along?"

The Power Broker smiled, a cold, knowing smile that seemed to reach into Daniel's very soul. "Not just pulling the strings, Daniel. I've been the one making sure the game stays in motion. Keeping the balance. Ensuring that those who understand the system are the ones who survive."

Daniel felt his knees go weak as the weight of the truth crashed down on him. The Power Broker—the puppet master, the one who had orchestrated it all—had been right in front of him, disguised as someone else, leading him to believe that he was on his side.

The man's smile grew wider. "And now, you've reached the final stage. The choice is yours. You can accept your place in this world, or you can let it consume you. But understand this, Daniel: There's no escaping it. Not now. Not ever."

Elias stood silently beside him, his eyes gleaming with something almost... approving. This was it. The final test. The moment when Daniel had to decide who he truly was—and whether he could become a part of a system that had been built on lies, manipulation, and greed.

Daniel's hand tightened around the coin, the weight of it no longer a symbol of hope but of power—of the power that had consumed him, his father, and the world he had never truly understood.

"I won't be your pawn," Daniel said, his voice fierce with defiance. "I won't be part of this game."

The Power Broker's gaze never faltered. "You don't have a choice, Daniel. You're already in it. And once the game is played, there's no going back."

The weight of those words hung in the air like a death sentence, and Daniel knew, deep down, that the game had only just begun.

Twenty-Four

Chased Through the Streets

The night air hit Daniel like a slap to the face as he bolted out of the warehouse, his heart hammering in his chest. Behind him, he could hear the pounding of footsteps—heavy, methodical, and growing louder with each passing second. Elias's voice still echoed in his ears, a reminder of everything that had just been revealed. The Power Broker. His father. The game. There was no escape from it. But at that moment, there was no time for contemplation.

"Move!" Daniel shouted, his voice hoarse as he grabbed Emily's arm and yanked her forward. She stumbled, but quickly regained her balance, her wide eyes locked on him. She didn't need to ask why they were running. They both understood. They were in danger now—not just from Raphael and his men, but from the very forces that had been controlling everything behind the scenes.

They reached the alley, the world around them a blur of shadows and cold concrete. Daniel's breath came in ragged gasps as his legs burned with the effort, but he pushed on. There was no choice now. No room for hesitation. Every part of him screamed for them to keep running, to stay ahead of the looming threat that was closing in.

Behind them, the sound of boots slapping against the wet pavement rang out, too close for comfort. Daniel's instincts kicked in, and he glanced over his shoulder. A figure—tall, ominous—appeared at the edge of the alley, moving with eerie precision. His face was hidden, but the silhouette was unmistakable. One of the men from the warehouse.

"They're coming!" Emily gasped, her voice barely audible over the sound of their frantic footsteps.

Daniel didn't answer. There was no time for words, no time for plans. He could feel the weight of the coin in his pocket, its cold edges pressing against his thigh. The key. The power. It was all too much. Too dangerous. And the more they ran, the more Daniel realized the truth—there was nowhere left to hide.

They tore down the alley, their footsteps muffled by the wet pavement, their breath coming in sharp gasps. The lights of the city seemed distant now, the glow of neon signs barely visible through the twisting maze of narrow streets. Daniel's heart pounded in his chest as he navigated the streets, his mind a blur of strategy, of survival. But the only thing that mattered now was escaping.

Emily was close behind him, her breath ragged, but her pace never faltering. She wasn't asking questions anymore. She was moving because she had no other choice. They were both in this together. And together, they would survive.

"Left!" Daniel shouted, veering sharply down another alley. He could hear Emily's footsteps quicken as she followed him without hesitation. The sound of pursuit was still there—louder now, more urgent. They were getting closer.

Daniel didn't know how much time they had. Minutes? Seconds? It didn't matter. What mattered was staying ahead of them.

They reached another street, this one wider and more populated. For a moment, Daniel thought they might be able to blend into the crowd, disappear into the flow of people. But then, from the corner of his eye, he saw them. Two men—one of them from the warehouse—emerged from the alley they had just exited, their eyes scanning the crowd with dangerous precision. They hadn't lost them. Not by a long shot.

"Keep moving!" Daniel barked, grabbing Emily's hand and pulling her along. He could see the panic in her eyes now, the realization settling over her like a weight. They were being hunted.

But Daniel wouldn't stop. He couldn't. Not when everything was at stake.

They turned another corner, but this time, Daniel's gut told him they were running out of options. The street was crowded with cars and pedestrians, but there were no clear exits, no alleys to duck into. Their pursuers were too close, too persistent. They had nowhere to go but forward.

The sound of a car engine roared behind them, the screech of tires tearing through the night air. Daniel's heart jumped into his throat as he whipped around, just in time to see a black SUV speed toward them, its headlights cutting through the crowd like a blade.

"Shit!" Daniel swore, pulling Emily to the side as the car sped past them. But it didn't stop. It didn't veer off the road. It kept coming.

Before Daniel could react, the SUV slammed to a halt in front of them, blocking their path.

"Get in!" a voice shouted from the driver's side, and Daniel froze, his mind racing.

The door to the SUV swung open, and the driver—another one of Raphael's men—gestured violently for them to get inside. Daniel's instinct was to resist, to run, but the reality of the situation hit him like a ton of bricks. They were surrounded. The alleyways, the streets—they had nowhere left to escape.

"Now!" the man barked, his gun raised, eyes scanning the crowd. "Get in, or we make this worse for you."

Daniel's stomach twisted as he made a split-second decision. He grabbed Emily's arm, pulling her toward the car. There was no time to hesitate. The choice had already been made for them.

They slid into the back of the SUV, the door slamming shut behind them with a jarring thud. The engine roared to life, and the vehicle shot forward, weaving through the streets as if it knew exactly where to go.

Daniel's heart raced, his breath coming in sharp bursts as he turned to Emily. Her face was pale, her eyes wide with fear, but she didn't say anything. She didn't need to. They both knew what was happening. They had been caught.

The SUV sped down the street, its engine growling like a beast in pursuit. Daniel kept his eyes on the road, but he couldn't shake the feeling that they were being led into a trap. The men in the front seats, the driver and the passenger, didn't speak. They were calm, too calm, as if they knew exactly what they were doing. They knew where they were going.

Daniel's fingers tightened around the coin in his pocket. The power. The key. It felt like a ticking time bomb, a weight that was growing heavier by the second.

The city blurred outside the window as the SUV accelerated, taking sharp turns with the precision of a well-oiled machine. Daniel knew they were getting closer to whatever it was that had been set in motion. The trap was closing in around them, and there was no escaping it now.

The streets grew quieter as they moved farther from the crowded downtown, the tall buildings giving way to darker alleys and quieter, more isolated streets. Daniel's mind raced, his thoughts spinning with the realization that they were heading deeper into enemy territory. They were no longer in control. They were pawns, driven by forces far greater than themselves.

As the SUV turned down another narrow road, Daniel's eyes flicked to the rearview mirror. For a brief moment, he thought he saw something move—something that shouldn't have been there.

It was another car. A black sedan, following them from a distance.

His blood ran cold.

"Keep your head down," Daniel whispered to Emily, his voice barely audible.

The sedan was too far behind to be a threat for now, but Daniel's instincts were screaming at him. They weren't just being chased. They were being watched. Tracked. This was no accident. Someone was orchestrating all of this from behind the scenes, and Daniel knew that they had just entered the heart of a much larger game.

The SUV rounded another corner, and Daniel's stomach dropped. They were heading toward a dead end—a narrow street flanked by warehouses on either side. The vehicle slowed as it approached a set of gates, guarded by two men standing in front of a towering, rusted fence. It looked like some kind of compound, but Daniel had no idea what lay behind those gates.

The car came to a stop, and the doors to the compound opened with a mechanical screech, allowing them to pass through. Daniel's mind raced, but he forced himself to remain calm. There was no going back now. Whatever awaited them on the other side of those gates, they had no choice but to face it.

As they crossed the threshold into the compound, Daniel's thoughts turned to the coin in his pocket. The weight of it felt like a burden, and yet, it also felt like their last hope. The cryptic key. The key to everything. But what was the price for unlocking it?

The SUV slowed, coming to a stop in front of a large, unmarked building. The men in the front seats didn't move, their eyes scanning the area with an unsettling calm. Daniel glanced at Emily, and for a brief moment, they locked eyes. They were in this together. And whatever happened next, they would face it side by side.

The doors to the SUV swung open, and the armed men

gestured for them to step out. Daniel hesitated for only a moment before he followed their orders, his heart pounding in his chest as he and Emily were led into the compound, the walls of the building looming over them like a prison.

They were trapped. And the real game—one that no one could escape—was just beginning.

Twenty-Five

A Heartfelt Confession

The cold steel door clanged shut behind them, the sound reverberating through the empty hallway like a death knell. The sudden silence was suffocating, thick and dense, as if the walls themselves were closing in. Daniel's heart pounded in his chest, each beat a reminder that he was no longer in control of his fate. His mind raced with questions, each one more pressing than the last, but one thought dominated them all: how had they ended up here?

The compound felt like a maze. A place designed to trap. There were no windows, no signs to guide them, just long corridors lit by flickering overhead bulbs. The air felt heavy, weighed down by the endless layers of secrecy that seemed to saturate the very walls of the building. It was a place designed to break spirits, to make those within forget what

From Dust to Diamonds

it meant to hope.

The armed men had ushered them inside without a word, their faces unreadable. There was no need for threats. They didn't need to speak. The oppressive air and the cold, silent authority of their presence spoke volumes.

"Stay close," Daniel murmured to Emily, his voice barely audible, as they walked down the narrow hallway. His hand brushed against hers, a small gesture, but one that seemed to reassure him. She was still here. Still with him.

Emily's breath was shallow, but her eyes never wavered from the path ahead. The moment they had crossed the gates into the compound, she had known the game was up. There was no escape. No last-minute plan. No miraculous solution. They were in this together, and that fact, in its raw honesty, kept her grounded.

The guards moved ahead of them, silent and deliberate, and soon they arrived at a small, unmarked door. The one who had led them here, a tall man with a scar that ran down the left side of his face, glanced back briefly before motioning for them to enter.

Daniel hesitated for a split second. What awaited them behind this door? The uncertainty gnawed at him, a constant companion ever since they had crossed into the unknown world of the compound. He looked at Emily again, her face pale but determined.

A Heartfelt Confession

This was it.

He took a step forward, opening the door with a creak that sounded impossibly loud in the silence. Inside was a small, sparsely furnished room. A low wooden table sat in the center, surrounded by four chairs, two of which were already occupied. On one side of the table, his father sat, his hands folded in front of him, his face inscrutable.

And across from him, sitting with an air of detached authority, was the Power Broker.

Daniel's chest tightened as the realization hit him. The man who had been pulling the strings, the one who had orchestrated everything, the one who had seemed so distant, so untouchable—he was now staring at them as if they were mere players in a game he controlled.

The room felt small, claustrophobic even, as Daniel and Emily stepped inside. The door closed softly behind them, sealing them in with the two men who had played pivotal roles in the collapse of everything Daniel had once believed in. His world had become a labyrinth of lies, of manipulation, and it seemed as though there was no exit.

"Sit," his father commanded, his voice low but steady. The words weren't a request—they were an order. A directive that left no room for refusal.

Daniel exchanged a glance with Emily before moving toward one of the chairs. She followed, her eyes still trained on the two men at the table. They both sat down, though the tension between them and the men across from them was palpable. Daniel felt the weight of it in his chest, a pressure that threatened to crush him.

"Do you know why you're here?" the Power Broker asked, his voice smooth, almost too calm. His eyes were fixed on Daniel, watching him with an intensity that felt like it could pierce through him.

Daniel swallowed, his throat dry. The room felt too hot now, the air thick and suffocating. "I have a few ideas," he said, his voice rough, though he tried to keep it steady.

The Power Broker's lips curled into a faint, knowing smile. "You've been running for so long, Daniel. Always chasing something. Always thinking that you were in control. But you never were."

Daniel's jaw tightened. "You've been controlling everything from the start. Everything."

His father didn't react, but the slight tightening of his hands on the table spoke volumes. The tension between them was palpable, an invisible force that pulsed through the room.

"What do you want from us?" Emily finally spoke, her voice cutting through the silence. Her eyes were sharp, her gaze focused on the Power Broker.

The man's smile remained. "What I want is irrelevant. What

A Heartfelt Confession

you do now matters. You see, you've both been brought to this point for a reason. The power—the coin, the vault—it was never meant for you, Daniel. It was meant for someone else."

Daniel's heart skipped a beat. "Someone else?"

The Power Broker's gaze flicked to his father for just a moment before returning to Daniel. "Yes. Someone else who would have understood what was at stake. Someone who knew how to use the power to reshape everything."

Daniel's breath caught in his throat. "You mean Raphael?"

"No," his father interrupted, his voice colder than before. "Not Raphael. Not anymore. You, Daniel, were always meant to be part of this. The key—the coin—it was meant to be in your hands."

The words hung in the air, suffocating him. The coin. The key to the future. And the weight of it seemed to settle in his chest, a crushing reminder of the responsibility, the power, and the danger that came with it.

"But why me?" Daniel asked, his voice barely above a whisper. "Why me? What makes me different from the others?"

His father's expression softened, just for a moment. "Because you're my son, Daniel. You were always meant to carry the legacy. The Laurent family isn't just about wealth.

It's about control. About shaping the world, about making decisions that will affect everyone."

Daniel's eyes widened, the realization crashing over him like a tidal wave. "You wanted me to be your successor. You wanted me to take your place."

His father nodded slowly. "It's more than just about succession, Daniel. It's about the greater good. The world can't function as it is. People need guidance, leadership. And someone with the right vision—someone who understands the system—can bring about the changes we need."

Daniel's chest tightened as the words sunk in. This was it—the truth he had been chasing. His father had wanted him to take over, to control the game. To become part of a system that was built on manipulation, power, and secrecy. And Daniel had been too blind to see it until now.

"No," Daniel said, his voice shaking. "I won't do it. I won't be part of this anymore."

The Power Broker's smile never wavered. "It's not about what you want, Daniel. It's about what you were born into. You're already in this. There's no turning back."

Daniel felt the weight of those words as if chains wrapped around him, pulling him into a future he never chose. But as the words settled in, something else surged inside him—an anger, a refusal to accept this twisted destiny that had been thrust upon him.

A Heartfelt Confession

"I don't have to accept this," Daniel said, his voice stronger now, filled with defiance he hadn't felt in years. "I will never be part of this game. I don't want this power. I don't want to be a part of a system that uses people like pawns."

His father's eyes darkened, a flash of something cold and dangerous passing through them. "You don't have a choice, Daniel."

"You're wrong," Daniel said, standing up suddenly. His legs shook with the intensity of the moment, but he stood firm. "I have a choice. And I choose to walk away. I choose to end this."

For a moment, the room was still. Daniel's breath was heavy, his heart racing in his chest. He had said it. He had made his choice. And the power that had controlled him for so long suddenly felt like a distant memory.

But then, as if to shatter his newfound resolve, his father's voice cut through the air, low and steady. "You think you can walk away from this? Do you think you can turn your back on everything we've built? You're not just walking away from the family, Daniel. You're walking away from the future itself."

Daniel's chest tightened, the weight of his father's words pressing down on him. But there was something else there too—a flicker of something deeper. A truth he hadn't realised until now.

"Maybe I'm not meant to control the world," Daniel said, his voice filled with a quiet but undeniable certainty. "Maybe I'm meant to be free from it."

Emily stood beside him now, her hand resting on his arm. "We're in this together, Daniel. Whatever happens, we'll face it together."

For the first time in what felt like forever, Daniel felt the weight of the world lift, just slightly. The path ahead was unclear, the danger still looming, but the truth had finally been spoken.

His father's gaze remained cold, but there was a flicker of something else in his eyes—perhaps regret, or the recognition that Daniel had just taken the first step toward something that had been buried long ago.

"You may think you've chosen your path," his father said, his voice softer now, tinged with a strange finality. "But the consequences of that choice will be greater than you can imagine."

Daniel met his father's gaze one last time before turning toward the door.

"Then I'll face them," he said quietly. "Because it's my life to live."

And with that, they walked out of the room, side by side, ready to face whatever came next.

Twenty-Six

Secrets in the Mansion

The mansion loomed before them, its silhouette cast in shadows by the late evening light. The air was thick with anticipation, the quiet of the surroundings only amplifying the weight of the moment. Daniel's heart thudded in his chest as they approached the front gates, their metal bars ornate and twisted like something out of a forgotten dream. This place—this house of secrets—was where it all began, where the answers had been buried under layers of lies and manipulation. Now, it was time to uncover them.

His hand gripped the coin in his pocket, the weight of it a constant reminder of everything they had been through. The vault, the ring, the cryptic key—each piece had led them here, to this mansion that seemed to hold the key to everything. But what lay within its walls? The truth? Or another trap waiting to snap shut on them?

"Are you sure this is the right place?" Emily's voice broke through his thoughts, sharp and laced with uncertainty. She had been quiet for most of the journey, her gaze fixed on the mansion as they walked. The weight of what they were about to face was heavy on both their shoulders.

Daniel nodded, though his own doubts lingered at the back of his mind. "We don't have a choice. The answers are here. Everything we've been looking for."

As they passed through the gates and up the grand stone steps leading to the massive front door, Daniel couldn't help but feel the strange sense of dread creeping up his spine. It wasn't just the mansion that unsettled him; it was the feeling that the game was about to reach its final stage, and there would be no turning back once they entered.

He pushed the door open with a creak, and they stepped inside, the dim light from outside barely reaching the darkened hallway. The interior was cold, the air stale as if it hadn't been disturbed for years. The grand chandelier overhead was draped in dust, its once brilliant crystals now dulled by time. Portraits of unknown figures lined the walls, their eyes seeming to follow every movement, their faces frozen in time, as though they had been here long before Daniel's family had ever set foot in this house.

"This place feels wrong," Emily whispered, her voice barely audible in the vastness of the entryway.

Daniel didn't answer. He didn't need to. He could feel it too—the weight of centuries of secrets that had been hidden in these walls, the lives that had been shaped by this mansion and the power it represented.

"Stay close," Daniel said, his voice low but firm. They had no idea what they would find inside, but whatever it was, they couldn't afford to be caught off guard.

They walked down the hallway, their footsteps muffled by the thick carpeting beneath them. The silence was suffocating, broken only by the occasional creak of the floorboards. As they moved deeper into the mansion, the air grew colder, the shadows seeming to stretch further with every step.

At the end of the hallway, Daniel stopped in front of a set of large double doors. The ornate carvings on the wood were intricate, almost grotesque, depicting scenes that seemed to shift in the dim light. He hesitated for a moment before pushing the doors open, the hinges groaning in protest.

The room beyond was vast, filled with towering bookshelves that stretched all the way to the ceiling. A massive fireplace took up one wall, its hearth long cold and unused. In the center of the room, a large desk sat covered in dust, papers scattered across its surface like forgotten remnants of another time. The walls were lined with mirrors, their surfaces cracked and warped, reflecting distorted images of the room around them.

Daniel stepped inside, his gaze sweeping the room, looking for anything that could offer a clue. He could feel Emily close behind him, her presence a comfort, even if they both knew the danger that lurked in this place.

"This is it," Daniel said quietly, his voice tense. "This is where it all ends."

Emily stepped beside him, her eyes scanning the room. "But where are the answers? What do we do now?"

Before Daniel could respond, the sound of footsteps echoed from behind them, sharp and measured. He whipped around, his hand instinctively reaching for the knife at his side, but he relaxed when he saw the figure standing in the doorway.

It was his father.

For a moment, time seemed to freeze. Daniel's mind raced as he tried to process what he was seeing. His father, the man who had abandoned him years ago, the man who had been the mastermind behind everything, stood before him in the doorway, his expression unreadable.

"Father," Daniel said, his voice tight with disbelief and a rising sense of anger. "What are you doing here?"

His father's eyes met his, and for a moment, there was something in them—a flicker of recognition, of sorrow, but also something else, something darker. "I didn't want you to find this place, Daniel," his father said, his voice rough. "But now that you're here, there's no turning back. You need to understand everything."

Daniel felt a knot form in his stomach. "Understand what? All these years, you've been playing me. You've been using me as a pawn in your game, and now you want me to just sit down and listen?"

His father's gaze softened, just for a moment, before his features hardened again. "You don't understand the full picture. You've never understood why I did what I did. But you will, once you see the truth."

Daniel's blood ran cold. "What truth?"

His father stepped into the room, his movements deliberate, his eyes flicking over the desk and the scattered papers. "The truth about the family. About what we've been trying to build. You're standing at the heart of it now, Daniel. The mansion, the vault, the coin—they're all part of something much larger than you've been told."

Daniel's mind raced as he tried to piece together the fragments of information he had gathered over the years. His father's words were like a jigsaw puzzle, but the pieces didn't quite fit.

"You've been working with Raphael," Daniel said, his voice low, the words coming out like venom. "You've been manipulating everything—me, the family, the world."

His father's expression faltered, just for a moment. "I've done what was necessary," he said, his voice strained. "I've done it for the family. For the future."

"Future?" Daniel laughed bitterly. "You think you're building something better by tearing everything down? By controlling people, by using them like chess pieces?"

His father didn't answer immediately. Instead, he walked toward the desk, his hands moving to the scattered papers. "You don't understand the stakes, Daniel. This isn't just about wealth or power. It's about survival. About creating a new world—one where we control the future."

Daniel stepped forward, his anger flaring. "And you think this is how to do it? By lying to me? By keeping me in the dark?"

His father's gaze snapped to his. "It wasn't supposed to be this way. You were always meant to take control. To lead the family into a new era. But you've been too caught up in your own sense of morality to see the bigger picture."

Daniel's heart pounded in his chest, the weight of his father's words sinking in. "You're sick," he said, his voice raw with emotion. "You've ruined everything. And now you want me to follow in your footsteps?"

His father's eyes darkened. "You think you can change things? You think you can walk away from all of this? You've already made your choice, Daniel. You've already taken the coin. And now you must decide what to do with it."

Daniel's pulse quickened. The coin. The key. He felt its weight in his pocket, the cold metal pressing against his skin like a curse.

"You have to understand," his father continued, his voice quieter now, but filled with a sense of urgency. "The world is changing. The system is collapsing. What we've built, everything we've worked for, it's all coming apart. But you, Daniel, you can fix it. You have the power to control it."

Daniel's vision blurred, his mind spinning with the weight of his father's words. The power to control it? What was he really asking? Was this what his father had wanted all along—to use him as a puppet, to continue a legacy of manipulation and control?

He glanced over at Emily, her face pale and drawn, her eyes wide with the realization of what was unfolding. She stepped forward slowly, her voice trembling but resolute. "Daniel… this isn't you. You don't have to be part of this. You don't have to choose this life."

Daniel's heart clenched as he looked back at his father, the man who had raised him, who had taught him to fight, to survive. But now, all of that felt like a lie. Everything he had been taught had been a means to an end. His father's vision of the future wasn't the future he wanted.

"No," Daniel said firmly, his voice filled with a quiet determination. "I won't be a part of this. I won't let you control me. Not anymore."

His father's eyes flashed with a dangerous mix of fury and disappointment. "You'll regret this, Daniel. You don't understand what you're throwing away."

Daniel stepped back, his heart pounding. "No. The only thing I'm throwing away is the life you've tried to force on me. I'm done with this. I'm done with you."

For the first time, Daniel saw something flicker in his father's eyes—a brief, fleeting moment of sadness. But it was gone in an instant, replaced by the cold resolve Daniel had grown so familiar with.

"You'll see, Daniel," his father said softly, his voice cold as ice. "You'll see that you can't escape the world we've built. Not ever."

And as his father turned and walked out of the room, leaving Daniel and Emily alone in the suffocating silence of the mansion, Daniel knew that the true battle was just beginning. The key, the coin—it wasn't just

Twenty-Seven

The Newspaper Clipping

The mansion was alive with the echoes of their footsteps as Daniel and Emily moved through the labyrinth of its vast corridors. The walls seemed to pulse with the weight of the secrets they held, and every creak of the old floorboards made the tension in the air thicker. The events of the past few days had sent Daniel's mind into a whirlwind. His father's words, the ominous power of the coin, and the decisions he had yet to make all played like fragments of a dream, blurring together in a haze of confusion and fear. But one thing was clear—he couldn't stop now. They had come too far.

As they navigated the long hallways, the flickering lights cast unsettling shadows on the faded portraits of long-dead relatives that lined the walls. It was as if the house itself was watching them, judging them, reminding them of the weight of the legacy they had inherited.

"What are we looking for, exactly?" Emily whispered, her voice barely audible as she glanced at the portraits, her eyes scanning the walls with a nervous energy.

"I don't know," Daniel admitted. "But we need something. A clue. A way out."

Emily's eyes softened, and she nodded, her hand brushing against his as they continued forward. The bond between them had only deepened in the wake of everything that had happened—since the first moments of their escape from the compound, when they had been thrust into the unknown. They were no longer just running from enemies or the weight of a family's twisted legacy. They were running toward something—toward truth, toward answers, toward freedom.

They reached the library at the far end of the mansion, a massive room filled with towering bookshelves that stretched all the way to the ceiling. Dust had settled thick on the leather-bound books, their spines cracked with age. The musty smell of old paper filled the air, the quiet hum of the mansion's isolation pressing in on them.

Daniel walked slowly toward a large wooden desk in the center of the room. It was cluttered with papers, photographs, and old books, the chaotic mess giving the impression that whoever had worked here had long since abandoned the space. As he sorted through the papers, his

The Newspaper Clipping

fingers brushing over their fragile edges, his gaze landed on something that immediately caught his attention—a yellowed newspaper clipping, partially hidden under a stack of books.

He lifted it slowly, as though afraid that touching it might break the fragile paper. The headline was bold, but faded with time, and as his eyes scanned the words, he felt a chill run down his spine.

"Mysterious Disappearance of Laurent Heiress: Foul Play Suspected"

Daniel's pulse quickened as he read the article more closely. The clipping was old—decades old, it seemed. The story was about a woman, a member of the Laurent family, who had vanished without a trace. There were no details, only speculation. But the implication was clear. Something had happened, something dark and twisted, to one of their own. And as Daniel read on, he recognized the name.

Isabelle Laurent.

His breath caught in his throat. Isabelle. His aunt, the woman who had mysteriously disappeared when Daniel was just a child. She had been the family's golden child, the one who was set to inherit everything, the one who had been groomed for power. And then, one day, she was gone. Just like that. No explanation, no trace.

But the article was a lie. The disappearance wasn't an

accident. It wasn't an unsolved mystery. It was something far worse.

Daniel's hand shook as he folded the clipping, his mind racing with questions. Isabelle's disappearance had never been solved. The police had done their best to find answers, but in the end, it was all swept under the rug. The Laurent family had moved on, just as they always did. But now, the answers were here. And they were darker than anything Daniel had imagined.

"Emily…" Daniel's voice was hoarse, his mind scrambling to process what he was holding. "This is about Isabelle."

Emily walked over to him, her eyes scanning the clipping with a growing sense of unease. "What does this mean, Daniel? What's going on?"

"She didn't disappear," Daniel said, his voice barely above a whisper. "She was taken. And I think I know who did it."

The realization hit him like a bolt of lightning. His father. The man who had spent his life hiding the truth, manipulating the family to maintain control. Isabelle's disappearance hadn't been an accident. It had been part of a larger plan, one that involved eliminating anyone who threatened the family's power. Isabelle had been a threat. She had been too smart, too capable, too driven to follow the family's corrupt path. So she had been removed.

Emily's gaze flicked from the clipping to Daniel's face, her eyes filled with concern. "But why? Why would your father do that?"

Daniel's stomach churned as the answer came crashing into his mind. His father had always been obsessed with control. Isabelle's death was part of his plan to maintain his grip on the family's wealth and influence. She had been the heir. And if she had disappeared, Daniel would be the one to take her place.

He shook his head, trying to shake off the horrifying thoughts that plagued him. "It's all connected," he muttered. "The vault, the coin, Isabelle's disappearance. They're all part of his plan."

Suddenly, there was a noise—a soft creak of the floorboards behind them. Daniel's heart skipped a beat as he turned, his hand instinctively going to his side, ready to draw the knife. But when he saw who it was, the tension in his body didn't ease. Instead, it deepened.

His father stood in the doorway.

For a moment, neither of them moved. The silence between them was suffocating, as if the air itself had frozen in anticipation of the next words. Daniel's hand tightened around the newspaper clipping in his grasp, his mind racing as he tried to process everything. His father had found them. Had been watching them. Waiting for them to uncover the truth.

"Well, well," his father said, his voice smooth, but with a hidden edge. "It seems you've found what you were looking for."

Daniel's grip on the clipping tightened, and he stepped forward, his chest rising with each shallow breath. "I know what you did. I know about Isabelle. And I know about the truth you've been hiding."

His father's eyes flickered, a momentary flash of something—guilt, maybe, or regret—but it was gone as quickly as it had appeared. "You're wrong, Daniel," he said quietly, his voice softer now, almost too calm. "You've been chasing shadows. Isabelle's disappearance was not what you think. It was necessary."

"Necessary?" Daniel spat, his anger rising with each passing second. "She was your daughter, and you killed her! You took her life to protect your own power!"

His father didn't flinch, but there was something in his eyes—something almost sad. "Isabelle was never meant to inherit anything. She was too… independent, too rebellious. She would have ruined everything. And I couldn't allow that. The family needed to survive, and to survive, we needed control. I did what was necessary."

Daniel's vision blurred with anger, his breath coming in sharp bursts. "You're a monster," he hissed. "And I've been part of your plan all along."

The Newspaper Clipping

His father stepped closer, his movements slow and deliberate, like a predator closing in on its prey. "You've always been part of the plan, Daniel. From the moment you were born. You were groomed to take my place, to carry on the legacy. The vault, the coin—they were always meant for you."

Daniel shook his head, trying to push past the rising wave of anger and disgust. "You've manipulated everything. My entire life has been a lie."

"You don't understand," his father said, his voice almost pleading now. "It was never about the money. It was about creating something that would last. You have the power, Daniel. The power to change the world."

Daniel's chest tightened. "I don't want your power. I don't want any of this. I'm not part of your system, and I never will be."

His father's face hardened, the sorrow gone, replaced with a cold, calculating expression. "You think you can escape it? You think you can walk away?"

Daniel didn't answer. Instead, he turned to Emily, his eyes locking with hers. They didn't need words. They both knew what had to be done. This was the moment they had been working toward. The truth was out, and they could no longer let it control them.

With a final glance at his father, Daniel turned and moved

toward the door. Emily followed, her steps light but determined. There was no turning back now.

His father's voice, cold and filled with finality, followed them as they left the room. "You can't outrun your destiny, Daniel. It will catch up with you."

But Daniel didn't stop. He didn't look back. He and Emily were walking away from the past, from the lies, from the darkness that had defined their lives. The future was theirs to shape.

And this time, they would do it on their own terms.

Twenty-Eight

A Nighttime Rescue

The night had fallen heavy, its dark veil blanketing the mansion and surrounding grounds in an eerie, almost suffocating silence. The mansion's imposing silhouette loomed like a silent sentinel, watching as Daniel and Emily carefully made their way toward the rear gate, their steps quick but deliberate. The weight of the decisions they had made and the secrets they had uncovered pressed down on Daniel like a thousand-ton weight. His mind raced as he replayed the conversation with his father, the man who had always been his mentor, his guide, now revealed to be the architect of all the pain and manipulation that had shaped his life.

His father's words echoed in his mind: You can't outrun your destiny, Daniel. It will catch up with you. The threat had been more than just words; it had been a warning. One that Daniel knew they couldn't ignore.

They had escaped the library, but the mansion was no longer a place of refuge. It was a cage, a place where their pasts were inescapable, where every corner hid more secrets, more lies. Their path forward was clear: they had to leave before it was too late.

The rear gate was a small, inconspicuous entryway, tucked away behind the overgrown ivy that clung to the stone walls. From here, they could make their way into the woods that bordered the property, a maze of trees that could provide cover and a route to safety.

"Stay quiet," Daniel whispered, his voice barely audible against the low hum of the wind rustling through the trees. "We're almost there."

Emily nodded, her breath coming in shallow gasps as she kept pace with him. Her hand clutched his tightly, the silent comfort of their bond the only thing that steadied her nerves. They had come this far together, and there was no turning back now.

The gate was just ahead. Daniel's fingers wrapped around the cold metal handle, turning it slowly, careful not to make a sound. The gate creaked in protest as it slowly swung open, revealing the dark, overgrown path beyond. The moonlight barely pierced through the thick canopy of trees above, casting long shadows across the ground. Every step they took seemed amplified in the quiet of the night, as if the world was holding its breath.

But as they stepped through the gate, a sudden rustle from behind them sent Daniel's heart into overdrive. He whirled around, his breath catching in his throat. The mansion loomed behind them, its windows dark, but in the distance, he saw movement.

A figure emerged from the shadows.

"Move!" Daniel hissed, grabbing Emily's arm and pulling her along as he sprinted down the narrow path, his legs burning with the effort. He didn't need to look back to know they were being followed. The figures at the mansion had seen them. They had been discovered.

"Go, go, go!" Daniel urged, his voice tight with fear as he pushed Emily forward, his own steps heavy and hurried. The trees around them blurred, the path a twisting maze of roots and underbrush that made every movement feel like they were running through molasses.

Behind them, the sound of pursuit grew louder. They weren't alone. The guards were coming, their footsteps heavy and relentless. It was too late to turn back now. The only choice they had was to run.

The dense woods swallowed them whole as they barreled through the underbrush, branches whipping at their faces and hands. Daniel's breath came in ragged gasps as he pushed through the thicket, his thoughts racing.

"We can't outrun them," Emily panted beside him. "They're faster, they're more prepared—"

"We don't need to outrun them," Daniel said, his voice strained. "We just need to get to the river. We're not far. Once we're there, we can cross, and they'll lose us in the current."

Emily's eyes met his in the darkness, a glimmer of hope flashing in her gaze despite the overwhelming danger. The river. It was their only chance. But it was a dangerous gamble, one that could easily end in disaster. Yet, there was no other option.

As they ran deeper into the woods, the sound of the guards' pursuit grew louder, closer. Daniel could hear their voices now, their shouts carrying through the trees, the unmistakable click of boots on the forest floor. They were gaining on them.

Then, ahead, Daniel spotted a clearing. The faint sound of rushing water echoed through the trees. The river.

"We're almost there," Daniel breathed, adrenaline flooding his veins as he pushed himself harder, faster. He could feel Emily's hand trembling in his, but he didn't slow down. They had no time to waste.

They broke through the trees and into the clearing, the moonlight reflecting off the fast-moving water below. Daniel's heart raced as he looked at the river. It was wide,

A Nighttime Rescue

but the current wasn't as strong as he had feared. There were rocks scattered along the surface, creating a makeshift bridge that could give them a way across.

Without hesitation, Daniel grabbed Emily's hand and plunged into the river. The icy water immediately soaked through his clothes, the cold biting into his skin as they struggled to keep their footing. The current was strong, pulling at their legs, but Daniel fought against it, his focus solely on getting across.

"Stay close!" he called to Emily, his voice almost drowned out by the rush of water around them. "Don't let go!"

They scrambled over the rocks, the water rising higher with every step they took. Daniel's legs were trembling from the cold and the effort, but he pushed forward, unwilling to stop now. Emily was right behind him, her breath labored but determined.

As they neared the far bank, the sound of the guards' voices reached them, echoing through the trees on the opposite side of the river. Daniel's pulse quickened. They weren't far behind.

Just as they reached the other side, Daniel heard a shout from the clearing. A guard had reached the edge of the river. He could hear the man's voice, shouting orders into the night.

"Faster!" Daniel urged Emily, pulling her up the muddy

bank. He could feel the weight of their situation closing in on him, the realization that they were not free yet sinking deep. They were still being hunted.

They staggered up the bank, their legs shaking from the cold and the exertion. Daniel glanced behind them as they reached the tree line. The shadows in the clearing were moving. The guards were coming.

"Go!" Daniel barked, his voice hoarse. They didn't have time to look back now. They needed to get to cover, to find somewhere safe before the guards could spot them.

They ran deeper into the forest, their legs burning, the sound of the river fading behind them as they pushed forward into the dark, uncharted woods. They had to lose their pursuers, had to find a way to disappear into the night.

Daniel's heart raced as they moved, the shadows of the trees seeming to close in around them, but the familiar sense of danger didn't go away. He kept glancing over his shoulder, expecting to see the flash of a flashlight or hear the crack of a twig breaking underfoot. But the night was still, and they were alone—at least for now.

"How much farther?" Emily gasped, her voice strained with exhaustion.

"Not much," Daniel said, his voice tight with determination. "We just need to get to the cabin. It's up ahead."

A Nighttime Rescue

The cabin. The small, hidden refuge that had once belonged to his uncle, a place where he and Emily had spent time as children, unaware of the danger that lurked in the shadows of their family. Now, it was their only hope. The last safe place.

They stumbled forward through the woods, their breath coming in ragged gasps. Daniel's mind raced, the pressure of everything weighing heavily on him. His father, Raphael, the truth, the lies—it all seemed like a blur now. But there was one thing that remained clear: they couldn't stop. Not yet.

Finally, after what felt like an eternity, they broke through the trees and into a small clearing. The cabin stood before them, a simple, weathered structure that seemed almost out of place in the midst of the dark forest. But it was theirs, for now. It was their refuge.

Daniel pushed open the door, the old wood creaking in protest as they stepped inside. He didn't bother with the light; the faint glow of the moon outside was enough to reveal the basic furnishings inside. The air smelled musty, untouched for years, but it was shelter. And for now, that was all they needed.

He turned to Emily, her face pale and drawn from the exertion. "We're safe," he said, his voice soft but filled with relief.

Emily nodded, but there was something in her eyes—a

flicker of uncertainty, of fear. "Are we really safe, Daniel? How long before they find us again?"

Daniel didn't have an answer. He wanted to tell her they were free, that they had escaped. But deep down, he knew they weren't. The game wasn't over. It was only just beginning.

He moved toward the window, peering out into the darkness. The faint sounds of the forest filled the air, but nothing else. He closed his eyes for a moment, trying to steady his racing heart. They had made it this far, but the journey was far from over.

For now, they were safe. But the night was far from over.

Twenty-Nine

The Code of Betrayal

The cabin's silence was broken only by the faint crackling of the fire in the corner of the room. Daniel's eyes darted from the window to the door, his mind racing with the weight of their escape. They had made it out of the mansion, out of the clutches of his father and the shadowy forces that had tried to control their lives. But even in the safety of the small cabin, deep in the heart of the woods, Daniel could feel the oppressive weight of the past pressing in on him.

Emily sat across from him, her face pale and drawn. She hadn't said much since they had arrived, too exhausted to speak, too shaken by the events of the night to form coherent thoughts. Her eyes, however, told a different story—one of fear, of uncertainty, and of the deep well of betrayal that seemed to pool between them.

Daniel couldn't shake the feeling that the game was far from over. The events of the past few days—his father's cryptic words, the discovery of Isabelle's fate, and the relentless pursuit of the people who wanted to control them—were still too fresh in his mind. The truth, if it could even be called that, was not as simple as they had once hoped. The mansion, the coin, the key to it all—it was all connected, but the pieces of the puzzle refused to fit.

"Do you think we're safe here?" Emily's voice cut through the thick silence, her tone quiet but filled with an undertone of fear.

Daniel's gaze flicked to the door once more. It was locked, as it should be, but the feeling of being watched, of being hunted, never quite left him. "For now," he muttered, running a hand through his hair in frustration. "But they're still out there, Emily. I can feel it."

Emily's shoulders slumped, her eyes falling to her lap as if the weight of the world had descended upon her. "They'll find us eventually," she whispered. "They always do. You can't outrun the people who've been in control for so long. Your father… Raphael… they won't stop until they have everything back."

Daniel's chest tightened at the mention of his father. The man who had once been his guiding force, the man who had shaped his life, was now the source of all his pain. The twisted legacy of the Laurent family had become a prison, one from which Daniel couldn't escape. And yet, despite all the hatred that brewed inside him for his father and the corruption that ran through his veins, he couldn't deny that there was something deep inside him—a flicker of doubt—that made him wonder if he was doing the right thing. Was it possible that his father had been right all along? That the world needed a leader who understood the rules, who could bend them to ensure survival?

"No," Daniel whispered to himself, shaking his head. He couldn't go down that path. He wouldn't.

Emily raised her eyes, her voice soft. "What are you thinking, Daniel?"

Daniel swallowed hard, his thoughts swirling like a whirlwind. "I don't know," he said finally. "I'm thinking that we don't have a choice. We can't keep running. We can't keep hiding forever. I need to know the truth. The whole truth. And I need to put an end to this. We both do."

Emily was silent for a long moment, her gaze unwavering as she studied him. Finally, she nodded. "I'll stand by you. But you need to know… we're not the only ones after the truth. If we go after it, it could destroy us."

Daniel's mind flickered back to the newspaper clipping they had found—the story about Isabelle. The more he thought about it, the more it became clear. His father's obsession with control, his family's legacy, and the fate of Isabelle all seemed to be woven into one dark tapestry of lies, deceit, and betrayal. And the key—the coin—was the final thread.

The clock on the wall ticked steadily, the sound a constant reminder of how little time they had. Every moment they stayed here was a moment closer to being found. Daniel knew they couldn't stay hidden forever. They needed answers. But where would they find them? And who could they trust?

He stood up suddenly, the firelight casting strange shadows on the walls. "We need to get to the vault. That's where the answers are. We can't keep running from this. It's the only way."

Emily stood as well, her expression hardening with determination. "Then we go after it. But we can't do it alone. We need help."

Daniel shook his head. "No. We can't trust anyone. Not after everything. I won't risk it."

Emily frowned, but she didn't argue. Instead, she turned and moved toward the small table in the corner, her hand brushing over a piece of paper that had been left there. As she picked it up, Daniel's eyes narrowed. It was a letter—folded and old, the paper yellowed with age.

"What's that?" Daniel asked, crossing the room to stand beside her.

Emily turned the letter over in her hands, her fingers trembling as she unfolded it. The ink was smudged in places, the handwriting uneven, but the words were unmistakable.

The Code of Betrayal

It was a letter—written in haste—addressed to Isabelle Laurent.

Daniel's breath caught in his chest. "Isabelle."

Emily's voice trembled as she began to read aloud.

"Isabelle, if you're reading this, then I've failed. I've failed to protect you from them. The family, your father, they are not what they seem. There's a code—an ancient code—that governs everything, every decision. You were right to question it, but I fear that even you won't be able to change it now. The vault holds everything. It is the key to understanding the truth, to ending this madness once and for all. But it is also a curse. Beware those who seek it. Beware your own blood. They will stop at nothing to keep it hidden."

Emily's voice faltered, her hands shaking as she finished reading the letter. "This... this isn't just about the family. It's about something bigger."

Daniel's mind raced as the pieces began to fall into place. "The code," he muttered, his voice barely above a whisper. "The code of betrayal. This letter... it's warning her. Warning us."

"Your father..." Emily began, her eyes wide with realization. "He's part of this code. The Laurent legacy. It's built on lies, on betrayal. And Isabelle knew it."

Daniel clenched his fists at his sides. "But she didn't just disappear. She tried to expose the truth. She paid the price for it."

Emily met his gaze. "And now we're paying the price too. If we go after the vault, we'll have to face everything your father's built. All the lies. All the blood."

A cold shiver ran down Daniel's spine as he thought of the vault. The key. Everything they had been searching for. It was all tied together by one thing: betrayal. The truth had been buried under a veil of lies, hidden behind a code that no one had ever dared to break. But Isabelle had tried. And now, it was up to Daniel to finish what she had started.

"We don't have a choice," Daniel said, his voice quiet but firm. "We can't run anymore. We have to face this head-on."

Emily nodded, her expression resolute. "Then we go. But we do it together. And we do it smart. We can't let your father get to us first."

Daniel turned away, walking toward the door. He had made his decision. There was no turning back now. The vault held the answers. The code of betrayal, hidden in the heart of the Laurent family, would finally be uncovered. And nothing—no one—could stop them.

As he stepped into the night, the cold wind biting at his skin, he could feel the weight of the past pressing down on him. But the future was theirs to shape now. The code, the betrayal, the lies—it all ended here.

And with Emily by his side, Daniel knew they would face whatever came next, together.

Thirty

The Accidental Kiss

The night was closing in, the thick dark of the woods surrounding them like a suffocating blanket, pressing in on all sides. The weight of what had just happened—escaping the mansion, finding the vault, and confronting Daniel's father—still hung heavy in the air. Daniel's heart was still racing, the adrenaline coursing through his veins, but there was no time to rest. Not yet. Not until they were out of here.

The fire in the small cabin had long since died down, leaving only faint embers to cast a low, flickering light on the walls. Daniel moved about the room, not really focused on anything but his own thoughts. The truth, the vault, the betrayal—it was all too much. His father's face kept flashing before his eyes, his cold, calculating stare, the same man who had once been his mentor, the man who had shaped

The Accidental Kiss

Daniel's world and then twisted it beyond recognition. The man who had murdered his sister, Isabelle, in order to maintain control.

There was no escaping it. The past would never truly let him go.

Emily had been quiet for most of the night, sitting on the far side of the room, her hands clasped in her lap, her eyes distant. She had been through just as much as Daniel, maybe even more. She had faced the terror of being hunted, of having the world collapse around her, and now, she was forced to navigate the labyrinth of lies and secrets that Daniel's family had built.

Daniel's thoughts drifted to her now. He hadn't realized how much he had come to rely on her presence. She had been a constant source of strength, the one person who hadn't turned away from him when everything else fell apart. They were in this together—no matter how dark it got.

"Emily?" Daniel's voice was soft, his throat tight as he tried to break the silence that had settled between them.

She looked up slowly, her eyes flicking to him before she shifted her gaze away, as though searching for something in the shadows of the room. "Hmm?"

"I—" Daniel hesitated, his mouth dry. "I don't know what to do next. I thought that finding the vault, unlocking the truth would… I don't know, would give me some clarity. But it's like I'm drowning in it all." His voice wavered at the end, the frustration and confusion that had been building inside him spilling out in an unguarded moment.

Emily studied him for a long moment, her eyes softening. Then she stood, moving toward him with deliberate steps. Her eyes never left his as she came closer, until she was standing right in front of him.

"You don't have to have all the answers," she said quietly. "You don't have to carry all of this alone."

Daniel's heart skipped a beat, the weight of her words settling deep inside him. He had spent so much of his life trying to solve everything by himself, trying to protect those he loved, but now, in this moment, he realized something. He didn't have to do it alone. He couldn't. Not anymore. And he didn't want to.

"I… I don't know what I'd do without you," Daniel murmured, his voice barely above a whisper. It was the truth. There was something in the way Emily had stayed by his side, no matter how dark things got. It wasn't just her bravery or her strength—it was her willingness to stand with him when everything else seemed to be crumbling.

Emily's breath hitched slightly at his words, and for a moment, Daniel thought he had said too much. But before he could retract his statement, she stepped closer, her face only inches from his. Her eyes searched his, and in the dim light of the cabin, the world outside seemed to vanish entirely. There was nothing but the two of them—silent, suspended in a moment that felt too charged to ignore.

And then it happened.

As if guided by some invisible force, they both leaned forward at the same time. The tension between them grew unbearable, the space between their lips shrinking with every passing second. Daniel's heart hammered in his chest as his mind screamed in protest, telling him to stop, to pull away, to think. But his body didn't listen. He was too caught up in the heat of the moment, in the raw, unspoken connection that had been growing between them for days, for weeks.

The kiss was not planned, not premeditated. It wasn't the product of romantic intention, but something deeper—something born out of shared pain, loss, and the unrelenting need for solace in the face of chaos. It was soft at first, tentative, a question between them, unspoken but undeniably present. And then, as if the world had been waiting for it, the kiss deepened, and everything else faded away. There was no vault, no betrayal, no secrets—only the heat of the moment, the feeling of Emily's lips against his, and the way her breath mingled with his in the dim light of the cabin.

Daniel's hand moved, almost without thought, to rest on her waist, drawing her closer. He could feel the rapid beat of her heart against his chest, her hands trembling slightly as they settled on his shoulders. The world outside the cabin felt so distant now, so irrelevant, as if time itself had stopped.

But just as quickly as it had started, the kiss broke. They pulled away from each other, their breaths ragged, their faces inches apart, their eyes wide with a mixture of surprise and confusion. The air between them was thick with unspoken thoughts, with the realization of what had just transpired.

Daniel's chest heaved as he tried to process the whirlwind of emotions that had just overtaken him. "I... I'm sorry," he whispered, his voice strained. "That wasn't—"

But Emily cut him off, her fingers lightly grazing his lips as if to silence him. She didn't say anything, but the look in her eyes spoke volumes. There was no judgment, no shock. Just understanding, a quiet acceptance that what had just happened was inevitable. The kiss was a momentary escape from the crushing weight of everything they had been through, and, in its own way, it was the only thing that made sense.

"You don't have to apologize," Emily said softly, her voice filled with a tenderness that made Daniel's heart ache. "We're both just trying to survive this. We're both lost in this mess, but we're here. Together."

Daniel nodded, his chest tight. He didn't know what to say. What could he say? This wasn't just about the kiss—it was about everything that had led them here. The trauma, the secrets, the betrayals. The truth that had been buried beneath years of lies.

"I didn't expect this," Daniel admitted, his voice low. "I didn't expect to feel this way."

Emily smiled faintly, her hand still resting gently on his chest. "Neither did I," she said, her eyes never leaving his. "But here we are."

Daniel swallowed hard, the weight of the moment settling in. He had always believed that emotions—especially in the midst of chaos—were distractions. But in that moment, he realized how wrong he had been. It wasn't a distraction. It was a lifeline. A reminder that even in the darkest of times, they weren't alone.

For a moment, they simply stood there, their bodies close, the soft glow of the fire casting flickering shadows across their faces. Time seemed to stretch and bend, and for the first time in days, the tension in Daniel's chest loosened, just a little. The weight of the world had not been lifted, but in Emily's presence, in the quiet understanding between them, there was a glimmer of hope.

"We'll figure this out," Emily whispered after a long pause, her voice steady, though the exhaustion was clear in her eyes. "Together."

Daniel nodded, his heart thumping in his chest. Together. They had been through so much, and yet, somehow, they had made it this far. The kiss hadn't changed anything—it hadn't fixed everything. But it had brought them closer, reminded them of what they meant to each other. They were in this mess together, and together, they would face whatever came next.

For the first time in a long time, Daniel felt a flicker of hope. It was small, fragile, but it was there.

And for now, that was enough.

Thirty-One

Emily's Doubts

The night stretched on, the silence in the cabin becoming suffocating as Emily stared at the flickering fire. The low crackle of the embers was the only sound in the room, and yet, in the heavy stillness, it felt as if the entire world was holding its breath, waiting for something—waiting for them to make the next move.

She hadn't said much since the kiss. Words seemed unnecessary, yet they hung in the air, just out of reach. She didn't want to make things awkward, to complicate the fragile truce they had found between them in the chaos of their flight. But something about the way Daniel had looked at her, the way his body had responded to the unspoken tension between them, made her question everything she thought she knew.

Was this real? Was it just a momentary lapse in judgment, a result of the stress, the danger, the fear that gripped them both? Or was it something more? Something deeper?

Emily couldn't deny the pull she felt toward Daniel. It wasn't just the kiss—it was everything. The way he had protected her, how they had fought side by side, how his pain mirrored her own. She had always believed that survival was a solitary thing, something you did alone. But with Daniel, she realized that wasn't true. Not anymore.

But as much as she wanted to believe in them, in the possibility of something more, doubt gnawed at the edges of her mind like a constant, gnawing hunger. She had seen what power, betrayal, and deception could do to people. She had seen how quickly relationships could turn toxic when built on lies. And that was what Daniel's world was— a world of lies, manipulation, and secrets that ran so deep, they threatened to drown everything in their wake.

Emily shifted uneasily on the couch, her gaze shifting from the fire to Daniel, who was pacing near the window, his back to her. She watched the way the shadows played across his face, how his shoulders were tense, his posture guarded. He had always carried the weight of the world on his shoulders, but now it felt different—he wasn't just trying to protect her, or keep his family's secrets hidden. He was unraveling, and Emily wasn't sure she could follow him into that darkness.

Her fingers tightened around the edge of her blanket as she tried to push the doubt away. Don't overthink this, she told herself. Just be here. Be with him.

But the doubts lingered, clawing at her from within. She had been part of this world for far too long—had seen how easily people could be consumed by it. And Daniel? He was no different. He was just as much a product of the lies and the darkness that ran through his family as anyone else.

Her mind kept returning to the kiss. She couldn't shake the way it had felt. The way he had kissed her with a kind of urgency, a need she couldn't quite place. And yet, in the moments after, as they had pulled away from each other, there was something in Daniel's eyes that unsettled her—a flicker of something deeper, something unreadable.

She needed to know. She needed to understand what that moment had meant, what had sparked it, and whether it was something she could trust.

"Daniel," Emily said quietly, breaking the silence, her voice softer than she intended. "Can we talk?"

Daniel stopped pacing, his eyes flicking over his shoulder to meet hers. His face softened, but the tension in his posture didn't ease. He nodded, but Emily could see the exhaustion in his eyes. He hadn't been sleeping well, had barely eaten anything, and it was starting to show. His jaw was tight, his face drawn, and his eyes had a haunted look to them, as though he was constantly fighting against something that threatened to consume him.

"What's on your mind?" he asked, his voice low, though there was a hint of concern in his tone. He sat down across from her, the distance between them somehow feeling too wide now.

Emily hesitated, chewing on her bottom lip. She didn't want to hurt him, didn't want to shatter the fragile bond they had formed, but the questions, the doubts, they wouldn't leave her. They couldn't be ignored any longer.

"I don't know if I'm ready for this," she said, her voice barely a whisper. Her heart pounded as she forced the words out, but once they were spoken, it felt like a weight had been lifted.

Daniel's expression softened further, and he leaned forward, his hands resting on his knees. "I know," he said simply, his voice quiet but understanding. "I know this isn't easy. We're not in a normal situation, Emily. I'm not pretending to have all the answers. But you're here. We're here together. And that means something."

Emily shook her head, her chest tightening as she tried to articulate the storm of emotions swirling inside her. "It's not just that. It's…" She faltered, trying to find the right words. "It's everything, Daniel. You're… you're different. I've seen what your family's done, what they're capable of. And I've seen you. The way you've been caught up in all of this. The way you've been trying to keep everything together. But I can't help but wonder if it's already too late for you. For us."

Emily's Doubts

Daniel's eyes flickered with hurt at her words, but there was something else there too—something guarded, something resigned. He looked away, his jaw clenching as though he were fighting against something within himself.

"I don't have a choice, Emily," he said, his voice quiet but edged with frustration. "I can't change what's been done. What my family's done. All I can do is keep moving forward. Keep trying to find a way out of this mess. For both of us."

Emily's heart ached at his words, but the doubt still lingered. She could see the weight of the past pressing on him, could see how it had shaped him into someone who was both strong and fragile at the same time. But she couldn't ignore the fear that had settled in her chest. Fear that he might become just like them. Fear that the darkness of his family would consume him, just as it had consumed so many others.

"I know you feel like you're trapped, like you have to fix everything, but Daniel… we're not the same as them," Emily said, her voice cracking slightly. She reached out, her hand brushing his, trying to close the distance between them. "We're not like them."

Daniel's eyes softened as he turned back to her, his hand closing over hers in a gesture that spoke more than words ever could. But there was something else in his eyes now—something uncertain, something that made Emily's stomach tighten with dread. Was he starting to believe that he was like them? That he was bound to follow the same path of darkness and betrayal?

"I'm not like them," Daniel whispered, as though trying to convince himself. His grip on her hand tightened, but his voice wavered, betraying the uncertainty inside him. "But the truth is, Emily, I don't know if I can be anything else. I don't know if I can outrun this. Outrun what's already been set in motion. The code, the vault, the family... it's all tangled up in me now. And I don't know how to untangle it."

Emily's chest tightened, her pulse quickening as the weight of his words settled over her. She had known that Daniel had been carrying a heavy burden, but hearing him say it out loud—hearing the self-doubt, the resignation in his voice—shook her to her core. Was he already lost? Was it too late for him to change? For them to change?

"Maybe we can't change everything, but we can change this," Emily said, her voice steady despite the turmoil she felt inside. She leaned forward, her eyes locking with his. "You don't have to carry this alone, Daniel. We're in this together. No matter what happens next."

Daniel's eyes searched hers for a long moment, and Emily could see the conflict within him. The war between the man he wanted to be and the man he thought he had to be. It was like watching a storm brew on the horizon, knowing that the calm would soon break.

"I don't want to lose you," Daniel said, his voice barely a

whisper. "But I can't promise you anything. I can't promise I'll be the person you think I am. I can't promise I'll be the person I want to be."

Emily's heart ached, but she didn't pull away. "I don't need promises, Daniel. I just need you to be here. With me. With us."

For a long moment, they sat there, locked in a silence that was both comfortable and suffocating. Emily could feel the weight of the doubt that hung between them, like a tangible thing. The kiss, the closeness, the unspoken feelings—they all seemed so fragile now, as if the smallest shift in the air could tear them apart.

But she wouldn't let it happen. Not yet. Not when they were so close.

"Let's just take it one step at a time," Emily said finally, her voice calm, even though the doubts still churned inside her. She squeezed his hand, trying to reassure him, and herself. "We don't have to have all the answers right now. We just need to stick together. We can figure this out. Together."

Daniel nodded slowly, his eyes searching hers for something. A promise. An answer. A way forward.

"I'm not giving up on you, Daniel," Emily said softly, her words a quiet vow. "And I'm not giving up on us."

For a long moment, they simply sat there, the weight of their words sinking in. The doubts, the fears, the uncertainty—they were still there. But in that moment, with her hand in his, Emily knew one thing for sure. They weren't alone. And maybe, just maybe, that was enough to start rewriting their story.

Thirty-Two

A Race Against Time

The first light of dawn was creeping over the horizon, casting faint golden hues across the dark forest. It was a beauty that seemed out of place in the midst of the chaos, but Daniel barely noticed. His mind was elsewhere, his thoughts tangled in a web of doubt and urgency. The hours of running, the constant danger—they had all led to this moment.

The weight of the past, of everything his family had done, was like a stone in his chest, pressing against him with each breath. He couldn't outrun it. But now, with the vault within their reach and his father's betrayal so fresh in his mind, the only thing that mattered was getting to the truth. The code, the vault, the coin—it was all connected, and it had to end today.

Daniel's eyes flickered to Emily, sitting across from him in the dim light of the cabin, her face pale, her eyes clouded with worry. She had been by his side through it all, and yet, even now, he could see the doubts lingering in her gaze. She had seen what his family was capable of, and it was hard for him to shake the feeling that Emily was starting to see him differently. That maybe she was beginning to question whether he was just another Laurent, trapped in the same cycle of lies and deception.

But he couldn't afford to focus on that now. They had one chance. One shot to take control of their fate, to break free from the grasp of his family's dark legacy. And time was running out.

"Are you ready?" Daniel's voice broke the silence. He didn't look at her, but he could feel her eyes on him, as though waiting for some sign that everything would be okay.

Emily didn't answer right away. Instead, she stood up slowly, her eyes narrowing with determination. She wasn't the type to give up, not ever. And yet, there was something in the way she held herself that made Daniel's heart ache. The weight of everything had worn her down too. The danger, the uncertainty, the constant threat from his family—it was all too much.

"I don't know if I'm ready," she said quietly, her voice tinged with uncertainty. "But I'm with you. We're in this together, remember?"

A Race Against Time

Daniel nodded, though his chest tightened at her words. Together. It was the only thing he had left to cling to, the only thing that kept him from falling apart. He couldn't afford to let her slip away now—not after everything they had been through.

The silence stretched between them, but it wasn't uncomfortable. It was just the weight of the moment, the weight of the choice they were about to make.

"We're not just running anymore," Daniel said, his voice steady, but tinged with a sense of urgency. "We're racing against time. If we don't make it to the vault before they do, if they get their hands on the coin, it'll all be over."

Emily's eyes flickered with fear, but she nodded. "We won't let that happen."

Daniel turned toward the door, his mind already calculating the distance to the vault. They had planned everything out, memorized every turn, every possible escape route. But nothing could prepare them for the last stretch of the journey—the part where they would face the inevitable confrontation.

The vault. The key. The answers to everything that had been hidden for so long.

They had been followed. Daniel knew it. His father's men would be close behind, watching every move, ready to pounce the moment they made their move. They were the last line of defense, the final obstacle standing between Daniel and the truth.

They couldn't waste any more time.

Daniel pulled the jacket tighter around his shoulders, and with one last glance at Emily, he pushed the door open. The world outside was still shrouded in the half-light of dawn, but he knew that the clock was ticking. They had to get to the vault, and they had to do it fast.

"Stay close," Daniel warned as he stepped out into the cool morning air. "Don't let them get too close."

They moved swiftly through the woods, the underbrush crunching beneath their feet. The clearing was just ahead—the vault wasn't far. The trees were dense, their branches reaching toward the sky, but in the distance, Daniel could just make out the faint outline of the stone structure where the vault lay hidden.

They were close.

But just as they approached the clearing, Daniel's senses went on high alert. There was something wrong. The hairs on the back of his neck stood up, his pulse quickening. He could feel eyes on him. They're here.

Without warning, a shout echoed from behind them. It was too late. They had been spotted.

"Run!" Daniel yelled, grabbing Emily's hand and pulling her toward the clearing. The sound of heavy footsteps and shouting filled the air, and Daniel didn't need to look back to know they were being pursued. The guards were closing in fast.

The vault was within sight, but it might as well have been a mile away as Daniel pushed himself harder, faster, the weight of Emily's hand in his sending a jolt of energy through him. They couldn't let them catch up.

The clearing was just ahead, the stone doors of the vault barely visible through the trees. They were almost there.

But the sound of boots crunching against the dirt reached Daniel's ears, growing louder by the second. He glanced back over his shoulder. The guards were right behind them—too close. They had to get to the vault before they were overtaken.

"We're almost there!" Daniel shouted, his voice filled with urgency. "Just a little further!"

He could see the outline of the vault now, the stone door barely visible in the dim light. There was a sense of finality about it—this was where everything would either come together, or fall apart.

Emily's hand tightened around his, and he could feel her pulse in her grip. She was scared, but there was something else in her—determination, grit. She wasn't about to let go now. They had come too far.

They reached the vault just as the first guard broke into the clearing. Daniel didn't waste a second. He reached for the coin, still clenched in his pocket, and with trembling hands, inserted it into the keyhole. The mechanism in the stone door clicked, and for a moment, everything seemed to stop. The guards were just steps behind them. The door began to turn, the heavy stone grinding against itself as it opened.

Emily grabbed the door with both hands, pulling it open wider. The moment the door was fully ajar, Daniel shoved her inside. He didn't look back. He didn't have time. He could hear the guards shouting, their footsteps too close for comfort.

"Get inside!" he yelled, his voice hoarse.

Emily stumbled into the darkness of the vault, but she didn't hesitate. She turned, pulling Daniel in after her. The stone door slammed shut behind them with a deafening thud, cutting off the sounds of the outside world. They were inside.

But it wasn't over yet.

The air inside the vault was cool, musty, and heavy with the scent of old stone. The room was dark, save for the faint light coming from the cracks in the stone door and the distant corners where dust had settled. But there was something else in the air—a sense of weight, of finality.

The vault was not just a place of secrets. It was a tomb, a resting place for the darkness that had been buried here for generations.

Daniel's heart hammered in his chest as he scanned the interior of the vault. The stone walls were lined with shelves, some filled with old books and scrolls, others with items whose purpose seemed lost to time. But at the far end of the room, a pedestal stood, covered in dust. And on that pedestal, there it was. The box.

It was small, ancient, and sealed with a wax emblem that matched the one on the coin.

Daniel took a step forward, his breath shallow. This was it. The truth. The answers they had been searching for. But as he approached the pedestal, something inside him shifted. He felt the weight of it—the box, the legacy, the lies—and suddenly, he wasn't sure if he was ready to face what lay inside.

Emily's hand found his again, pulling him back to the moment. "We don't have time to hesitate, Daniel," she whispered, her voice urgent. "Open it."

Daniel nodded, but the uncertainty lingered in his chest. He didn't have a choice. Not anymore.

With a deep breath, he reached for the box, his fingers trembling as he broke the seal. The moment the lid was lifted, the room seemed to breathe with him—an ancient, oppressive energy filling the air. Inside the box was a single piece of parchment, aged and fragile.

Daniel's hands shook as he unfolded the paper, the words on it scrawled in a language he barely recognized.

And then, as the realization hit him, he knew. The race wasn't over. The real challenge had just begun.

Thirty-Three

The Family Heirloom

The silence in the vault was oppressive, each second stretching endlessly as Daniel's trembling fingers held the parchment. The paper crackled softly in his grip, the ancient ink on it dark and unfaded despite the years it had spent hidden away. The vault itself seemed to close in on them, the weight of its centuries of secrets pressing on their shoulders. He couldn't help but feel that every step they had taken had led them to this moment, and yet, it was only now that he realized the true cost of what they had done.

Behind him, Emily stood motionless, her breath shallow in the suffocating stillness of the room. Her hand hovered near his, but she didn't touch him. She knew as well as he did that this was the moment that would either give them the answers they sought or bury them in even more lies.

"Do you know what it says?" Emily's voice was barely a whisper, but it felt loud in the quiet room, filled with anticipation.

Daniel swallowed hard, his mouth dry as he glanced at the delicate parchment again. The language was ancient, the letters curled in a way he could barely decipher. He could make out a few words, fragments of phrases, but they were not enough. He had no way of knowing if they were the answers they sought—or just another twisted riddle.

"No," he muttered, shaking his head. "But we have to find out."

He spread the paper flat on the pedestal, his hand hovering over it, unsure of the next move. It felt as though the vault was holding its breath, the very air pregnant with expectation. The parchment was old, fragile; it could fall apart with a wrong touch. But they had no choice but to read it, to take this last step toward uncovering the truth.

"Help me," Daniel said, his voice steady despite the racing thoughts in his head.

Emily stepped forward, her eyes locked on the paper as if she, too, could feel the weight of the moment. They both leaned over the pedestal, their faces inches apart as they studied the text. It was in an archaic language, one Daniel barely recognized. It was a form of Laurent family script, but older—much older. The letters were too jagged, too twisted, to be anything that could be understood easily.

"This is..." Emily began, but the words died in her throat. She reached forward carefully, her fingers grazing the ink as if afraid it might fade away beneath her touch. "It's a warning."

Daniel's heart skipped a beat as he read a few more lines, the translation slowly forming in his mind. The script was familiar but distorted, almost unreadable. But then the meaning began to clear.

"The heirloom is the key, not just to the vault, but to the family's true legacy. The one who seeks must first understand the blood that binds them. The key to the legacy is not in the coin but in the heirloom, the blood-bound ring that has held the family's power for generations. It must be returned to its rightful place. To open the vault is to expose the truth, but to wear the ring is to accept the weight of the family's sins."

Daniel felt a cold chill run down his spine as the words began to sink in. The heirloom. The ring. It was more than just a piece of family history—it was the key to everything. The vault, the coin, the power—it had all led them here. But what did it mean? What had this ring done to his family, to his bloodline?

He looked up at Emily, his mind racing. "The ring... it's not just a symbol. It's the power. The key. But where is it?"

Emily stepped back, her eyes wide, her hand instinctively clutching her chest as if she had been struck. "What do you mean, Daniel? The ring… we've never seen it before. Where could it be?"

Daniel's mind raced, the words of the parchment repeating over and over in his head. It had to be somewhere. The ring was the family's true legacy, the symbol of their power. If they were going to understand what was happening, they needed to find it. It was the missing piece, the thing that had been hidden all this time. But where could it be?

"Wait—" Emily's voice broke through his thoughts. She was staring at the pedestal, her eyes focused intently on something Daniel hadn't noticed. "There's something… hidden."

Daniel's breath caught in his throat as he turned to look at what Emily had noticed. She was pointing at the base of the pedestal, at a small indentation in the stone. It was barely visible, hidden beneath layers of dust and cobwebs. But as she cleared away the dirt with her fingers, Daniel's heart stopped. The indentation was shaped like a ring.

"A hidden compartment," Emily said, her voice hushed. "The ring must be inside."

Daniel nodded, his pulse quickening. This was it. He could feel it—the final puzzle piece. The legacy of his family, the darkness that had been hidden for generations, was within their grasp.

He reached down, his hand trembling slightly as he traced

the outline of the compartment. A soft click echoed through the vault as the mechanism inside the pedestal released, and the compartment opened with a grinding sound. Inside, nestled in a velvet-lined box, lay the ring. It was unlike anything Daniel had ever seen. The metal was dark, aged with time, and it glowed faintly, as if it were imbued with some ancient energy. The family crest was carved into it—a symbol of a hawk and a dagger crossed, twisted in a way that seemed almost... alive.

Daniel felt a strange pull as his fingers brushed against the ring. It felt both cold and warm at the same time, as if it had been waiting for him to find it. He hesitated for a moment, but there was no turning back now.

"It's the key," Daniel murmured, his voice thick with realization. "This is what we've been looking for. The legacy... the power."

Emily's eyes widened as she took a cautious step forward. "Daniel, you don't know what that means. What it could do."

"I have to," he said, his voice steady but filled with a mix of dread and determination. "We have to understand what's really been happening. What my family's been hiding."

He picked up the ring, the cold metal sending a jolt through his fingers. As he held it in his palm, he felt a strange surge of energy, something ancient and primal that seemed to call to him. The weight of the ring felt heavy—heavier than any piece of jewelry had a right to be.

Without thinking, he slid the ring onto his finger. The moment it touched his skin, the air in the vault shifted. The stone walls seemed to hum, a low, vibrating sound that rattled through his bones. The room felt as though it was breathing, alive with a force Daniel couldn't explain.

"What's happening?" Emily asked, her voice rising in panic. She reached for him, but he couldn't pull his gaze away from the ring, from the strange power it seemed to exude.

The vault walls shifted, the stone creaking as if they were awakening after centuries of slumber. Daniel's heart raced as the room seemed to close in on him, the air thick with a presence he couldn't place. And then, the light from the cracks in the walls shifted, illuminating something he hadn't noticed before.

On the far wall, an image began to take shape. It was faint at first, but then it became clearer—etched into the stone was the family crest, the hawk and the dagger, and beneath it, the words Daniel had read in the parchment:

"He who wears the ring inherits the truth and bears the sins of the past. The power is bound to blood, and the legacy is eternal."

Daniel's chest tightened as he understood the meaning. The legacy. The truth. It wasn't just a story, a piece of family history. It was real. And the weight of it had now fallen squarely on his shoulders.

Suddenly, the doors to the vault slammed shut with a deafening thud. The stone walls shook, the light flickering as if something inside was being unlocked. A voice, low and ancient, seemed to whisper through the vault, its tone both commanding and mournful.

"You have claimed the heirloom," the voice said. "Now, you must decide—will you accept the burden, or will you let the legacy die?"

Daniel's heart pounded in his chest, his mind racing. This was it. The moment of truth. The moment where he had to make a choice that would shape not only his future but the future of everything his family had built.

Emily stepped closer, her voice trembling as she spoke the words he had been dreading to hear.

"Daniel... what are you going to do?"

Thirty-Four

A Spy Among Us

The air in the vault still vibrated with the heavy, oppressive energy of the heirloom, the ring Daniel now wore. The stone walls felt closer than before, their ancient weight pressing in on him like a forgotten secret, trying to break through the thin veil of the present. Daniel could feel his heart pounding, the blood rushing in his ears as he stood frozen before the shifting shadows of the vault.

Emily stood beside him, her eyes wide with unease, her hand clutching his arm as if to ground herself, to steady herself against the strange pulse of energy emanating from the ring.

The voice, that low, disembodied whisper, had faded, leaving behind an unsettling silence. The stone doors, which had slammed shut behind them moments ago, were now closed with a finality that felt as though they were trapped, held in place by some unseen force. The walls groaned, shifting slightly, and in the distance, a faint light flickered from the cracks in the stone, a promise of something more—but Daniel didn't dare approach it. Not yet.

"We need to get out of here," Emily said, her voice trembling slightly as she took a hesitant step toward the door. The fear in her eyes was clear. She had always been the one to hold onto the clarity of their situation, but now, it was as if the weight of the vault was dragging both of them under.

Daniel's mind was still racing. The voice, the ancient presence—everything was shifting too quickly. The vault had opened its secrets to him, but there was something off. Something he couldn't quite grasp.

"Stay close," Daniel muttered, his voice low, as he turned his head, his eyes darting between the door and the walls. The air felt thick now, like they were being watched. Like someone else was here with them.

As he turned, a sudden noise from the shadows caught his attention. A rustle, a faint whisper of movement that didn't belong to either of them.

He froze, his hand instinctively reaching for the knife at his side. His senses, already heightened by the events unfolding around him, sharpened to a razor edge. Emily's breath hitched in her chest as she looked toward him, her body tensing, the fear palpable in her eyes.

"Who's there?" Daniel's voice was low but demanding. He had no time for games, no time for uncertainty. His eyes scanned the room, but everything was cloaked in shadow, the vault too vast and too dark to see beyond the dim light spilling through the cracks.

The rustling came again, but this time, it was louder. Closer. A deliberate movement, one that was unmistakable.

"Daniel…" Emily's voice was barely a whisper, her eyes wide, searching the shadows for any sign of who—or what—might be lurking just beyond their reach.

"I heard it too," Daniel whispered back, his pulse quickening. The vault was large, but it was a trap. A perfect place for someone to hide, to watch. His instincts screamed that they were not alone.

Suddenly, a figure stepped from the shadows, emerging slowly from the far corner of the room where the stone met the darkened alcove. Daniel's hand went to the knife, his fingers gripping the hilt tightly, ready to act. But the figure didn't move toward them. Instead, it raised its hands in mock surrender.

"No need for weapons, Daniel," the voice that spoke was calm, even amused—familiar, yet somehow different. The tone made Daniel's skin prickle with recognition. He hadn't heard that voice in years. He knew it all too well.

"Raphael?" Daniel's voice dropped to a low growl, his grip on the knife tightening. His heart skipped a beat. This wasn't supposed to happen. Not here, not now. But Raphael's face, hidden in the shadows of the vault, grinned back at him—a chilling, knowing smile.

"Did you think you could get away from us, Daniel?" Raphael stepped further into the light, revealing his face—older, more hardened, but still unmistakably the man Daniel had grown up with, his cousin, his family. A man who had long been entrenched in the web of lies and corruption Daniel was trying to escape. "You think you can just walk in here and take what doesn't belong to you?"

Emily moved beside Daniel, her eyes narrowing. She recognized the threat in Raphael's stance, the underlying arrogance in his posture, as if the vault, and the power within, had already been claimed.

"Why are you here?" Daniel demanded, his voice raw, edged with anger. His hand remained tight around the knife, his body coiled, prepared for a fight. "You've already tried to take everything from me."

Raphael chuckled softly, stepping closer with that unsettling grin still fixed on his lips. "I should be asking you that question. You think you can unlock the truth and take control of the Laurent legacy? It's not so simple, Daniel. The family doesn't just let anyone waltz in and change the game."

"Enough with the games, Raphael!" Daniel snapped. "What do you want?"

Raphael raised an eyebrow, his smile deepening into something far darker. "You really don't get it, do you? You've been so focused on your little vendetta against your father, but you've forgotten the most important lesson. The one I'm here to teach you."

The words hit Daniel like a punch to the stomach. He had been so focused on getting to the vault, on finding the answers, that he had neglected the deeper, darker truth about his family. About Raphael.

"You've been following us," Emily said, her voice growing colder, more accusatory as she stepped forward. Her eyes fixed on Raphael with a fierce intensity. "You knew what we were after. You've been tracking us this entire time."

Raphael's grin faltered for a split second, and in that moment, Daniel realized something that made his stomach churn. This wasn't just about the vault. It never had been. Raphael wasn't just an obstacle in their way. He was the one pulling the strings, watching them from the shadows, waiting for the right moment to strike.

"I didn't just follow you," Raphael said, his voice low, measured. "I'm the one who set this in motion."

Daniel's blood ran cold. "What are you talking about?"

Raphael stepped closer now, the shadows in the room seemingly wrapping around him like a cloak. He looked almost... pleased. "Your father might think he's the mastermind behind everything. He might think he's the one who's been controlling the game. But the truth is—he's a puppet, just like you. And I'm the one who's been pulling the strings from the beginning."

Emily's breath caught in her throat, her hand unconsciously reaching out to grasp Daniel's arm. The realization hit her too—the same horrifying truth. Raphael was more than just another member of the Laurent family. He was a part of the very web of lies that had ensnared them all.

Daniel's chest tightened. "You're the one who led us here. You're the one who's been manipulating everything."

Raphael's eyes glinted with something dangerous. "Not just everything. Everyone."

Daniel's mind reeled as the weight of his words sank in. Everything. Raphael had known from the beginning that they would find the vault. He had been watching them, orchestrating events, leading them to this moment as if it was all part of a game. The pieces had been set up perfectly, and Daniel and Emily had unknowingly played into his hands.

"You're here for the ring, aren't you?" Daniel asked, his voice suddenly cold, realization flooding through him.

Raphael's lips curled into a smile, but it wasn't one of triumph. It was a smile of possession, of entitlement. "The heirloom is the key to everything, Daniel. It's what ties our family together. It's the power we've all been fighting for. Your father's too weak to see it, but I know what it's worth. I've always known."

The air in the vault seemed to thicken, and for a moment, everything fell silent. Daniel could hear his heart pounding in his ears. Emily's hand tightened on his arm as she whispered, "You're one of them, Raphael. All this time, we thought you were helping us, but you were just using us to get closer to the heirloom."

Raphael's smile widened as he took another step forward. "I'm not just one of them, Emily. I am them. And now that I have the heirloom, it's all over. The Laurent legacy will be mine. No one else can stand in my way."

Daniel's grip on the knife tightened. "You won't get away with this, Raphael. I won't let you."

Raphael's eyes narrowed, and for a moment, the room seemed to pulse with an almost electric tension. It was as if the air itself was waiting for a confrontation. "You don't have a choice, Daniel. The game is over."

Before Daniel could react, Raphael moved swiftly, a blur of motion, and with a flick of his wrist, he produced a gun. The cold metal gleamed in the dim light, its presence a reminder of the stakes.

Daniel's mind raced. They were caught. Trapped in the vault with no way out. The only thing that mattered now was survival.

And the game had just gotten deadly.

Thirty-Five

A Life Saved

The cold metal of the gun pressed against Daniel's chest, and for a moment, everything seemed to freeze. Time stretched, seconds turning into eternity as his eyes locked onto Raphael's. The gun in Raphael's hand gleamed, the barrel dark and foreboding in the dim light of the vault. The air was thick with tension, and Daniel could hear the slow, steady beat of his heart in his ears. Emily's breath came in sharp, ragged gasps beside him, her presence a constant reminder that they were in this together.

But the weight of the situation was suffocating. Raphael had them trapped—there was nowhere to run, nowhere to hide. The vault's stone walls seemed to close in on them, their ancient presence pressing against Daniel, as though the vault itself was holding its breath, waiting for the inevitable.

A Life Saved

"Do you really think you can just take the heirloom, Daniel?" Raphael's voice was calm, cold, but there was something else behind it—something darker. His smile had faded, replaced with a look of cold determination. The gun in his hand never wavered, its presence a reminder of the power he held. "This was always part of the plan. I've been watching you, setting you up from the beginning. The moment you found the vault, the moment you picked up the ring... it was already over."

Daniel's breath caught in his throat, his mind racing to make sense of everything. Raphael had orchestrated this from the start. From the beginning, he had been a part of the game, manipulating the pieces without Daniel even realizing. All of the lies, all of the twists—they had all led them here.

"You think you can control everything, Raphael?" Daniel said, his voice steady, despite the storm of fear and rage swirling inside him. "You've been watching us, manipulating us, but you're wrong. You'll never control the legacy."

Raphael's lips twitched into a smirk, the gun still steady in his hand. "You don't understand, Daniel. This isn't about control. It's about survival. The Laurent legacy isn't just some family story. It's power. It's everything." He stepped closer, the gun never leaving Daniel's chest. "And I will do whatever it takes to ensure that power is mine."

The vault, with its ancient stones and hidden secrets, seemed to pulse with an eerie energy, as if the walls were alive with the weight of everything Raphael was about to claim. Daniel's mind raced, but his body remained still, calculating. He couldn't make a wrong move. One wrong gesture, and the consequences would be catastrophic.

He glanced at Emily, whose face was pale, her eyes wide with fear. She stood frozen beside him, her hand gripping the edge of the pedestal, but there was a determination in her gaze that Daniel couldn't ignore. She wasn't just going to stand by and let Raphael take everything from them.

"Don't do this," Emily said, her voice trembling, but her words were sharp, filled with conviction. "You don't have to do this, Raphael. You don't have to be like them. You've always had a choice."

Raphael's gaze flicked to her, his eyes narrowing with contempt. "A choice?" he laughed bitterly. "You really think I had a choice? The Laurent family doesn't leave room for choices. It leaves room for power, for control. And now, I'm taking what's mine."

The tension between them grew, the gun in Raphael's hand a constant reminder of the danger they were in. Daniel could feel his heart pounding, but his mind was still racing, looking for any way out. If they didn't act now, everything would be lost.

"Raphael, you don't have to do this," Daniel said again, his voice rising slightly. "You don't have to destroy everything. There's still time to stop."

A Life Saved

For a moment, Raphael hesitated, his finger hovering over the trigger. The gun wavered slightly, and in that brief moment of uncertainty, Daniel saw a flicker of doubt in Raphael's eyes. A doubt he had never seen before.

But before Daniel could seize the opportunity, the door to the vault suddenly crashed open with a deafening bang, making them all jump. The air seemed to shift in an instant, and Daniel's heart skipped a beat.

A figure stepped into the vault, silhouetted by the light streaming through the doorway. The sound of heavy footsteps echoed in the space, and as the figure moved closer, Daniel's breath caught in his throat.

It was his father.

"You!" Daniel gasped, his voice a mixture of anger and disbelief. His heart slammed in his chest as he tried to process the presence of the man who had betrayed him, the man who had played the role of his enemy from the beginning. But now, standing in the doorway, there was something different about him. Something had shifted.

"I knew you'd come for the heirloom, Raphael," his father's voice was cold, but there was a quiet authority in it. "But I didn't expect you to betray the family like this. Not so soon."

Raphael's eyes widened with shock, the gun dropping slightly as he faced Daniel's father. "What are you doing here?" he asked, disbelief in his tone. "You… you were supposed to be out of the way. This was supposed to be mine."

"You never understood, did you, Raphael?" Daniel's father stepped further into the vault, his eyes narrowing with anger as he took in the scene before him. "The Laurent legacy isn't just about power. It's about family. You think you can take control by using the ring, by using the vault. But you've lost sight of what's important."

Daniel's father's words hung in the air, and for the first time, Daniel saw something in his father's eyes that wasn't the usual cold calculation. There was something more—something almost desperate, like a man trying to hold onto the last remnants of something he had lost.

"Put the gun down," Daniel's father commanded, his voice steady and firm. "You've already done enough, Raphael."

Raphael's hand shook slightly as he held the gun, but there was something in his posture that betrayed his growing uncertainty. He wasn't prepared for this—wasn't prepared for his uncle, the patriarch of the Laurent family, to show up and challenge him in this way.

"No," Raphael spat, his voice filled with venom. "This is mine! The legacy is mine! I deserve it!"

His father stepped closer, his gaze hardening. "You've failed, Raphael. You've made a grave mistake. And now, you'll pay the price."

The air in the vault seemed to snap with tension as the two men faced each other, their family history hanging like a dark cloud between them. Daniel could feel the weight of the moment—the legacy, the power, the betrayal—all of it coalescing in one final act.

Then, as if the universe itself had decided to intervene, the door behind Raphael suddenly slammed shut with a deafening crash, trapping him inside with Daniel and his father. The vault was no longer just a place of secrets—it had become a battleground.

"Stay away from him!" Emily shouted, her voice cutting through the chaos like a knife. She moved to stand in front of Daniel, her eyes fixed on Raphael, but there was something new in her gaze. Something fierce.

Daniel's father turned toward Emily, his expression shifting. For the first time, he looked uncertain, as if he were seeing her for the first time, realizing the depth of the situation.

"You're a spy, aren't you?" Daniel's father asked, his voice low, his eyes narrowing in realization. "You've been working with them this whole time. With Daniel."

Emily stiffened, her posture betraying her surprise. "What are you talking about?"

But before she could say anything else, Daniel's father

stepped forward, his hand reaching into his coat pocket. The air was thick with a sudden, sharp fear. He pulled out a small, intricate device, which began to beep softly in his hand.

"I knew you'd never betray me, Raphael," Daniel's father said. "But I knew you'd bring someone else. A spy."

Daniel's stomach lurched as his father turned toward Emily, holding the device out as the beeping intensified. His father had known all along. He had known they weren't just being hunted by Raphael—there was someone else in play, someone working against them from the inside.

Emily took a step back, her eyes wide with shock. "What… what is that?"

Daniel's mind reeled as the beeping grew louder, more insistent. It was only then that he understood.

A spy. Among them.

And time was running out.

Thirty-Six

The Hidden Diary

The vault was alive with the hum of tension, a thick, suffocating air that pressed in on Daniel, Emily, and his father. The stone walls, once cold and imposing, now seemed to pulsate with the weight of the revelations unfolding in the shadows of this forgotten room. The beeping from his father's device echoed, a relentless reminder that time was slipping away. Daniel's thoughts swirled, each one more frantic than the last, as he tried to make sense of what was happening.

The device his father had pulled out—a small, almost inconspicuous object, barely larger than a matchbox—was now a blaring siren in the oppressive silence of the vault. The beeping grew louder, more urgent, as though it were signaling something far more dangerous than any of them could have anticipated.

"Stop it," Daniel said, his voice tight with frustration. "What is that thing, and why the hell do you have it?"

His father's eyes remained cold, his fingers clutching the device as though it were a lifeline. There was something calculating in his expression, something that hinted at the deeper layers of deceit Daniel had been trying to uncover all along.

"You've been too focused on the coin, the ring, the vault, Daniel," his father said slowly, his voice almost sympathetic, as though trying to justify the chaos they were all caught in. "But there's one thing you still don't understand. One thing you've overlooked in your desperation to take control."

"What are you talking about?" Daniel demanded, his heart pounding in his chest as the words his father spoke echoed in the vast, oppressive space. "Tell me what it is."

His father didn't answer immediately. Instead, his gaze flickered over to Emily, then back to Daniel. His face, usually so unreadable, now showed the slightest hint of weariness. It was a flicker of vulnerability, one Daniel had never seen before, and it sent a shiver down his spine. There was more to the story than he could have ever imagined.

"You think the Laurent legacy is just about power, wealth, and bloodlines," his father continued, his tone colder now, as though he were speaking to someone much younger, much more naive. "But it's about something else. Something far more dangerous. There's more to the family than you realize. More than just the heirloom, the vault, the coins. A far deeper connection."

Daniel's mind raced as the puzzle pieces began to shift. He had always known that his family's history was steeped in shadows, that the Laurent legacy was far darker than anyone had ever admitted. But the words his father spoke now felt like a revelation—a deeper truth that had been hidden for years.

"Enough with the cryptic nonsense," Daniel snapped, his hand clenched tightly around the knife at his waist. "What are you really hiding?"

His father's expression softened, almost imperceptibly, but there was something in his eyes that made Daniel's breath catch. His father wasn't just trying to protect the legacy. He was protecting something far more personal—something that had been buried deep within the family for generations.

"I'll show you," his father said, his voice almost a whisper now. "But you're not going to like it."

Before Daniel could react, his father moved swiftly toward the far wall of the vault, his footsteps echoing in the stillness. He pressed his hand against one of the stone bricks, and with a quiet grinding noise, a hidden panel slid open in the wall, revealing a small, dusty shelf. Daniel felt a strange unease wash over him as his father retrieved an old, weathered leather-bound book from the shelf.

The book looked ancient, its cover cracked and faded with time. The pages inside, though, seemed pristine, untouched by the years. His father walked back toward Daniel, holding the book out to him.

"This," his father said, his voice low, "is the key to everything. The true legacy of the Laurent family."

Daniel took the book, the weight of it pressing into his hands, and for the first time in years, he felt the full burden of his bloodline. He had thought the coin, the ring, the vault were the only things that mattered, the things that could unlock the secrets of his family. But this book… it was something else entirely.

"What is this?" Daniel asked, his voice barely a whisper, as though afraid the walls might hear him. He turned the book over in his hands, searching for some clue, some indication of what it contained.

"It's a diary," his father said, his voice now heavy with something Daniel couldn't quite place—guilt, perhaps, or something darker. "A record of the Laurent family's true history. It's been passed down through generations, hidden from everyone who could never understand. Only those with the bloodline are meant to read it. Only those with the right knowledge."

Daniel's fingers trembled as he opened the diary to the first page. The handwriting was elegant, but the ink was faded, the letters flowing in a way that made the words difficult

The Hidden Diary

to read. His eyes scanned the first few lines, trying to make sense of the strange language.

It wasn't just a diary. It was a testament. A record of things that had been deliberately hidden, buried beneath the weight of time.

"The Laurent legacy is not just bound by blood," the words began, scrawled in a tight, deliberate hand. "It is bound by a pact, a promise made long ago. A promise to protect what we have built. What we have done. There are things that cannot be undone, choices that cannot be erased. But we, the true heirs, will always be bound to our fate. To the blood."

The words sent a chill down Daniel's spine, and he could feel his father's eyes on him, watching him carefully. There was something in the air now, a thick, oppressive force that seemed to push them all toward a terrible truth.

"Who wrote this?" Daniel asked, his voice barely above a whisper.

His father didn't answer right away. Instead, he stepped closer, his eyes on the diary. "It was written by my great-grandfather. He knew the truth about the family, the real reason the Laurent legacy exists. He made sure it was passed down, generation to generation, hidden from those who could never be trusted to understand."

Daniel's mind raced as he absorbed his father's words. The

Laurent family was built on secrets, on things that had been buried deep in the past. But this book—this diary—was the key to understanding everything. It wasn't just about power. It was about control, about a promise made long ago to protect something far darker than Daniel could have imagined.

As Daniel continued to read, the words grew more cryptic, more ominous. "The heirloom must be returned. The bloodline must be preserved. The pact must be kept, or everything will be lost. Only the chosen will stand at the gates, and only the chosen will be able to see the truth."

"What truth?" Daniel asked, his voice raw with desperation as he looked up from the diary.

His father took a deep breath, his face hardening. "The truth about your family's real power, Daniel. The truth about why the Laurents have always held influence, why we've always been untouchable. It's not just about money or status—it's about something far more dangerous. Something that has kept us all alive for generations."

Daniel's heart pounded in his chest as he absorbed the weight of his father's words. His family wasn't just wealthy. They weren't just influential. There was something darker, something more sinister behind everything.

"You knew all along," Daniel said, his voice trembling with a mix of anger and betrayal. "You knew what this was. What the heirloom really means."

His father nodded slowly, his eyes fixed on the diary. "I didn't want you to know. I didn't want you to carry the burden. But you're the heir now, Daniel. You're the one who will have to decide."

"Decide what?" Daniel asked, his voice thick with frustration. "What do you expect me to do with all of this? With this legacy?"

His father's gaze met his, and for the first time, Daniel saw something almost human in his eyes—something vulnerable, something raw. "You'll have to decide whether you want the power, the legacy, or whether you want to destroy it. You have the choice, Daniel. But the bloodline will always find you. It's your inheritance, whether you want it or not."

The words hung in the air like a death sentence, and Daniel felt the weight of the decision settling on him. He had spent his whole life trying to escape his family's shadow, but now, he realized, there was no escaping it. The legacy was his—whether he accepted it or rejected it.

And as he looked at the diary, at the faded pages and the cryptic words, he knew that this was only the beginning. The truth was out there, but whether he was ready to face it—or whether it would consume him like it had consumed so many before him—remained to be seen.

Daniel closed the diary with a soft snap, his hands shaking. "We're not done yet," he whispered, more to himself than anyone else. "The game is just beginning."

Thirty-Seven

A Growing Threat

The vault felt suffocating, its ancient stone walls closing in as the weight of Daniel's father's words hung heavy in the air. The heirloom. The bloodline. The pact. Everything Daniel had believed to be true about his family, his legacy, had been turned on its head in an instant. He hadn't expected this—he hadn't expected any of it. But now, as he stood with the leather-bound diary in his hands, he could feel the growing weight of a truth far darker than he could have imagined.

His father's eyes never left him, a mixture of caution and expectation in his gaze. The air around them was thick with tension, the silence pressing in like a vise. Daniel's mind was still reeling from the discovery, from the cryptic warning in the diary that had been passed down through generations. The Laurent family had always been more than just powerful—it had been bound by something far more insidious. And Daniel was the one who would have to bear the burden.

"Do you understand now, Daniel?" his father asked, his voice low but filled with a quiet authority. "This is more than just money or power. This is about survival. About protecting the family. The bloodline."

Daniel swallowed, his throat dry. His hand tightened around the diary, but it felt as though it was slipping from his grasp—like the very legacy it represented was trying to pull him under. "I understand that you've been lying to me all these years," he said, his voice tight with anger. "You've been hiding this from me. From all of us."

His father's eyes flickered, a flash of something—regret, perhaps—passing across his features. But it was gone almost as quickly as it had come. "I did what I had to do," he replied, his voice steady. "You think I wanted to protect you from this? From the truth? No, Daniel. I wanted to protect you from what it would cost."

"And what is that?" Daniel asked, his voice thick with disbelief. "What exactly is it going to cost me, Dad? Because I'm not sure I want anything to do with this… legacy."

His father's expression hardened. "It's not a choice, Daniel. You are the heir. You've always been the heir. The Laurent bloodline is yours to carry, and with it, you will carry the weight of everything our family has done. The mistakes, the sins. The power."

Daniel's stomach churned at his father's words. His mind raced, trying to process everything. The bloodline. The heirloom. The pact. He felt like he was sinking into a dark, endless abyss. How had it come to this? How had he gotten caught up in a legacy that was so far removed from what he had ever imagined?

A distant noise broke through the silence—the sound of footsteps approaching from the hallway. Daniel's heart skipped a beat, the sudden noise pulling him from his thoughts. His father's face grew more guarded, his posture straightening as he turned toward the entrance to the vault.

"Who's there?" Daniel's voice was sharp, his hand instinctively reaching for the knife at his side. He had learned by now that no one could be trusted—not even his father.

His father's face tightened with concern, but before he could respond, the door to the vault creaked open. A figure stepped inside, shrouded in shadow, blocking out the light from the hall. For a brief moment, Daniel thought it was one of Raphael's men, or perhaps someone else who had come to seize the heirloom—but then the figure stepped fully into the light, and Daniel's breath caught in his throat.

It was Emily.

"Emily," Daniel breathed, a mixture of relief and confusion flooding through him. She looked disheveled, her clothes torn and dirt-streaked from their time in the forest, but her face was pale, her eyes wide with something that Daniel couldn't quite place. "What are you—"

She cut him off, her voice urgent, breathless. "Daniel, we don't have much time. There's someone else. Someone who's been watching us."

"What do you mean?" Daniel's heart began to race, fear creeping into his chest as he took a step toward her. "Who's been watching us?"

Emily stepped forward, her eyes scanning the vault as if she were expecting someone to step out of the shadows at any moment. "I don't know yet, but they're close. Too close. I saw them. They've been tracking us. Following our every move since we left the mansion."

Daniel's stomach dropped. He knew it was too good to be true. They had spent so much time focused on the vault, on the heirloom, that they hadn't considered the possibility of being pursued. His mind raced as he thought of the implications. If they had been watched all this time, then there was no telling who else might be involved. No telling how deep the conspiracy ran.

His father's voice broke through the tension. "You were followed, Emily?" There was a note of disbelief in his voice, but it quickly shifted to something more menacing, more protective. "Who? Who's been watching us?"

A Growing Threat

Emily hesitated, her eyes flickering to Daniel before she spoke again, her voice trembling with uncertainty. "I don't know. I just know they're dangerous. Whoever they are, they've been keeping track of everything we've done. And they won't stop until they get what they want."

Daniel's mind was spinning. The heirloom. The vault. The ring. Everything they had fought for could be undone by this unknown threat. They were being hunted—and worse, they didn't know who by. But one thing was certain. The threat was real, and it was closing in fast.

"We need to get out of here," Daniel said, his voice low but urgent. He turned to his father. "We can't stay in this vault any longer. We're sitting ducks in here."

His father didn't move, his expression unreadable as he looked between Daniel and Emily. There was something in his gaze—something calculating—as if he were weighing his options, trying to decide whether to trust his son or not.

"You don't understand," his father finally said, his voice low and filled with an edge of desperation. "You think you can just walk away from this? From your birthright? From the legacy?"

Daniel's heart pounded in his chest. "I don't want the legacy, Dad. I want out. I want to get out of this family, out of this nightmare. I'm not taking the reins of the Laurent empire. Not like you."

His father's eyes narrowed, and for a moment, Daniel thought he saw a flicker of anger flash across his face. But then it was gone, replaced with something darker. "You're making a mistake. You think running from it will save you, but it won't. The Laurent family is in your blood. There's no escaping it."

Before Daniel could respond, Emily grabbed his arm, her fingers cold against his skin. "We don't have time for this," she said, her voice urgent, her gaze darting to the door. "They're here. And they're getting closer."

Daniel felt the blood drain from his face as he looked at the door to the vault. The distant sound of footsteps had stopped, but in its place was an eerie silence, one that felt far too still. And then, just as quickly as it had arrived, the silence was shattered by the sound of a door slamming open down the hall.

"They're here," Emily whispered again, her voice shaking with fear.

Daniel's pulse quickened as he looked back at his father. There was no time left. They couldn't hide in the vault any longer. They had to move.

"Dad, we need to go. Now," Daniel said, his voice firm, though his mind was screaming with uncertainty. "We don't have a choice."

His father hesitated for a moment, his eyes searching

A Growing Threat

Daniel's face as if trying to read something in his expression. Then, finally, he nodded, his gaze hardening. "Fine. But we do this my way. Understand?"

Before Daniel could respond, the sound of footsteps came again, but this time, they were closer. Too close. The door to the vault was about to be breached.

"Move!" Daniel shouted, grabbing Emily's arm and pulling her toward the back of the vault. The room was too small, too confined. They had to find another way out. His mind raced, and in that instant, he saw it—the small, hidden passage at the back of the vault, one he had missed before. It was narrow, barely wide enough for them to crawl through, but it was their only chance.

"Get in!" Daniel barked, pushing Emily toward the entrance of the passage. "Hurry!"

Emily didn't hesitate. She ducked into the passageway, and Daniel followed closely behind. His father brought up the rear, his hand gripping the knife at his side as they moved quickly, their footsteps muffled by the damp stone walls of the tunnel.

But as they crawled through the narrow passage, Daniel couldn't shake the feeling that they were being led into something worse. Something darker than they had ever imagined.

And as they reached the end of the passage, Daniel knew—

whatever was waiting for them outside would be more dangerous than anything they had faced so far.

The growing threat was real.

And it was closing in.

Thirty-Eight

The Conflicted Choice

The passage was cold and narrow, the damp stone pressing in from all sides. Daniel's breath came in quick, shallow bursts, the claustrophobic space making it harder to think clearly. Behind him, Emily's footsteps echoed faintly, the sound of their hurried movement the only thing breaking the eerie silence of the tunnel. His father, ever vigilant, brought up the rear, his movements cautious but deliberate.

The further they moved through the cramped tunnel, the more Daniel felt the weight of the situation pressing down on him. His mind was a storm of conflicting thoughts—emotions swirling in every direction, none of them offering a clear path forward.

They had been running for what felt like hours, but the

sense of urgency had only grown stronger with every step. The footsteps they'd heard earlier, the sound of pursuers, had stopped. But the tension in the air had not. Whoever—or whatever—was coming after them was still out there. They weren't safe yet.

Finally, the tunnel opened up into a wider chamber, a small cavern-like room, still damp and filled with the smell of earth and decay. A faint light from the cracks in the walls illuminated the space just enough for Daniel to see the way forward. But the moment they emerged into the room, Daniel stopped.

He could feel it—an almost tangible pressure in the air. It wasn't just the threat of their pursuers. It was something else. Something older. Something that made the hairs on the back of his neck stand up.

"Where does this lead?" Emily's voice broke through his thoughts, her words careful, but full of the same tension Daniel was feeling.

Daniel scanned the room, his mind searching for any signs of a way out. The light that filtered through the cracks barely touched the edges of the chamber, leaving most of it shrouded in shadow. The walls were covered in ancient markings, symbols Daniel didn't recognize, but the shape of them felt strangely familiar, as though they had been left behind by the Laurent family's forebearers.

"I'm not sure," Daniel muttered, his voice tense. He moved

closer to one of the walls, running his fingers lightly over the carvings. The symbols felt like they were pulsing with energy, but the sensation was faint—almost like the walls themselves were waiting for something to happen.

"You can feel it, can't you?" Emily's voice was low, almost reverent. "The energy in this place. It's... powerful."

Daniel nodded, his fingers still tracing the strange symbols. The sense of history and power in the room was overwhelming, as though the very stones beneath their feet were saturated with secrets that had been buried for centuries. His heart pounded in his chest, the realization that they were standing on the precipice of something much larger than they had ever anticipated sinking in.

"We have to keep moving," his father's voice came from behind them, harsh and commanding. "This place is a trap. It's designed to keep us in the dark."

Daniel's father stepped forward, his face hard as stone, his eyes scanning the room. He had always been the one in control, the one who made the decisions, but for the first time, Daniel could see the weariness in his father's eyes. The weight of what had been done, the bloodline they were all bound to, was evident in every line of his face. There was no escaping it now. There was no way to go back.

"What is this place?" Daniel asked, his voice edged with curiosity, but also a growing sense of fear.

"It's an old family secret," his father replied, his words clipped. "A place where the Laurent family's true power was forged. Where the pact was made." He paused, looking at Daniel with a piercing gaze. "But it's more than that. It's a place where you'll be forced to make a choice."

Daniel turned to face his father, his brow furrowed. "A choice? What do you mean?"

His father didn't respond immediately. Instead, he stepped toward the center of the room, where an altar-like stone table stood. The surface was smooth, worn down by time, but there was something about it that felt significant. Something that drew Daniel's gaze. As he moved closer, his father placed a hand on the stone, his fingers brushing across its surface with reverence.

"This is where the legacy began," his father said, his voice almost reverent. "This is where the first Laurent made the pact, where the bloodline was sealed. And this is where the true power of the family resides."

Daniel's heart skipped a beat. The weight of the words hit him like a hammer, the pieces of the puzzle finally clicking into place. The legacy wasn't just about wealth or influence. It was about something far deeper, something far darker.

"Power," Daniel whispered, his voice thick with disbelief. "This is about power."

"Yes," his father said, his voice quiet but firm. "And now, it's your turn. You must choose. The bloodline is yours. The legacy is yours. But what you do with it… that's up to you."

Daniel's mind spun as he processed his father's words. He had always believed that the legacy was something he could choose to reject, something he could walk away from. But now, standing here, in this dark chamber filled with the echoes of the past, Daniel understood that there was no walking away. The bloodline ran too deep. It had claimed him before he was even born, and now, it was demanding his allegiance.

The power was there. The choice was there. But Daniel wasn't sure if he was ready to make it. He wasn't sure if he could bear the weight of what it meant.

"What kind of choice are you asking me to make?" Daniel asked, his voice barely above a whisper. His heart was racing, his thoughts jumbled, as he tried to understand the magnitude of what his father was offering.

"Do you want the power, Daniel?" his father asked, his eyes intense, fixed on him. "Do you want to be the one to lead this family into the future? To wield the power that has been passed down through the generations? Or do you want to walk away, to let everything crumble, to let the family fall into oblivion?"

Daniel's stomach twisted at the words. The choice seemed impossible, the weight of it threatening to crush him. How could he choose? How could he walk away from everything he had ever known? From everything his family had worked for? But at the same time, how could he accept the power that came with this legacy, knowing what it had cost them all?

"I can't," Daniel said, his voice thick with emotion. "I don't want to be like you. I don't want to carry this burden."

His father's eyes softened for a moment, but the hardness quickly returned. "You don't have a choice, Daniel. You were born into this. The power is yours whether you want it or not."

"But I don't want it," Daniel said, his voice firm now, the frustration bubbling to the surface. "I don't want any part of this family, of this legacy. You've spent your whole life building this empire, but it's built on lies, on manipulation. I won't be a part of that."

Emily stepped forward, her eyes locked on Daniel, her hand reaching out to him. "Daniel, listen to me," she said, her voice trembling but full of urgency. "This isn't just about the power. This is about you. About who you are. You don't have to be bound by the choices your father made. You don't have to carry this legacy if you don't want to."

Daniel's gaze flickered to her, and for a moment, the tension in the room seemed to fade. She was right. He didn't have to accept the legacy. He didn't have to carry the weight of the bloodline if he didn't choose to.

The Conflicted Choice

But as he looked back at his father, he could see the storm brewing in his eyes. His father's face was hard again, his posture rigid as if preparing for a battle. This wasn't just a family legacy. It was a war. A war that Daniel was being forced into, whether he wanted it or not.

"You'll regret this," his father said, his voice low, almost a threat. "You think you can walk away? You think you can reject the legacy and leave everything behind? You're wrong, Daniel. You'll never escape it."

Daniel's heart pounded in his chest, the pressure of his father's words pressing in on him. This wasn't just about power anymore. It was about survival. The family's survival.

"I'm not you," Daniel said, his voice steady despite the storm raging inside. "I'll never be you."

The words hung in the air, heavy with the weight of the decision he had just made. He had chosen. He had rejected the legacy.

But as he stepped back, the air around him seemed to shift. He had made his choice, but it was clear that this wasn't over. The legacy would not let him go so easily.

And the choice he had made, the path he had taken, would come at a cost. One that would haunt him forever.

The vault seemed to darken around them, the walls closing

in as the shadows of the past reached out for him.

There was no escaping the Laurent legacy now.

The real battle had just begun.

Thirty-Nine

The Safehouse Encounter

The night had fallen thick and heavy around them, the sky an ink-black expanse, dotted only by the occasional flicker of distant stars. The woods surrounding the safehouse were silent, save for the whisper of wind rustling through the trees, as if nature itself were holding its breath, waiting. Daniel stood at the edge of the property, his back to the weathered wooden fence that marked the boundary of the small, hidden compound. The safehouse had been their refuge—a place to regroup, to lick their wounds after the chaos in the vault. But now, even here, there was no peace. No safety.

The decision he had made earlier, the rejection of his family's legacy, weighed heavily on him. The tension between him and his father, the unspoken threat that had lingered in the vault, had only intensified as they fled to the safehouse. It felt as though his very existence was now a betrayal—not only to his father, but to everything he had ever known. He had chosen the harder path, the one that led away from the Laurent family's power, and toward something that felt—what? Freedom? Escape? He wasn't sure anymore.

He had heard the stories, the warnings about the safehouse: how it was meant to be impenetrable, a place of refuge for those who knew the secrets of the Laurent legacy. And yet, as Daniel stood at the perimeter, something felt wrong. The hairs on the back of his neck prickled, a chill creeping over him despite the warmth of the night.

"You okay?" Emily's voice cut through the stillness, soft but filled with concern.

Daniel turned, his eyes catching hers in the dim light from the house. She stood in the doorway, her silhouette framed against the yellowish glow from inside. Her eyes were wary, searching his face for answers that he didn't have. He knew she could feel it too—that lingering unease, that subtle sense that something wasn't quite right.

"I don't know," Daniel admitted, running a hand through his hair as he looked back out over the woods. "It just doesn't feel right, Emily. We've been here for hours, and it's too quiet. Too still."

Emily moved toward him, her footsteps light on the dirt path, her breath misting in the cool air. She came to stand

The Safehouse Encounter

beside him, her gaze following his out into the woods. "You're not the only one who feels it," she said, her voice barely above a whisper. "But we've been through worse. We can't let paranoia get the best of us now."

Daniel glanced at her, her calm demeanor a stark contrast to the roiling storm inside him. She was right, in a way. They had fought their way out of far more dangerous situations. But something about the safehouse, something about the night, unsettled him. Maybe it was the knowledge that they were not just running from his father anymore. The danger had grown beyond familial conflict. There were forces at play here, forces that neither of them fully understood.

"We've got a lot to unpack," Daniel muttered, his eyes flicking back to the safehouse. "The diary. The pact. Everything my father said in there. The choice I had to make—it's not over, Emily. It's just beginning."

Emily didn't respond immediately. She stood by his side, her eyes trained on the same darkened woods, as if listening to the silent warning that hung in the air. After a moment, she spoke again, her voice steady but tinged with uncertainty.

"You know what that means, don't you? It's not just your father you're up against anymore. There are other people—people who know about the pact, about the power. Whoever's been tracking us… they're not just after you. They're after what you know."

Daniel's chest tightened at her words. She was right. His decision to reject the Laurent legacy had put him in direct opposition to far more dangerous forces than his father. They were not just fighting for control of the Laurent fortune—they were fighting for control of something older, something far more dangerous. The family's secrets had never been meant to be uncovered, and now that they were, there was no telling who would come for them next.

"I know," Daniel said, his voice barely audible. "And I don't know who I can trust anymore. There are too many enemies, too many people who want to see me fail. Too many people who want to keep the legacy intact."

As they stood there in the silence of the night, the tension between them palpable, the feeling that something was about to happen—something imminent—grew stronger. They were not alone. The woods surrounding the safehouse were not as still as they seemed. The sense of being watched had returned, and it was worse now, closer than before.

Just then, the sound of a twig snapping underfoot broke through the stillness. The hairs on the back of Daniel's neck stood on end. He instinctively pulled Emily closer, his body tensing as he scanned the shadows around them. There was something moving out there.

"Did you hear that?" Emily whispered, her voice low, her breath shallow.

Daniel nodded, his eyes narrowing as he focused on the

The Safehouse Encounter

darkened edges of the woods. "We're not alone."

They both froze, straining their ears, waiting for the next sound. Another rustle, followed by the faintest echo of a footstep on the ground. The noise was unmistakable. Someone was coming toward them. Slowly. Stealthily.

"We need to get inside," Daniel said, his voice sharp with urgency. "Now."

But before either of them could make a move, a shadow detached itself from the trees. A figure stepped into the dim light of the safehouse's doorway, its outline vague but unmistakably human. Daniel's hand instinctively went to the knife at his side, his grip tightening.

"Who's there?" Daniel called out, his voice firm, though his pulse was racing.

The figure didn't answer immediately, standing just beyond the edge of the light, as if gauging their response. Then, as if deciding something, the person stepped forward, revealing a face that made Daniel's blood run cold.

It was a woman. Tall, with sharp features and dark eyes that gleamed with an intensity that Daniel couldn't ignore. She was dressed in dark clothing, her movements fluid and calculated. She looked like someone who had been trained to blend into the shadows—and someone who could kill without hesitation.

"I think you know who I am," she said, her voice calm and authoritative. Her accent was faint, but her words were unmistakable, carrying a chilling sense of familiarity.

Daniel's heart skipped a beat as recognition slowly crept over him. "You—" he started, his voice faltering for a moment. "You're one of them."

The woman smiled faintly, a knowing, almost pitying smile. "Yes, Daniel. I am one of them. And you've been a thorn in our side for far too long."

Before Daniel could respond, Emily stepped forward, her eyes narrowed, her posture tense. "Who are you working for?" she demanded, her voice sharp. "What do you want with us?"

The woman's gaze flickered to Emily, her eyes flicking over her with disinterest. "You're smart. I'll give you that. But the answer to your question doesn't matter. Not anymore."

Daniel's mind was racing. They had been followed, and now this woman was here, blocking their way to safety. But there was more to her words—more to what she had said than just a simple threat. "You're not just a hired gun," Daniel said slowly, his voice filled with realization. "You're part of something bigger. Who are you really working for?"

The woman's smile widened, but there was no warmth in it. "I'm working for the Laurent legacy, just as you are. And I'm here to make sure it survives."

The Safehouse Encounter

The words hit Daniel like a punch to the gut. The Laurent family's influence wasn't just a matter of inheritance. It was far more complex, more insidious. And the woman standing before him—this agent of the family—was a force in that machine. She wasn't just here to stop him; she was here to ensure that the legacy remained intact, regardless of the cost.

"Why don't you come with me, Daniel?" the woman said, her voice soft, almost coaxing. "There's no need to make this more difficult. You can't run forever. You're tied to the family, no matter how hard you try to escape it."

Daniel's fists clenched at his sides. "I'll never be a part of your legacy," he spat. "I've made my choice."

The woman's gaze turned colder, the corners of her lips twitching in what might have been amusement. "I think you'll find that your choice isn't yours to make. Not anymore."

A sudden, loud crack broke the tension in the air. A shot rang out, echoing through the stillness of the woods.

Everything went black.

Forty

The Undercover Billionaire

The sound of the gunshot echoed through the safehouse like a thunderclap, sending a shockwave of fear through Daniel's chest. The world seemed to slow for a moment—his pulse hammering in his ears, his breath caught in his throat. The woman, standing just feet away, froze for a heartbeat, her hand still steady at her side. Daniel's hand shot out instinctively, pulling Emily behind him, his body a barrier between her and the danger that was now in their midst.

The silence that followed the shot was deafening. The air in the room was thick with tension, so thick it felt like it could suffocate them. Daniel's eyes flicked frantically to the source of the sound, but everything was shrouded in shadow, impossible to decipher. The figure of the woman standing in front of them was momentarily blurred, her posture unchanging, but the coldness in her eyes was unmistakable.

For a moment, Daniel could only hear his own breathing, shallow and fast, his mind racing, trying to process what was happening. The shot had been aimed at them—or had it? His eyes darted between Emily and the woman, but before he could make sense of it, the woman's lips curved into a cold, knowing smile.

"You weren't expecting that, were you?" she said, her voice as smooth as silk, but with a bite beneath it. "You thought you were safe here. That you could outrun it all. But you're wrong, Daniel. No one is ever truly safe."

Daniel's heart pounded harder, and his mind was already shifting into overdrive. Whoever this woman was, she wasn't just any enemy—they had no idea who she really worked for, what her true purpose was. She was more than a mere obstacle. She was the beginning of something much larger. And the fact that she had fired a warning shot— without hesitation—spoke volumes about the stakes they were facing.

But Emily was still behind him, her presence grounding him, and Daniel knew he had to keep his head clear. One wrong move and it would all come crashing down.

"You think you can intimidate us?" Daniel said, his voice sharp, but controlled. "You think you can silence us just like that?"

The woman raised an eyebrow, her expression still unreadable. "I don't need to intimidate you, Daniel. I need to get your attention. And trust me, you've got mine."

She took a slow step forward, the heels of her boots clicking ominously against the wooden floor, the sound eerily amplified in the quiet room. Each step felt like a countdown, the space between them growing heavier with every inch. Daniel didn't dare move, his hand still holding Emily tightly, his eyes never leaving the woman's face.

"What do you want?" Daniel demanded, trying to steady his breath, to quell the panic rising within him. "Who are you really?"

For a moment, the woman didn't speak, her gaze fixed on Daniel. The silence stretched between them, thick with the weight of unspoken words. Then, with deliberate slowness, she reached into her jacket pocket and pulled out a small, black wallet, the leather worn but well-kept. She opened it, revealing an ID card with a name Daniel didn't recognize—nothing about it felt ordinary.

"Who am I?" she repeated, almost as though the question itself bored her. "I'm someone who has the resources to find anyone. And I have no problem showing up when necessary."

She flipped the ID closed, her movements almost fluid, precise. "But you're not here to know who I am. Not yet. You're here to understand why I'm here."

Daniel's brow furrowed, but before he could respond, the woman's eyes flickered toward the doorway of the safehouse. A sudden movement caught his attention—another shadow—much larger this time, but it was gone too quickly to pinpoint.

A chill ran down Daniel's spine. There was someone else here. Someone else who had been watching. He felt a deep sense of urgency settle into his chest.

"I didn't come alone," the woman continued, her voice carrying a dangerous undertone. "You should know that by now. The world you're trying to escape from—this 'safehouse' you've been hiding in—it's never going to keep you safe. Not from what's coming."

The door behind her creaked open, and Daniel's instincts flared. Without a word, he shoved Emily back into the shadows, his body protective, keeping her from being in the line of sight. The woman barely blinked as the door fully opened, but it was the figure that stepped into the room that made Daniel's heart leap into his throat.

A tall man, dressed in a sharp, tailored suit, entered the room. His presence was commanding, every inch of him exuding power and control. But it was his face—the way his features were set in an almost unearthly calm—that sent a ripple of recognition through Daniel.

This wasn't just a random hired gun. This man, Daniel could tell from the way he moved, from the way his very stance radiated influence, wasn't just anyone. He was someone important. Someone who knew exactly what was at stake.

And then it hit Daniel—the man wasn't just anyone. He was someone who had been missing from his life for years. The realization hit like a punch to the gut, leaving him winded.

"Mr. Laurent," the man said, his voice smooth, rich, and confident. "I see you've met my associate."

The world seemed to tilt, the blood draining from Daniel's face. The man's smile didn't reach his eyes, but there was no mistaking the familiarity in his voice. The coldness. The precision. The way he carried himself—it was unmistakable.

"Levi," Daniel whispered, the word slipping from his lips before he could stop it.

The man's eyes gleamed with cold amusement, but his lips remained in a tight, controlled smile. "I'm surprised you remember me, Daniel. After all, you've been busy trying to hide the family name, haven't you?"

Daniel's heart pounded in his chest, his pulse quickening as the weight of everything settled over him. Levi Laurent. His older cousin. The one person he had never expected to see again. The one person whose disappearance had always been a source of quiet rumors in the family. The stories of his 'tragic fall' into the shadows of the Laurent empire, of his sudden retreat from the public eye, had always been a mystery. But now, standing in front of Daniel, Levi wasn't the man he remembered.

Levi was more than just a ghost of the past. He was alive. And worse, he was standing here, inside the very walls Daniel had believed would be their sanctuary.

"I see you've been doing well for yourself," Daniel said, his voice tight, masking the shock and the bitterness that threatened to break through. "Or maybe I should say, for them."

Levi's smile only widened. "You don't have to be so hostile, cousin. I'm not here to fight. I'm here to help you, in my own way."

Daniel didn't buy it. Levi was never a man to 'help' anyone, especially not him. The way he spoke, the way he moved—it was all a performance. A show. A game. And Daniel wasn't about to fall for it.

"I don't need your help," Daniel said, his voice low and dangerous. "Not from you. Not after everything."

Levi's eyes flashed, but he didn't lose his composure. "I understand your frustration, Daniel. Believe me, I do. But whether you like it or not, I'm part of the family. I've always been a part of this legacy—just as you are. And I'm here to remind you that running won't save you. You can't escape what you are."

"Don't tell me what I am," Daniel growled. "You know nothing about me."

Levi's gaze darkened, the underlying threat in his voice clear now. "You think you're different? You think you've broken free from the family? You haven't. You can never break free, Daniel. The Laurent name is in your blood. And it always will be."

The silence that followed his words was suffocating. Daniel could feel the weight of the family's history bearing down on him, the legacy that had been thrust upon him now more than ever. His choices, his rejection of the name—none of it mattered. The Laurent bloodline would always find a way to pull him back in.

The woman who had accompanied Levi stepped forward, her eyes narrowing as she assessed Daniel. "The longer you fight it, the harder it will be," she said, her voice low, her words laced with cold authority. "You think you've been playing this game by your rules, Daniel, but it's never been up to you. This is bigger than you."

Daniel's mind raced. He had rejected everything the Laurent family stood for. But now, standing in the face of Levi's unyielding presence, he realized something. He was only just beginning to understand how deep the ties ran. And just how much the family was willing to do to ensure its survival.

The stakes had never been higher. And Daniel knew, deep in

his bones, that the choice he had made—to walk away—had just become the most dangerous decision of his life.

But he wasn't going down without a fight. Not now. Not when everything he had fought for was on the line.

"Then let's see how much of a fight I have left," Daniel muttered, his eyes locked onto Levi's with a defiant fire that couldn't be extinguished.

The game was far from over. And now, it was time to make them realize just how deep Daniel Laurent could dig in.

Forty-One

Emily's Shock

The safe house had never felt this suffocating before. As the seconds stretched on, each one feeling longer than the last, Emily's senses were overwhelmed by the presence of Levi Laurent in the room. The man standing before them was not the cousin Daniel had once spoken of with an air of disdain and avoidance—he was a force, powerful and dangerous, someone whose very presence seemed to alter the air around them.

The realization struck her in waves. Levi Laurent had been the one behind their pursuit. He had orchestrated everything. The woman who had emerged from the woods, the dangerous calm of Levi's voice, all of it had been part of a larger plan. They hadn't been running from the shadows of the Laurent family. They had been running from Levi himself.

Emily's Shock

Emily's mind raced, trying to process everything that had happened in the past few minutes. She could feel Daniel's tension, the anger simmering just beneath the surface, but there was something more. Something that neither of them had expected. Levi wasn't just another player in the game—he was the architect, the one who had been pulling strings all along.

And now, standing before them, Levi was smiling, his expression cool and almost detached, as though their very presence was a mere inconvenience. The air felt thick with the weight of what was happening. The very walls of the safehouse, the place that had promised them refuge, seemed to close in around them. The silence that followed Levi's last words felt like a death sentence, as if the walls themselves were holding their breath.

Emily's heart was still racing from the shock of seeing Levi. She had never seen a man so assured of his power, so in control of everything around him. There was no fear in him, no hesitation—only the certainty that Daniel, and by extension, she, were nothing more than obstacles in his path.

Daniel's hand had instinctively gone to the knife at his side, his fingers gripping it tightly. His body was taut, his muscles coiled like a spring, and his eyes were locked on Levi, the intensity of his gaze unwavering. Emily could feel the energy in the room, the invisible pull between the two men, as if they were on the brink of an explosion. But despite Daniel's apparent anger, there was something else in his eyes—a deep sense of betrayal, an understanding that their fight had just grown much larger than either of them had ever anticipated.

"We're not done here, Levi," Daniel said, his voice low and dangerous. "I don't care how much power you think you have. I will not be a part of your game."

Levi's smile didn't falter. He didn't move an inch, standing as if he owned the room, as though the words Daniel had spoken held no weight.

"You don't get it, Daniel," Levi said smoothly, his voice laced with an eerie calm. "This isn't your choice to make anymore. You can run, you can fight, but the Laurent bloodline will always find you. It always finds its way back."

Daniel's jaw clenched, his fingers tightening on the knife handle, but it was Emily who spoke this time, her voice trembling but firm. "What do you want from us?" she demanded, stepping forward. "Why are you here? You have everything—why chase us down like this?"

Levi's eyes flickered toward her, and for a brief moment, Emily thought she saw something in his gaze. A flicker of respect, maybe, or perhaps something more calculating.

"I don't need anything from you, Emily," Levi said, his voice smooth, almost dismissive. "But you're part of the package, aren't you? Daniel's weakness. You always were. He won't make the right choice without you."

Emily's Shock

The words hit Emily like a slap in the face. She stumbled back, the weight of his words sinking in. She had always known that Daniel's family was a force of manipulation, but hearing Levi say it so plainly, without a trace of remorse, made her feel like a pawn in a game that was far too dangerous.

"Stop it," Daniel said, his voice sharp. He stepped toward Levi, his fists clenched at his sides. "You don't get to use her. You don't get to manipulate us anymore."

Levi's expression shifted slightly, the faintest trace of amusement curling at the corners of his lips. "Manipulate? You think I'm manipulating you, Daniel?" He shook his head slowly, the smirk never leaving his face. "I'm offering you what you've always wanted. Freedom. Power. Everything you've been too afraid to accept."

Emily felt the bile rise in her throat at his words. Power. Freedom. Those were just illusions, promises designed to trap them in the same cycle of lies that had ensnared Daniel's family for generations. She had seen it before—how the Laurent family twisted everything they touched, how they preyed on the vulnerable to maintain their control.

"You think freedom means taking control of everything and everyone around you," Emily spat, her voice growing louder. "But all it does is trap you in a cage, just like the one your family has built around itself. You're no different from them."

Levi's eyes darkened, and for the first time, there was a flicker of something dangerous in his gaze. "You don't understand, Emily. You never will."

The tension in the room thickened, and Daniel moved to stand beside Emily, his body radiating with quiet fury. Emily could feel the weight of the moment pressing in on them, suffocating them. This was more than just a confrontation with Levi. This was the culmination of everything that had brought them here—the vault, the legacy, the decision Daniel had made to reject it all.

But Levi wasn't done. He wasn't finished with his game, and as much as Daniel wanted to fight, there was something in Levi's eyes now that made Emily's blood run cold. He wasn't just after Daniel's allegiance—he was after something else. Something far darker. And she could feel it.

"We've all been here before, Daniel," Levi said, his voice dropping to a low, dangerous whisper. "You think you can break free from your past? You think you can outrun it? You can't. You're part of this family, whether you like it or not. And I'll make sure you understand that—one way or another."

The last words hung in the air like a warning, an undeniable promise that rang with the weight of history, of bloodlines and decisions that had already been made long before either Daniel or Emily had been born. The sense of inevitability was suffocating. Emily could feel it pressing on her chest, drowning her in its sheer weight. She knew that, whatever happened next, their choices would never be entirely their own. They would never be able to outrun the Laurent legacy.

"I'll never be like them," Daniel said quietly, his words sharp and determined.

Levi tilted his head, a strange, almost admiring smile curving his lips. "You already are," he said softly. "The question is: how far will you go to fight it?"

The words struck like a blow to the gut, and Emily took a step back, her thoughts spinning. What was Daniel supposed to do? What could he do? Levi was right. The Laurent legacy was in his blood, in his veins, and no matter how far he ran, it would always pull him back. Emily had seen it in his eyes—his desire to be free of it, but also his fear that he could never truly escape.

But there was no time to dwell on it. The air had shifted again, and Emily could feel the presence of another figure—someone else was here. Someone who had been waiting in the shadows.

A figure stepped out from behind the doorway, a man dressed in dark clothing, his face obscured by the hood of his jacket. Emily's heart skipped a beat as he moved into the dim light, his expression unreadable.

"You're not alone," the man said, his voice low, almost growling. "And neither is Daniel."

The room went still. The tension was unbearable. Levi, for the first time, seemed taken aback, his eyes narrowing as he turned toward the newcomer. Emily felt the rush of fear and adrenaline flood her veins. Who was this man? Why was he here?

"I've come for what belongs to me," the man said, stepping forward with the confidence of someone who had already claimed victory.

The game was no longer just about Daniel's choice. There were forces far beyond his control that were converging on them. Forces that Emily had no idea how to fight.

The room seemed to close in around them, and in the stillness that followed, Emily's mind raced. They weren't just running from Levi anymore. They were running from a future that had already been written. A future where their every move had been calculated long before they had ever understood the stakes.

And in that moment, Emily realized just how high the cost was—how much she had underestimated the dark web that had been woven around them all.

Forty-Two

The Hidden Conspiracy

The room was suffocating, the air thick with the kind of tension that only came when a truth—dark and dangerous—was about to be uncovered. Emily stood frozen at the doorway of the safehouse, her heart pounding in her chest as she watched the scene unfold before her. The man who had just stepped into the room wasn't just some stranger. He wasn't another hired gun, another obstacle standing in their way. No, this man was someone far more dangerous. His presence radiated power, a chilling confidence that made her blood run cold.

He had spoken with such authority—his words measured, calculated, as though he were already ten steps ahead of them. As though he had known this moment was coming. He wasn't just after Daniel's life or the Laurent legacy. He was after something much more elusive. And Emily had the sinking feeling that, no matter how hard they fought, they were all pawns in a much larger game.

"I've come for what belongs to me," the man had said, his voice low and forceful, as he stepped into the dim light of the room. He moved with the grace of someone who had done this a thousand times, his every action deliberate, controlled. His face, still mostly obscured by the hood of his jacket, held an air of mystery. But Emily could feel it—the undercurrent of malevolence that lurked beneath his calm exterior.

The man paused, as if assessing the room, his sharp eyes flicking from Daniel to Levi, and then to Emily, who stood frozen by the doorway. It felt as though the weight of his gaze pierced straight through her. Emily swallowed hard, her mind racing, trying to make sense of the growing uncertainty that had engulfed them.

Levi had stiffened the moment the man entered, his eyes narrowing, but he didn't speak. Instead, he seemed to study the man with a mixture of wariness and calculation. This wasn't an ordinary encounter. This was something far more personal. And Emily realized, with a growing sense of dread, that they had walked right into the heart of a conspiracy far bigger than they had ever imagined.

"Who are you?" Daniel demanded, his voice laced with anger but tinged with the kind of confusion that came with being thrust into the unknown.

The Hidden Conspiracy

The man smiled faintly, the corners of his lips twitching as if he found Daniel's question almost amusing. "I'm someone who's been watching," he said, his voice calm, but each word seemed to hang in the air with an unsettling finality. "Someone who's been waiting for this moment for a long time."

Emily felt her pulse quicken, her thoughts racing. Watching. Waiting. What did that mean? Who was this man really? And how deep did his involvement run in everything they had been through? The safehouse, the chase, the cryptic warnings—it was all beginning to fit together in ways that terrified her. But she wasn't about to let the fear take hold. Not yet. She needed answers, and she needed them now.

"Waiting for what?" Daniel asked, his voice growing more defiant as he stepped forward, putting himself between Emily and the man. "Who are you really?"

The man tilted his head slightly, as though amused by Daniel's questions. "Who I am is less important than what I represent," he replied coolly. "You see, Daniel, you've been running for a long time. But what you don't realize is that you've been running in circles. Everything you've done has been predicted. Every move you've made has been part of the plan."

Daniel's eyes flashed with confusion, and for a brief moment, Emily saw the flicker of disbelief cross his face. "What the hell are you talking about?"

The man's eyes never left Daniel's. "You think the Laurent family is the only force you're up against. You think it's just a matter of rejecting your legacy, of walking away from your bloodline. But there's something much more dangerous at play here. Something that goes deeper than family. Something you haven't even begun to comprehend."

Daniel took a step back, his eyes narrowing in suspicion. "What do you mean?" he asked, his voice sharp.

The man paused for a long moment, as if weighing his words carefully before speaking. "The Laurent family has been involved in a conspiracy for generations, Daniel. But it's not just about power. It's about control. Control over something far greater than wealth. This isn't just a family affair. This is global. And you've unknowingly become a part of it."

The weight of his words hit Emily like a sledgehammer, and she felt her stomach twist with a mixture of fear and disbelief. A global conspiracy? What was he saying? She looked at Daniel, whose face had gone pale, his jaw clenched tight as he processed the information.

"You're lying," Daniel said through gritted teeth. "This is all just some elaborate game. You're trying to intimidate me, but it won't work."

The man smiled, but there was no warmth in it. "I'm not lying, Daniel. You've been fed lies your entire life. The Laurent legacy isn't just a family affair. It's the cornerstone of something much bigger. A secret society that has been pulling the strings behind the scenes for centuries. And now, you're the key to its future."

Emily's heart pounded as the truth began to dawn on her. A secret society. A conspiracy that stretched across the globe. And somehow, Daniel was at the center of it. She had always known that his family was entangled in something dangerous, but this... this was beyond anything she could have imagined. And the realization hit her like a cold wave: they weren't just fighting for survival anymore. They were fighting against a force so entrenched, so hidden, that they had no idea how far it reached or how deep the roots ran.

"What are you saying?" Emily's voice trembled as she took a step closer to Daniel, her hand instinctively reaching for his. "What do you want with him?"

The man looked at Emily for a long moment before responding, his eyes cold and calculating. "You, Emily, have always been a part of this. You think you've been fighting for Daniel. For his freedom. But the truth is, you've been a pawn in this game just as much as he has. Whether you like it or not, you've already been marked. The family knows you, Emily. They've been watching you too."

Daniel's eyes flared with anger. "No," he said, shaking his head, his voice a low growl. "You're wrong. We've been fighting against them, not for them. You can't manipulate us into believing we're part of this. We won't fall into your trap."

The man's gaze never wavered. "You don't have a choice, Daniel. The conspiracy is already in motion. You're already in the center of it. The only question now is: will you join us, or will you fight it, knowing that you're fighting against a force that has no equal?"

There was a heavy pause in the room as everyone processed the man's words. It was as if time had frozen, the weight of the truth sinking in like a stone in Emily's stomach. The Laurent family had always been at the center of a power struggle, but this? This was something entirely different. And now, Daniel was part of it. They both were.

Emily felt a cold shiver run down her spine. She wasn't just fighting for Daniel's freedom anymore. She was fighting against a conspiracy that could shake the foundations of the world. She looked at Daniel, her heart aching with the fear of what lay ahead. They were no longer just running from Levi. They were running from something far larger, a force that had been lurking in the shadows for generations.

The man stepped forward then, his hand reaching into his jacket pocket. He pulled out a small, metallic object and held it up for them to see. It was a ring, much like the one Daniel had found in the vault, but this one was different. This one gleamed with an otherworldly sheen, its surface carved with intricate symbols that seemed to pulse with an eerie energy.

"This," the man said, holding the ring between them, "is the key to everything. The key to unlocking the future of the Laurent family. And you, Daniel, are the one who will decide whether it is used for good or for destruction."

Emily's breath caught in her throat as she stared at the ring, its gleaming surface reflecting the dim light of the room. She could feel the weight of its power, the danger that came with it. The stakes had never been higher. Daniel's choice wasn't just about rejecting his family's legacy anymore. It was about choosing between a future where power reigned supreme or a future where they fought to destroy the forces that had manipulated them all.

The man's eyes flicked to Daniel, his gaze unwavering. "The choice is yours, Daniel. But know this: whatever you decide, it will change the world. And there's no going back."

The words hung in the air like a sentence, heavy with the knowledge that whatever happened next, it would mark the beginning of the end.

Daniel's eyes never left the ring, his expression unreadable. Emily could see the struggle in him, the weight of his decision pressing down on him. They weren't just fighting for their survival anymore. They were fighting for the future of everything.

The truth had been revealed. And now, the conspiracy had begun.

Forty-Three

The Vault Opens

The room was colder than it had ever been, the temperature dropping steadily as if the very air inside had sensed the shifting balance of power. Daniel stood at the center of it, the weight of his decision pressing down on his shoulders, the realization of the moment heavy in his chest. The ring—the key to everything—glinted in his hand, its cold surface like an anchor tying him to something far beyond his understanding. Levi Laurent had always been a shadow in his life, but now, with the sudden appearance of the man who had orchestrated everything, Daniel knew that the shadow had grown into a full-on storm.

The safehouse, their supposed sanctuary, felt like a tomb now. The walls, once an unassuming barrier between them and the world outside, seemed to close in around them.

The Vault Opens

There was no escape. They had run, they had hidden, but now, everything had led them back here. Back to the vault.

The man who had appeared with Levi earlier—the one with the dark, calculating eyes—watched them from the shadows of the room. His presence was a constant weight, something unseen but always felt. The quiet was unnerving, oppressive, like the calm before a storm. And Daniel could feel it—whatever was coming next, it wasn't just a battle for survival. It was something far larger, far more dangerous.

The ring felt heavier in his hand, the cold metal pressing against his skin, as if it had a life of its own. He had rejected the Laurent legacy, but the choices in front of him now were no longer about personal freedom. They were about something much darker, something buried deep within the family's bloodline—a power that had never been meant to be unleashed.

"We can't let them have it," Emily whispered from behind him, her voice barely audible. Her words were more of a plea than a command, but they resonated in the quiet room. The weight of the world seemed to rest on those words. The vault. The power. They had to stop it.

Daniel turned to face her, his eyes dark with determination. "I won't let them. But I don't know if we can stop it. I don't know if we can stop him."

Levi's figure shifted in the corner of the room, his eyes never leaving them, his face unreadable. It was as though he were calculating every possible outcome, every move they might make, every breath they took. He wasn't just a man in this moment—he was the embodiment of the Laurent legacy itself: cold, manipulative, and full of secrets that had been buried for far too long.

"You don't understand what's at stake here," Levi finally spoke, his voice cool but laced with an underlying threat. He stepped toward Daniel, his every movement deliberate. "The vault is not just a vault. It's the key to securing the future. The Laurent legacy has always been tied to it. And now, it's time for the truth to be revealed."

Daniel's chest tightened as the words sank in. The truth? What truth? He had thought he understood it all—the betrayal, the manipulation, the lies. But this? This was something else. Something far darker.

The man beside Levi stepped forward now, his eyes glinting with a predatory gleam. "The vault is not just a symbol of the Laurent family's power," he said, his voice gravelly but authoritative. "It's the repository of everything we've built, everything we've worked for. And now, it's time for you to understand what it means to inherit it."

Emily moved closer to Daniel, her hand brushing against his arm in a silent show of support. She had been with him through every twist and turn, through every betrayal, and now, more than ever, he needed her by his side. The stakes had never been higher.

The Vault Opens

"You're wrong," Daniel said, his voice steady but filled with quiet rage. "I don't want any part of this legacy. You've been using it to manipulate everyone. To control everything. But I won't let you. I'll destroy it before I let you take it."

Levi's eyes glinted with a mixture of amusement and cold calculation. "You think you can destroy it? You think you can erase what's already been done? It's too late, Daniel. You've already made your choice. The vault will open, whether you're ready for it or not."

Daniel clenched his fists around the ring, his mind racing. He had been running from this legacy for so long, trying to escape the inevitable, but now, standing here, with the vault within reach, he understood. The vault wasn't just a treasure trove of wealth or secrets. It was something far more powerful, far more dangerous. And it wasn't just about him. It was about everyone. The Laurent family's power wasn't something that could be contained. It was something that, once unleashed, would tear everything apart.

He could feel the pull of the vault, the magnetic force of the power within it, urging him to open it, to unlock the truth. But that truth was something Daniel wasn't sure he could face. Not without risking everything he had left.

The tension in the room was unbearable. The air felt thick with anticipation, like the very walls were waiting for Daniel to make the next move. The vault, he realized, wasn't just a physical object. It was a test. A test of his strength, his resolve, and his ability to withstand the weight of the choices that lay before him.

"You don't have to do this," Emily said quietly, her voice filled with concern. She stepped closer to him, her hand reaching for his. "You can still walk away. We can still find a way out of this."

Daniel looked into her eyes, searching for the reassurance that he needed, but all he saw was fear. Not fear for herself, but for him. She knew, as he did, that there was no walking away now. There was no escaping what they had already set into motion.

"I can't," Daniel said softly, his voice filled with a quiet resignation. "I thought I could, Emily. I thought I could walk away from this legacy, but it's in me. It's always been in me. And if I don't face it now, if I don't open that vault, I'll never be free."

The silence that followed his words was deafening. The weight of his decision hung heavy in the air, the implications of it crashing down on him like a tidal wave. But there was no turning back. Not anymore. The vault was waiting. The secrets were waiting.

And then, with a sudden movement, Levi spoke again, his voice cold and final. "Do it."

Daniel's heart skipped a beat as he turned toward Levi. The command had been simple, but it carried the weight of

The Vault Opens

everything—the history, the family, the legacy. It was a call to action. And Daniel had no choice but to answer it.

Taking a deep breath, Daniel stepped forward, his hand gripping the ring tightly. He could feel its power, the strange energy that pulsed within it, as he moved toward the ancient stone structure that housed the vault. The room seemed to darken as he reached the door, the shadows closing in around him, the air thick with anticipation.

The vault had been sealed for generations. It had been hidden away, its secrets locked behind layers of time, but now, as Daniel stood before it, he understood the true purpose of the vault. It wasn't just about keeping something hidden. It was about protecting something—something so dangerous that it could change everything. And now, he was about to unlock it.

With trembling hands, Daniel placed the ring into the keyhole of the vault. The moment it made contact, the ground beneath him seemed to tremble, a low rumble reverberating through the floor, as if the vault itself were awakening from a long slumber. The air around them grew colder, the room filled with an electric charge, and Daniel could feel the very walls of the safehouse vibrating with energy.

Then, with a grinding sound, the vault door slowly began to open.

The light that poured from the vault was blinding, a sharp

contrast to the darkened room. For a moment, Daniel couldn't see anything but the brilliant glow that emanated from within. It was as though the vault was alive, breathing, waiting for its secrets to be revealed.

And then, as the door fully opened, the truth was revealed.

Inside the vault, lying upon an ancient pedestal, was a small, intricately carved box. It was unassuming at first glance, but Daniel could feel the power emanating from it, the dark, magnetic energy that seemed to draw him in. His heart raced as he took a step toward it, his hand trembling as he reached for the box.

But before he could touch it, a voice echoed from behind him.

"Don't."

Emily's voice was barely a whisper, but it carried the weight of a thousand unspoken fears.

Daniel turned toward her, his eyes filled with confusion. "What? What do you mean?"

She took a step forward, her face pale but determined. "You can't open it. Not yet. We don't know what it will do. We don't know what's inside."

Daniel's chest tightened as he looked at the box, the unknown truth inside it beckoning him. But Emily was right.

The Vault Opens

They didn't know what they were dealing with. And as much as he wanted to unlock the secrets of the Laurent family, as much as he needed to know the truth, he couldn't ignore the sense of danger that loomed over them.

The decision was now before him. The vault had opened. But was he ready to face what lay within?

The weight of the world seemed to press down on him as he stood there, torn between the truth and the consequences of uncovering it. The vault had opened, but the true test had only just begun.

Forty-Four

The Return of an Enemy

The silence that followed the opening of the vault was deafening. Daniel stood frozen, the glowing box before him casting an eerie light across his face. His mind was a whirlpool of conflicting emotions—fear, curiosity, dread—each emotion clawing at him, urging him to either approach or retreat. The box seemed so small, so unassuming, yet everything about it felt monumental, as if it were a trigger for something far more dangerous.

Emily stood by his side, her hand trembling as it hovered near his. She wasn't sure if it was from fear or the strange energy that had begun to fill the room, but she felt it too. The air had thickened, the sense of impending danger growing heavier with every second. She wanted to reach out, to take Daniel's hand, but she couldn't move. Every instinct told her that this moment was one that would change everything. And yet, she had no idea how.

"Daniel," she said, her voice low and cautious, "we don't know what's inside that box. We don't know what it will do."

Daniel's eyes flickered to her, the conflict evident in his gaze. He knew she was right. They had already been thrust into a world of darkness, manipulation, and power struggles. But now? Now they were standing on the edge of something far more dangerous, something that could tip the scales in ways they couldn't even fathom.

"I have to know," Daniel said, his voice hoarse with uncertainty. He took a slow, hesitant step toward the box, his fingers twitching at his sides, as though instinctively drawn to it.

"Daniel..." Emily's warning was soft but firm, and yet, it seemed futile in the face of his determination.

And just as he was about to reach out, a noise cut through the silence—a slow, deliberate step, followed by the unmistakable sound of a voice that sent a chill down his spine.

"Well, well, well. It's been a long time, hasn't it?"

The voice echoed from the doorway, low and mocking, with a tone so familiar that Daniel's blood ran cold. He whirled around, his heart pounding in his chest, his body tensing in a defensive stance. Standing in the doorway of the safehouse, framed by the shadows of the night, was a figure he had never expected to see again.

Kara.

Her silhouette was sharp against the dim light of the room, her long, dark hair flowing like a shadow behind her. She was older now, her face harder, her posture more commanding. The woman who had once been a part of Daniel's past—someone he had thought was lost to him forever—was now standing in front of him, alive, very much in control, and with a presence that seemed to demand submission.

Kara's eyes were locked onto him, and there was something cold in her gaze, something predatory. Daniel's throat tightened as he realized the truth—Kara had never truly disappeared. She had always been there, lurking in the shadows, waiting for the right moment to return.

"What are you doing here?" Daniel's voice was tight with anger, but underneath it, there was a layer of fear he couldn't suppress. Kara had always been a wildcard—unpredictable, dangerous. And now, seeing her again, he realized just how much he had underestimated her.

She stepped into the room, her eyes flicking between Daniel and Emily. "What do you think I'm doing here?" she said, her voice dripping with condescension. "I've been watching, waiting for the perfect moment. And here you are. The prodigal Laurent son, back at the heart of it all. The vault.

The power. The legacy. You really thought you could just run from it, didn't you?"

Daniel's chest tightened, his pulse quickening. "This isn't your fight, Kara. You don't belong here."

Kara chuckled, a low, dark sound that filled the room. "Don't belong? Daniel, I've always belonged. You just didn't know it." She took a few steps forward, her heels clicking ominously on the floor with each movement. "You've been so focused on the vault, so focused on rejecting your legacy, that you never once thought about who else was waiting in the wings. Who else had a hand in all of this. You really think you're the only one who's been watching? The only one who's been involved?"

The question struck Daniel like a blow to the chest. He knew, deep down, that Kara wasn't just a part of the Laurent family's web. She had been a player in it all along. The people who had always remained in the shadows, the ones whose motives were unclear—Kara had been one of them. And now, her return felt like a cruel reminder that they had all been pawns in someone else's game.

"What do you want from me, Kara?" Daniel asked, his voice low and edged with suspicion. His eyes never left hers, watching her every movement, waiting for the trap to snap shut.

Kara's lips curled into a smile, a smile that sent a shiver down Daniel's spine. "I want what's mine, Daniel. What's always been mine. The power. The control. Everything you've been hiding from."

"You're insane," Emily said, her voice shaking but defiant. "You don't have any claim to this. None of us do."

Kara's eyes shifted to Emily, a cold gleam in them. "You're still so naive, aren't you? This isn't about what we claim. It's about what's already been decided. The Laurent family doesn't just let go of power. It doesn't just disappear. It survives. It thrives. And you, Emily, you've been a part of that. Whether you like it or not."

Daniel took a step forward, his body tense, ready for whatever was coming next. Kara had always been a threat, but now, more than ever, her return meant that the game had changed. The vault had opened, but it wasn't just about uncovering the family's secrets. It was about something much more dangerous.

"Don't make this worse, Kara," Daniel said, his voice steady, though his heart was racing. "You have no idea what you're dealing with. This isn't just about control. It's about power that we can't even begin to understand."

Kara tilted her head, as if considering his words. Then, without warning, she moved faster than Daniel had anticipated. She reached for the box in the center of the room, her fingers brushing against its surface as if she had claimed it before. And in that instant, Daniel realized that whatever game they had been playing, it was now coming to an end.

Kara wasn't here just to talk. She was here to take control, to claim the power that had been sealed away for so long.

Before Daniel could react, Kara opened the box. The moment the lid cracked, a surge of energy filled the room, a crackling force that made the air hum with an electric charge. The walls seemed to tremble, and the temperature in the room dropped sharply. Daniel could feel it—like the vault itself was awakening, its secrets coming to life, ready to spill out into the world.

"What have you done?" Daniel shouted, his mind spinning as he realized that whatever was inside the box had been activated. The very air around them felt charged, as though the world itself were holding its breath, waiting for what would come next.

Kara held up the object inside the box, and for the first time, Daniel saw it clearly. It was a small, intricately carved artifact—shaped like a key, but with symbols and markings that seemed to shift with the light. It wasn't just a key to the vault; it was a key to something far more dangerous. A key to unlocking the Laurent family's deepest, darkest secrets.

"This," Kara said, her voice low with satisfaction, "is what I've been waiting for. The final piece. The key to everything. The power that has been kept hidden for centuries."

Daniel felt his stomach drop. It wasn't just a key. It was the source of the Laurent family's true power, and it was in Kara's hands now. There was no stopping her. No way to undo the damage that had been done.

"You've made a grave mistake," Daniel said, his voice steady but filled with resolve. He couldn't let this happen. Not now. Not after everything they had been through.

Kara's eyes met his, her expression unreadable. "No, Daniel. The mistake was yours. You had a choice. You could have joined me. You could have embraced the power. But you didn't. And now, you'll have to live with the consequences."

As Kara turned away, the object in her hand glowing faintly, Daniel realized with a sinking feeling that everything they had been running from was now closing in on them. There was no escape. The vault had opened. The conspiracy was no longer just a shadow in the distance—it was here. And now, they were in the eye of the storm.

Kara's return marked the beginning of the end, and there was nothing they could do to stop it. The Laurent legacy had claimed them all.

Forty-Five

The Ticking Clock

The clock on the wall ticked louder with every passing second, its rhythmic, mechanical sound reverberating through the safehouse like a constant reminder of the pressure they were under. Daniel's breath came in shallow bursts, his heart hammering in his chest as his eyes locked onto Kara. The object in her hand—still glowing faintly, like some forgotten relic of an ancient world—seemed to pulse with an energy that resonated deep within him, drawing him closer to it, even as his instincts screamed at him to run.

Kara's eyes never left him as she stood, poised and still, the air around her thick with the weight of everything she had just set in motion. The power, the ancient artifact, the consequences of their actions—everything had led to this moment. Daniel had thought he was prepared. He had thought that walking away from the Laurent legacy would be enough to sever the ties that bound him to this twisted family. But now, he saw the truth for what it was. There was no escaping it. Not for him. Not for Emily. Not for anyone.

The object in Kara's hand—the key—wasn't just an artifact. It was a key to unlocking something much darker, much more dangerous than Daniel had ever imagined. And Kara knew it. She had always known it. She had been waiting for this moment, waiting for the right time to strike, to take control of the very power that had haunted their family for generations.

"You know what this is, don't you?" Kara's voice cut through the thick silence, smooth as silk but carrying a weight of finality. "The final piece of the puzzle. The key to everything the Laurent family has built. The power we've been hiding for centuries."

Daniel didn't answer. He couldn't. His mind was racing, his thoughts scattered, trying to process the magnitude of the situation. The vault had opened. The secrets had been revealed. But the price they were all going to pay for it was more than he could comprehend.

"You've made a mistake, Kara," Daniel said, his voice hoarse with a mixture of anger and fear. "You don't know what you're tampering with. You don't know what will happen once you unlock this power."

Kara's lips curled into a smile, but there was nothing warm or reassuring about it. "I know exactly what I'm doing, Daniel. You're the one who doesn't understand. All this time, you've been so focused on rejecting the legacy, on trying to distance yourself from the family's power, that you've forgotten one simple truth: the Laurent bloodline is more than just a family. It's a legacy. It's a dynasty. And it doesn't just fade away. It resurfaces. It never dies."

Daniel's chest tightened as he realized the full extent of what Kara was saying. The power that the Laurent family had always wielded was more than just wealth or influence. It was a force, a malevolent energy that had been cultivated over generations, and now, with this key—this artifact—Kara was about to unleash it. The consequences were unthinkable. No one could control that kind of power.

Emily stepped closer to Daniel, her hand brushing against his as if seeking comfort, but Daniel could feel the same tremor in her fingers that he felt in his own bones. She, too, understood the gravity of what was happening. She had always known that the Laurent legacy was dangerous, but this—this was beyond anything either of them had imagined.

"We can stop this, Daniel," Emily said softly, her voice trembling with the weight of her words. "We have to stop her."

But Daniel knew, deep down, that it wasn't that simple. Kara wasn't just a rogue member of the family. She was a part of something much larger. And whatever was in that box—the object she held in her hand—was the key to the very heart of the family's power. It was the one thing they couldn't control. The one thing that would destroy them all if unleashed.

"Put it down, Kara," Daniel said, his voice firm but laced with urgency. "You don't know what you're doing. You don't know what's at stake."

But Kara wasn't listening. She lifted the object higher, her fingers tracing the intricate markings etched into its surface as if she were caressing a lover. The room seemed to grow colder with each passing second, the shadows in the corners of the room deepening, swallowing everything in their path.

"This," Kara whispered, her voice reverent as she held the object up to the light, "is the key to our future. And this is where everything changes."

As her words hung in the air, Daniel's mind screamed at him to act. He couldn't let her do this. He couldn't let her unlock whatever power lay hidden within that artifact. The consequences were too great. If Kara succeeded, everything they had fought for would be lost. The Laurent legacy would rise again, and this time, it would be unstoppable.

But there was something else—a feeling, a pull deep inside him—that made Daniel hesitate. It wasn't just the object. It wasn't just the power it represented. It was the truth. The truth about the Laurent family. The truth about his own bloodline. The truth that had always been there, buried deep beneath the surface, just waiting to be unearthed.

"You've always been part of this, Daniel," Kara said, her voice cutting through his thoughts. "You can't run from it. You can't deny it. It's in your blood. And once I unlock this power, once I claim what's mine, you'll be forced to join me. You'll see that there's no other way. The power will demand it."

Daniel's head was spinning, his thoughts a whirl of confusion and fear. Kara's words echoed in his mind, gnawing at him, pushing him to make a choice. A choice he didn't want to make. A choice that would change everything.

"I won't join you," Daniel said, his voice hoarse with determination. "I won't let you destroy everything we've worked for."

Kara's eyes narrowed, her smile fading into something colder, more predatory. "Then you'll be forced to watch. Watch as I take what's mine. Watch as I take control of the legacy you tried to reject."

Suddenly, the ground beneath them trembled, a low rumble vibrating through the floorboards. Daniel's heart skipped a beat as the room seemed to shift, the shadows growing thicker, pressing in on them. He could feel it—an ancient force awakening, something older than the Laurent family itself, something that had been waiting, buried beneath layers of time, to be unleashed.

The clock on the wall ticked louder now, the sound echoing in the room, its rhythmic ticking like a countdown to some unknown, inevitable conclusion. The power in the air was palpable, a thick, oppressive energy that made it difficult to breathe. It was as if the very walls were closing in on them, trapping them in this moment, this decision.

"Daniel," Emily whispered, her voice tight with fear. "We have to stop this. We can't let her open it."

But Kara was already moving, her fingers tightening around the artifact as she lifted it higher, her eyes locked onto Daniel with an intensity that made his stomach churn.

"It's too late," Kara said, her voice filled with dark satisfaction. "The power is already here. And nothing you do can stop it."

The room seemed to shudder as Kara pressed the artifact into a small indentation in the floor. The moment it made contact, a blinding flash of light erupted from the object, filling the room with a searing, almost unbearable glow. Daniel's heart raced as he shielded his eyes, but even through the blinding light, he could feel it—an overwhelming surge of energy, as if the very foundations of the world were shifting beneath his feet.

The ticking of the clock grew louder, faster, as if it were marking the final moments of their lives. Daniel's breath hitched as the air around them seemed to grow thick with power, an energy unlike anything he had ever felt before.

The Ticking Clock

The vault, the artifact, the Laurent family—everything was converging now, all leading to this moment.

And then, as the light reached its peak, a voice—low and ancient, filled with a weight that could crush mountains—echoed through the room.

"You have awakened me."

Daniel's chest tightened as the voice seemed to reverberate through his very bones. It wasn't just a voice. It was a presence. A force. The power that Kara had unlocked was more than just the Laurent family's legacy—it was something far older, something that had been waiting in the darkness for centuries.

The room seemed to shift again, the very walls trembling as the presence in the room grew stronger. And in that moment, Daniel realized the true cost of everything they had fought for. They hadn't just been fighting for survival. They had been fighting for control of something far beyond their understanding. And now, as the clock ticked down, they were about to witness the return of an enemy they could never defeat.

The vault had opened. The ticking clock had brought them to this point. And now, there was no turning back.

Forty-Six

A Betrayal Confirmed

The room was a whirlwind of chaos; every inch of it charged with the crackling energy of the artefact Kara had unleashed. The air was thick with power, an ancient force that seemed to seep into the very walls, bending them, warping the space around them. Daniel's heart thundered in his chest as the world seemed to stretch, the light from the artifact too bright to look at, yet impossible to avoid. He could feel it—an overwhelming, suffocating presence that crushed all the air from the room, leaving him gasping.

The walls, the ceiling, the floor—all seemed to vibrate, as if the very fabric of reality were being torn apart. Every tick of the clock sounded like a countdown to something more dreadful, more final. The voice that had boomed through the room still echoed in Daniel's mind, its words reverberating deep within him.

You have awakened me.

The darkness in those words was not just a threat. It was a promise. A promise of a return, of something older and far more dangerous than anything Daniel had ever encountered. His mind raced, trying to grasp what was happening. He had thought he understood the danger, but now he realized how little he truly knew. Kara's actions had torn open a door that should have remained closed forever. And now, they were all standing on the edge of something far worse than they could have imagined.

The blinding light from the artifact began to fade, but the oppressive energy in the room only grew stronger, thickening like a storm cloud overhead. Daniel's breath was shallow, his hands trembling as he reached out to steady himself against the nearest wall. His eyes flickered between Kara, who stood grinning in triumph, and Emily, who was still beside him, her face pale, her eyes wide with the terror that matched his own.

But as the light dimmed, a deeper darkness filled the room. A presence, vast and ancient, stretched out in every direction, its weight pressing down on them, suffocating them in its reach. And then, as if the air itself were charged with some supernatural force, it happened. The room's temperature dropped, a cold wind sweeping through the space despite the absence of any visible draft. It felt like a thousand icy hands were closing in around them.

Emily reached out to Daniel, her grip tight and frantic. "We need to stop her. We need to stop this," she whispered, her voice filled with a mix of fear and urgency.

Daniel shook his head, his eyes fixed on Kara. She wasn't just standing there triumphantly—she was basking in the presence of the power she had unleashed, feeling its weight and energy flow through her, as though it were a reward for her loyalty. But Daniel could see it now. She wasn't just a rogue element of the Laurent family—she was something far worse. She was part of something much more sinister, something that he had failed to realize until now.

"I never expected it to be this easy," Kara said, her voice cool and full of satisfaction. She stepped forward, her eyes locked on Daniel, as though savoring every moment of the victory that was about to unfold. "You always thought you were the one in control, Daniel. You thought you could run from this legacy. But I've been waiting for this. For this moment."

Daniel's stomach churned, his mind reeling as he began to piece together the truth. Kara had always been a part of this. The Laurent family's web of influence, the power that ran through their veins—it was more than just blood. It was control. It was manipulation. And Kara? She had known the truth all along. She had been working toward this moment. Every move she had made, every step she had taken, had been part of her plan to seize the power.

But what truly stung, what cut deeper than any betrayal,

was that Daniel realized something else: Emily had been caught in the crossfire of Kara's game. All along, Emily had been an unwilling player, dragged into this mess because of her connection to him. She wasn't just standing by his side—she had been a pawn in Kara's plan, just like he had been. It was all coming together now, and the realization hit him like a physical blow.

Kara smiled, her lips curling into a cruel smirk. "You really didn't understand, did you, Daniel? You thought you could reject the legacy, reject the family, but you're wrong. You never had a choice. No one ever does. Not when the power runs this deep."

"No," Daniel said, his voice low and furious, but there was a note of disbelief in it as well. "You've been playing us. This whole time. You—"

"Yes," Kara interrupted, her tone sharp, and there was no hesitation in her voice. "I've been playing you. I've been playing all of you."

The words hit Daniel like a punch to the gut. All this time, he had thought Kara was someone who had simply been lost to the family's web of deceit. He had thought she had been a victim too, that she had been just another pawn in the game. But she hadn't been a victim. She had been the mastermind, the one pulling the strings all along. She had never been lost. She had always known exactly where she was heading. And now, standing before him, she was about to claim the legacy that Daniel had tried so desperately to escape.

His chest tightened, and he felt the weight of his own helplessness crashing down on him. The ticking of the clock had slowed, but the ominous sense of finality grew with every passing moment. The energy in the room seemed to thicken, the air growing heavier as Kara stepped closer, her eyes never leaving Daniel's.

"You think I'm the enemy, don't you?" Kara said, her voice filled with a dark amusement. "But it's too late for that, Daniel. I'm just the one who's been chosen to bring it all back. To restore the Laurent dynasty to its true power."

Daniel's hands clenched into fists at his sides, his heart racing in his chest. He could feel it now—the weight of everything that had been hidden, the years of manipulation and lies, the dark secrets that had been buried for generations. He could feel the power of the Laurent legacy pulsing in the air around him, threatening to consume everything in its wake.

"No," Daniel said again, his voice sharper this time, his anger rising. "I won't let you do this. I won't let you take this power."

But Kara only laughed, her eyes gleaming with something cold, something predatory. "You don't get it, Daniel. You can't stop this. The legacy is alive. It's in your blood. It's in all of us."

A Betrayal Confirmed

And then it happened. The moment the clock struck again, the air in the room shifted, and the entire safehouse seemed to come alive with an energy that was almost tangible. The walls seemed to tremble, the floor vibrating beneath their feet, as the power Kara had unleashed began to grow stronger. The very fabric of the room seemed to warp, the shadows deepening and twisting around them.

Suddenly, the door to the safehouse burst open with a loud crash, sending a rush of cold air into the room. Daniel's head whipped around, his heart leaping into his throat, as another figure appeared in the doorway.

It was Raphael.

His eyes were cold, calculating, but there was something different about him now. The calm, controlled demeanor that had once marked him as a distant observer of the family's affairs was gone. His features were tense, and his posture was rigid. And in his hand, he carried a weapon—a sleek, black gun that glinted menacingly in the dim light of the room.

"I told you," Raphael said, his voice cold and full of finality. "This isn't your fight anymore, Daniel."

Daniel's heart stopped. The weight of Raphael's words settled into his chest, heavy and suffocating. Raphael had always been a part of the family, but this? This was a betrayal so deep, so dark, that Daniel could barely process it. He had known that the Laurent family was ruthless, but this? This was a line that Daniel could never cross.

"You were never meant to be free, Daniel," Raphael continued, stepping further into the room, his eyes scanning the chaos around him. "And now, you'll pay for trying to escape it."

Daniel's blood ran cold as he realized the full extent of the betrayal. The clock had stopped. The game had ended. And now, they were all caught in a web of lies, deceit, and manipulation that no one could escape.

The moment that Kara had unlocked—the moment when everything had shifted—had brought them all to this point. And now, with Raphael standing in the doorway, gun in hand, Daniel understood. There was no escape. There never had been.

The vault had opened. The ticking clock had stopped. And now, Daniel was trapped.

This was the end of the line.

And there was no way out.

Forty-Seven

A Broken Heart

The room was silent now. The only sound was the faint hum of the energy from the artifact, still vibrating in the air like an invisible force, its presence undeniable. The cold weight of what had just transpired pressed down on Daniel's chest, suffocating him, as the darkness in the room seemed to stretch and reach out for him. Kara, standing triumphantly by the artifact, her smirk never fading, was the source of that weight. And yet, it wasn't her presence that crushed him.

It was Raphael.

Daniel's eyes shifted from Kara to the man now standing in the doorway—Raphael, the one person who he had thought was a distant relative, someone who had never fully aligned with the family's schemes, someone who had seemed to want out just like him. But now, as the truth unfolded before him, Daniel realized how wrong he had been. How dangerously wrong.

Raphael's cold eyes never wavered, his stance rigid as he gripped the gun in his hands. The weapon, so out of place in the safehouse, seemed to embody the harshness of the reality that had been thrust upon them. The family. The legacy. The power. It was all too much, and for a moment, Daniel felt as if the walls of the room were closing in, the shadows creeping closer with every passing second.

"You…" Daniel whispered, his voice barely a breath, as his eyes locked on Raphael. "You were never on our side."

Raphael didn't flinch. His gaze remained as cold as ever, his lips pressed into a tight line. "I told you, Daniel. This isn't your fight anymore." His words hung in the air, thick with finality. "You chose the wrong path."

The weight of those words sent a chill down Daniel's spine. It wasn't just the weapon in Raphael's hand. It wasn't the betrayal that now cut so deep. It was the realization that, no matter how hard Daniel fought, no matter how much he had tried to escape the Laurent family, there had always been a part of him that belonged to it. A part of him that couldn't break free.

But it wasn't just the betrayal from Raphael that shattered him—it was the way Emily's gaze shifted, her expression turning pale as she looked from Raphael to Daniel. Her hand, still gripping Daniel's arm, trembled slightly. The fear in her eyes was unmistakable, but it was something deeper that tore at Daniel's heart. She wasn't just afraid for her own safety—she was afraid for him. For what was happening. For what had already been done.

The coldness in the room seemed to multiply as the truth settled between them. The clock that had been ticking ever so steadily seemed to stop altogether. The power that Kara had awakened was here, and now everything was beyond their control. Daniel felt the last vestiges of hope begin to slip away, his fingers tightening into fists at his sides, his breath coming in short bursts as he struggled to find a way to make sense of what was happening.

"Raphael," Emily spoke, her voice strained but firm. "Why are you doing this? Why would you betray us like this?"

Raphael's eyes flickered to her, but there was no warmth in his gaze—only a distant, calculating look. "You don't understand, Emily. You never could. The Laurent family doesn't operate on feelings. It operates on power. And you've all been pawns in a game you never understood. You don't belong here. None of you do."

Emily recoiled, her face a mixture of disbelief and pain. "But you do? You belong in this? After everything?"

The pain in Emily's voice—her raw, unguarded words—hit Daniel harder than anything he had felt so far. The way she looked at Raphael, the way she struggled to make sense of his actions, only reminded him of how deeply they had been deceived. All of them. She hadn't asked to be caught in the web of the Laurent family's power, yet here she was—entangled in it, struggling to break free. She had trusted Raphael, even when she had hesitated. Even when she had questioned his loyalties.

And now, Daniel realized with sickening clarity, he had failed her. He had dragged her into this world of darkness and deceit, only to watch it break her apart piece by piece.

The weight of his failure crashed down on him. He had always known that there was something insidious about the Laurent family's legacy—something that could never be outrun. But it wasn't until now, standing in this room with the artifact glowing ominously at Kara's side, that he truly understood the cost of his decisions.

"I never wanted this for you, Emily," Daniel said, his voice hoarse with regret. He reached out to her, his fingers brushing against her trembling hand, but she pulled away, her gaze flickering to the weapon in Raphael's hands. The unspoken message was clear—she was afraid, not just for herself, but for him. And it broke Daniel's heart.

"You don't get it, Daniel," she whispered, her voice barely audible, as her gaze met his. "None of us do. This… this was never just about the family. It was about you. About us. And we're all trapped in it now."

A quiet sob caught in Emily's throat, her face flushed with

emotion as she turned away from him, pressing her back against the cold stone wall of the safehouse. Daniel could hear her breath hitching, the weight of everything they had been through—the betrayals, the manipulation, the lies—crushing her in ways that were too painful to bear. It was as though she had suddenly realized something he had known all along: they were beyond saving.

Daniel took a step forward, his voice shaking. "Emily, please—"

But she couldn't look at him. She couldn't face him. And it hurt more than he could have ever imagined.

"I'm sorry," she whispered, her voice cracking as she wiped her eyes with the back of her hand. "I just don't know how to deal with this. You've changed. This... this isn't you. You're not the person I thought you were."

Daniel's heart shattered. He couldn't find the words to explain the storm of emotions tearing through him, the regret, the sorrow. He had always prided himself on being able to protect her, on being able to shield her from the truth. But now, he had exposed her to it all. The truth had broken them. He had been too selfish, too focused on his own desire to escape the family's grip, that he had never once stopped to think about the consequences for Emily.

Kara's voice sliced through the silence like a blade. "It's over. All of it. There's no going back now." Her voice was calm, detached, as if she were watching an inevitable tragedy unfold. She looked at Daniel with a strange mixture of pity and satisfaction. "You still don't get it, do you? This isn't about what you want. It's about what's already been set in motion. The Laurent legacy will rise again. It's not your family anymore. It's mine."

The words struck Daniel like a punch to the chest. The weight of them—the reality of what Kara was about to do—hit him all at once. He wasn't just fighting for his own survival. He wasn't just rejecting the legacy anymore. He was fighting for the soul of his family, for the future that Emily had fought so hard to build. And now, standing there in front of Kara, it felt like it was all slipping away.

He turned to her, the frustration and heartbreak in his eyes. "I'll never let you take this. You can't control it. You can't control me."

Kara laughed softly, a dark, hollow sound that sent a chill through the room. "You've already lost, Daniel. We all have. The legacy controls you. It always has."

And with that, the truth finally shattered him—Daniel wasn't fighting for freedom anymore. He wasn't even fighting for the truth. He was fighting for a way to undo the broken pieces of his heart, the pieces that had shattered in front of him. Because what he feared the most, what truly crippled him, was the realization that Emily might never look at him the same way again.

A broken heart, he realized, was a far more terrifying thing than any power the Laurent family could ever wield. And it was the one thing he could never escape.

The silence stretched out, painful and raw, as Daniel turned away from Emily, knowing in his heart that whatever came next, whatever they would face together or apart, nothing would ever be the same again.

The betrayal had been confirmed, but it was the broken heart—the heart of a man who had lost everything he held dear—that would haunt him the most.

Forty-Eight

The Confrontation

※

The safe house felt like a pressure cooker, every inch of it vibrating with an electric charge. The artifact in Kara's hand still pulsed with an eerie glow, and the room, once filled with the promise of secrecy and sanctuary, now seemed to crackle with a malevolent force. Daniel's chest was tight, the weight of everything pressing down on him, suffocating him in a way he had never felt before. The betrayal, the lies, the legacy—it was all too much. But it was the last, unforgivable betrayal that tore at him the most: Emily.

Her face, pale and stricken, her eyes filled with a mixture of confusion and fear, still haunted him. She had trusted him, followed him into this mess, believing they could fight it together. But now, standing in this room, surrounded by the remnants of a life he could never escape, Daniel realized the truth he had been running from all along. He was alone.

Kara's presence loomed over him like a dark cloud, and her every word seemed to chip away at the walls Daniel had built around himself. She stood at the center of the room, the artifact raised high, as though she were preparing for some kind of unholy coronation. Daniel's eyes flickered to Raphael, standing beside Kara, the gun still clenched in his hands. It felt like the walls were closing in on him, the silence stretching between them like a taut rope, ready to snap at any moment.

"What are you waiting for?" Daniel's voice was hoarse, barely a whisper. The room had grown colder, the air thick with tension, and every breath felt like it might be his last. He couldn't breathe, couldn't think. His gaze flickered between Kara and Raphael, his mind reeling with the gravity of the situation. "You've got what you wanted, Kara. You've got the artifact. You've got the power. So, what now?"

Kara's lips curled into a thin, humorless smile. She stepped forward, her eyes narrowing as she took in Daniel's shaking form. "You still don't understand, do you, Daniel?" Her voice was smooth, like venom dripping from every word. "It's never been about the artifact. It's not about the power it holds. It's about what's coming next. You've woken up something ancient, something that's been sleeping for centuries. And now? Now, you're part of it. Whether you like it or not."

Daniel's pulse quickened, his chest tightening as her words

sank in. He hadn't just been fighting for freedom from the Laurent family. He had unwittingly become part of something far older, something far more dangerous than he could have ever imagined. He was tangled in a web of power, manipulation, and ancient forces that stretched beyond his comprehension. There was no escape. There never had been.

"You've always been too proud to see the bigger picture," Kara continued, her eyes gleaming with a dark satisfaction. "The Laurent legacy isn't just about bloodlines. It's about the control of something far more powerful. And you—" She pointed at Daniel, her finger like an accusation, "—you're the key. The moment you rejected the legacy, you sealed your fate."

A cold sweat broke out on Daniel's forehead, his breath coming faster now. He could feel the walls closing in, the air growing thick with the weight of her words. The artifact in her hands wasn't just an object of power. It was a beacon, calling something ancient and terrifying. Something that, once awakened, would change everything. And he? He had been the one to unlock it.

"You're wrong," Daniel managed, his voice hoarse but defiant. "I never wanted any of this. I never asked for any of it."

Kara's gaze softened, but there was no warmth in it. It was the cold, calculating gaze of someone who had already made up their mind. "It doesn't matter what you wanted,

The Confrontation

Daniel. You don't get to choose. You never did. The Laurent bloodline has always had a purpose, and you're a part of that purpose now."

Daniel's chest ached with the weight of her words, but he wasn't about to let her break him. Not now. Not when Emily was watching. Not when everything was on the line.

"You've been playing me from the start," Daniel spat, his anger rising. "You never cared about me. You only cared about your own damn power."

Kara's lips tightened, but her eyes held a flicker of something almost—sorrow? Regret? It was gone so quickly that Daniel couldn't be sure. She had always been a mystery to him, a shadow in the background of the Laurent family's empire. But now, in the light of what had been revealed, Daniel could see her for what she truly was. A puppet master. And he was nothing more than her pawn.

"I did what I had to do," Kara said, her voice cold and resolute. "I didn't have the luxury of playing nice, Daniel. I'm doing what needs to be done."

As her words hung in the air, Daniel felt the ground beneath his feet tremble. It wasn't an earthquake. It wasn't some natural force. It was something else, something far darker, and the moment the tremor hit, Daniel knew that it was only the beginning. The artifact had awakened something, and the clock was ticking down to a final confrontation—one that would either destroy them or bind them to something they couldn't escape.

But it wasn't just Kara or Raphael he had to worry about anymore. It wasn't even the artifact. It was the darkness that had been waiting, hiding in the shadows, that had begun to stir. The ancient force Kara had spoken of—it was real. It was here.

Daniel's thoughts were interrupted by a sudden shift in the room. The temperature dropped sharply, the air growing thick and heavy, like the weight of a thousand years pressing down on them. He could feel it now—something in the air, something ancient and terrifying, as if the walls themselves were alive. It wasn't just the artifact glowing anymore. It was the entire room, pulsing with an energy that threatened to consume everything in its path.

He turned to look at Emily, her face pale, her eyes wide with fear. She hadn't said a word in what felt like hours, but Daniel could feel her fear, her desperation. She was trapped in this just as much as he was, but he couldn't protect her—not when the stakes had risen this high. Not when the darkness that Kara had awakened had begun to bleed into their world.

"Emily," Daniel said, his voice low, filled with the weight of his regret. "Get out. Run. Get as far away from here as you can."

But Emily didn't move. She didn't even flinch. Instead, her eyes met his, filled with something more than fear—

The Confrontation

there was understanding. There was something in her gaze that made Daniel's heart ache. She wasn't going to run. She wasn't going to leave him. She had stayed by his side through everything, and now, when the very world they had known was crumbling around them, she wasn't about to turn her back on him.

"No," Emily whispered, her voice barely audible over the growing hum in the room. "I'm not leaving you. We'll face this together."

The determination in her eyes, the resolve in her voice, made Daniel's chest tighten. She had always been his anchor, his strength when he couldn't find his own. But now, he was afraid. Afraid that everything they had fought for would be shattered, and that there would be no way back.

"Stay close," Daniel said, his voice low, his hands reaching for hers. His heart raced as he realized the truth—whatever happened next, they were in this together. They had always been together.

As he held her hand, the tremors in the room intensified. The artifact was no longer just a light. It was a force, an entity that had been released from its prison, and now, Daniel could feel it—its presence, overwhelming and suffocating. It was coming for them. And it would stop at nothing to claim what was its own.

"Do you feel it?" Emily's voice broke through his thoughts.

Her grip on his hand tightened, her face pale but resolute. "It's like the air is alive. Like the room is—"

"Alive?" Daniel finished for her, his voice strained. "It is. And we're standing at the heart of it."

The shadows in the room seemed to pulse, twisting in unnatural ways. The walls groaned under the pressure, and the air shimmered with an oppressive energy that made Daniel's skin crawl. The moment had arrived. The confrontation they had all been dreading. The culmination of everything they had fought against.

"Enough talk," Kara's voice cut through the tension. "It's time for the final act."

And with that, she raised the artifact high, her eyes locked on Daniel with a look of triumph. But it wasn't her triumph that filled the room—it was the overwhelming force that poured from the artifact, flooding the room with an energy that sent shockwaves through the very air around them.

Daniel closed his eyes for a moment, bracing himself for the chaos that was about to unfold. The clock had ticked down to this moment, and there was no escaping what was to come.

The battle for their survival was beginning.

And nothing would ever be the same again.

Forty-Nine

A Desperate Plea

The room had descended into chaos. The very air seemed charged with an energy that Daniel could feel deep in his bones. It wasn't just the artifact that Kara had raised above her head, glowing with an ominous light, or the weight of her cold gaze as she stood at the center of it all. No, it was something more. Something ancient, something dark. Daniel's breath came in short, desperate bursts, his eyes darting around the room, trying to make sense of what was happening. But nothing made sense anymore.

Emily's hand gripped his tightly, her knuckles white against his skin, her eyes wide with fear and uncertainty. He could feel her tremble, the force of the unknown crashing down on her, as it was crashing down on him. She had always been his anchor, the one person who kept him grounded in the midst of all the turmoil. But now, in this moment, she felt as lost as he did.

They were trapped in a storm they couldn't escape. The walls seemed to close in on them, the shadows in the room growing thicker, like a living presence. The once-familiar safehouse now felt alien, as though it had become a prison, and the world outside—whatever was left of it—had been swallowed by the growing storm inside.

Kara's laughter echoed through the room, cold and triumphant. "You really thought you could stop this, didn't you?" she taunted, her voice sharp with cruel amusement. "You thought you could break free of the Laurent family's grasp. But this… this was never something you could escape."

Her words cut through Daniel like a blade. The weight of them pressed down on him, drowning him in a sea of regret. He had thought that by rejecting the Laurent legacy, by running from the family's power, he could free himself from the chains that had bound him since birth. But it wasn't that simple. It had never been that simple.

He turned his gaze to Emily, searching her eyes for any hint of reassurance, but there was nothing but fear and helplessness there. The power Kara had unleashed, the ancient force that had been dormant for centuries, was pulling them all in. The clock was ticking. And the final act was about to unfold.

A Desperate Plea

"I'm sorry," Daniel whispered, his voice breaking under the weight of his own guilt. "I never wanted this for you. For us."

Emily squeezed his hand, her expression torn between anguish and determination. "We can't give up now. We've come too far to back down."

Her words were a lifeline in the storm. Daniel wanted to believe her, wanted to believe that they could fight their way out of this, but the reality was setting in. Kara had awakened something they couldn't fight with strength alone. This wasn't a battle of wills. It was a battle of forces beyond their comprehension, forces that had been waiting for centuries to be unleashed.

Kara's eyes never left them as she stepped closer, the artifact still raised high. The glow from it intensified, casting strange shadows across her face, turning her into a specter of something far more terrifying. She seemed to grow taller in the glow of the artifact, her presence swelling as though it was feeding on the energy she had awakened.

"You're just like the rest of them," Kara said, her voice low and venomous. "So eager to pretend you can outrun the legacy. But in the end, you're nothing more than pawns. Pawns in a game you don't even understand."

Daniel's fists clenched at his sides, the anger rising in him like a fire, but it was a hollow anger, born from helplessness. He wanted to fight, to lash out at her, to make her understand that she couldn't control him, that she couldn't control them. But as he stood there, frozen in the grip of the artifact's power, he knew that nothing he said or did would change the course of what was happening.

"You're wrong," Daniel said, his voice filled with a quiet resolve. "You don't control me. You never will."

Kara's laugh was sharp, cutting through the room like a blade. "Do you still not see it?" she asked, her voice laced with disbelief. "You've already chosen. You've already given in."

"No," Daniel replied firmly, shaking his head. "I chose to reject this. I chose to fight for something else."

Kara's expression darkened, and she lowered the artifact slightly, her fingers still wrapped around it, but her gaze now fixed intently on Daniel. "You think rejecting your birthright makes you strong? You think running from the family's legacy makes you different? You're wrong. You're just like your father. Just like the rest of them."

The mention of his father made something shift in Daniel's chest. He had spent years running from the legacy his father had left behind, but now, facing Kara, he realized that he wasn't just fighting for freedom. He was fighting to reclaim the part of himself that had been swallowed by the Laurent family's grip. And in that moment, Daniel knew what he had to do. He had to stop Kara. He had to stop the artifact's influence before it consumed them all.

A Desperate Plea

"I'm not like them," Daniel said, stepping forward, his voice growing stronger. "I won't be."

Kara's eyes narrowed, a flicker of surprise crossing her face, but it was gone in an instant. She raised the artifact higher again, the glow intensifying. "Then prove it."

The room seemed to tremble, the power in the air growing heavier, thicker. Daniel felt it pressing on his chest, suffocating him. He could see the shadows growing darker around them, their forms stretching toward the light as though they were alive. The very air seemed to hum with energy, and he knew that the final confrontation was at hand.

Emily's hand tightened around his, her grip almost painful now, but it was a reminder that they were still in this together. He couldn't give up. He couldn't let Kara have control over them. He had to act. But what could he do? How could he fight something so much older, so much more powerful than anything he had ever faced?

"Please," Daniel whispered, his voice barely audible. "You don't have to do this. You don't have to destroy everything."

Kara's gaze softened for a moment, but it was only fleeting. A flash of something in her eyes that he couldn't quite place. But it was gone as quickly as it had come, replaced by the coldness that had driven her to this moment. "It's too late for that, Daniel," she said, her voice flat. "It's too late for all of us."

Daniel's heart ached at her words. There was no reasoning with her. There was no turning back. She had made her choice. And now, it was time to make his.

His eyes flicked to the artifact again, the power that radiated from it still pulling at him, trying to bind him to it. The same pull that had claimed his father, that had claimed his entire family. But he wouldn't let it claim him. He couldn't.

"I won't let you control me," Daniel said, his voice steady now, filled with resolve. He wasn't running anymore. He wasn't going to let Kara win. Not like this.

But as he stepped forward, the air around him seemed to thicken, as though the very fabric of the room were alive, pushing against him. It was the artifact—its power was growing, spreading, trying to overwhelm him. He could feel the energy tugging at him, pulling him in, threatening to rip him apart.

And then, just as he thought he might give in to the force of it, a voice pierced the air—a voice that made his blood run cold.

"Stop."

The word was simple, but the weight of it stopped Daniel in his tracks. He turned toward the doorway, his eyes wide with shock as he saw a figure standing there—tall, cloaked in shadows, but unmistakable.

A Desperate Plea

It was his father.

The man Daniel had thought was long gone, buried in the past. The man who had betrayed him, who had been part of the very legacy he had tried to escape. Yet here he was, standing in the doorway, his eyes locked onto Daniel's, his face expressionless.

"Father," Daniel whispered, disbelief flooding his voice. "You... you're alive?"

His father nodded slowly, his face unreadable. "I've been watching," he said, his voice low and heavy with something Daniel couldn't quite place. "And I've been waiting for this moment."

The room seemed to hold its breath as Daniel's father stepped forward, his gaze flickering toward Kara. There was a moment of tension, an unspoken understanding between them.

"You can't stop this," Kara said, her voice filled with cold certainty. "You don't understand. The power is here. It's time to claim it."

But his father's eyes never wavered. "You're wrong," he said softly, but with a conviction that made Daniel's heart race. "This isn't the power you think it is. This isn't the legacy you want to claim. It's time to end this."

Daniel's breath caught in his throat. This was it. The final confrontation. But whose side was his father really on? Would he betray him again? Or had something changed? Was there still hope?

"Please," Daniel whispered, his voice trembling. "Don't let her win. Don't let this family win."

His father's eyes softened, just for a moment. Then, with one final movement, he reached out, grabbing the artifact from Kara's hands and ripping it away from her.

The energy in the room seemed to shudder, the walls vibrating with a deep, resonant hum. And in that instant, Daniel realized: this wasn't just about the artifact. This wasn't just about power or legacy.

It was about breaking the cycle. And maybe, just maybe, this was the moment when everything changed.

The light from the artifact began to fade, but the tension in the room remained. And in the midst of it all, Daniel found the one thing he hadn't expected: hope.

The clock was ticking. And the fight for the future had only just begun.

Fifty

The Final Showdown

The room was suffocating, the air thick with tension, as the heavy silence settled in after the artifact had been ripped from Kara's grasp. Daniel's chest tightened, his breath shallow, as the reality of what had just happened began to settle in. His father—his estranged, distant, and once-betrayed father—had just intervened. He had taken the artifact from Kara, and with that, the balance of power had shifted. But what did this mean? Was this a moment of salvation, or had they just stepped deeper into the web of deception?

Kara stood frozen, her eyes wide with a mixture of fury and disbelief, her hand still outstretched toward the place where the artifact had once been. Her lips parted as if she were about to speak, but no words came. The world around them seemed to hold its breath, waiting for the inevitable explosion of conflict that was bound to follow.

Daniel's father, once a towering figure in the Laurent family, was now just a man—his face creased with age, his expression hardened by years of betrayal and guilt. But there was something else in his eyes. Something that felt like a long-awaited revelation. The weight of his presence seemed to loom over them all. He stood there, unmoving, the artifact now clenched in his hands, the power it held humming softly, almost as if it were alive.

For a long moment, the room seemed to stretch out, as if time had slowed, and all that mattered was the artifact—the force that had once bound them all together, and the one thing that now stood between them and freedom.

"You—" Kara finally broke the silence, her voice low and venomous. "You dare to take it from me?" Her eyes darted from Daniel's father to him, and then back to the artifact, now held securely in his hands. The madness in her voice was unmistakable. "You don't understand! This power is what's going to save us! This is what has been promised to us, to the family!"

Daniel's heart raced as he stepped forward, standing beside his father, the weight of the moment pressing down on him. His mind was a storm of conflicting thoughts—relief, confusion, fear. He wanted to believe that his father had finally chosen a different path, but deep down, a nagging fear lingered. What if his father was only playing a new game? What if Kara's words were true, and the power that they had all sought was inevitable?

"Do you really believe that?" Daniel's voice was steady, though his heart pounded in his chest. He glanced at his father, trying to read the expression on his face. "Do you think this power is the answer? The same power that's torn our lives apart?"

His father's gaze didn't waver, though the faintest flicker of something—guilt? Regret?—passed across his face. "This isn't about power, Daniel. It never was," he said, his voice low but filled with a weight that seemed to resonate through the room. "This is about breaking a cycle that has lasted far too long. The Laurent legacy isn't what you think it is. It's not about wealth or control. It's about something darker— something that has been controlling us all for generations."

Kara let out a harsh laugh, shaking her head in disbelief. "You're a fool," she spat. "You think you can stop it? You think you can just—" She stopped herself, taking a step back as if trying to steady herself. The air between them had grown thick, and the intensity in her eyes had shifted from defiance to something darker. "You can't stop it, Daniel. You can't stop me."

Her words were like a slap to the face. They were the same words she had said before, when she had first entered the room, when she had made her intentions clear. But now, there was a sense of desperation in her voice, a crack in the armor of the confident, powerful woman who had orchestrated this entire plan. The artifact in Daniel's father's hands wasn't just a tool—it was a key, a piece of a much larger puzzle. And now, for the first time, it seemed that Kara was beginning to understand that she had no control over it.

"The artifact doesn't belong to you, Kara," Daniel's father said softly, his voice filled with finality. "It never did."

Daniel's heart twisted as he heard his father's words. He had spent years running from the family's legacy, from the pain and betrayal it had caused, but now, standing here with the artifact in his father's hands, he realized that there was still so much he didn't understand. His father's words were heavy with meaning. The artifact—this power—wasn't just about the Laurent family's history. It was about something far greater. Something that neither Kara nor anyone else could control.

Kara's eyes narrowed, and her lips curled into a dangerous smile. "You're weak," she hissed, her voice dripping with contempt. "You always have been. You're afraid of the power because you know it will consume you. You know that you'll be nothing without it."

Daniel could feel the anger rising within him, bubbling to the surface. He had spent so long fighting against the Laurent legacy, fighting against the idea that power and control defined who he was, but in this moment, in this room, he realized that it was more than just that. It was about survival. It was about understanding who he was meant to be in this broken family.

The Final Showdown

"I'm not afraid of it," Daniel said through gritted teeth, his voice unwavering. "But I will stop you."

The energy in the room seemed to shift again, and Daniel could feel it. The very air seemed to grow heavier, thick with the weight of the decisions being made in that moment. This wasn't just a battle for power. It was a battle for their very survival.

Kara's lips tightened, and she took a step forward. "You think you can stop me?" she taunted. "I'm already in control. You can't fight what's been set in motion. Not now."

Her voice was a cold wind against Daniel's resolve, but his father's hand on his shoulder steadied him. The power in the room was rising, but this time, Daniel could feel something else—something more potent than fear. It was clarity. He had been running for so long, afraid of the legacy that had defined his family, afraid of the darkness that had been passed down through the generations. But now, standing in this room, with Emily at his side, and his father finally taking control of the artifact, Daniel realized something else.

He wasn't running anymore.

"You may have awakened the power, Kara," Daniel said, his voice low and steady, "but it doesn't belong to you. You've never understood it. And neither did I. But I do now."

Kara's eyes flashed with anger. "You're too late."

Her voice rang out in the room, but before she could move, a powerful surge of energy erupted from the artifact in Daniel's father's hands. The room seemed to quake as the power exploded outward, rippling through the walls, shaking everything in its path. The very ground beneath their feet felt like it was about to give way.

Daniel's heart raced as he stepped forward, the weight of the moment sinking in. The energy was overwhelming, pulling at him, as if the artifact were alive, and it wanted him—wanted all of them—to be a part of it. But it wasn't just about power anymore. It wasn't just about who controlled it. It was about how they chose to fight it.

The light from the artifact flickered, its pulse growing stronger as Daniel's father spoke one final word.

"Enough."

The command was simple, but the energy it carried was like nothing Daniel had ever felt before. It wasn't just his father's will—it was something more. Something ancient and deep, buried within the family's legacy, but now being wielded for the first time by someone who understood it.

The energy from the artifact began to dissipate, the walls trembling as if the very foundation of the safehouse were being torn apart. Kara's eyes widened, her mouth opening as though to speak, but no words came.

And then, as quickly as it had started, the power receded,

The Final Showdown

leaving the room still and silent. The artifact in Daniel's father's hand had dimmed, its once-brilliant glow fading to nothing.

Kara stood frozen in disbelief, her eyes wide, her lips parted, as if the very world had shifted beneath her feet. "This isn't possible..." she murmured, her voice trembling.

Daniel's father stepped forward, the weight of the moment settling in as he looked at Kara with an expression of finality. "It's over," he said simply.

For a long moment, the room was still. The air was heavy with the aftermath of the final showdown, the battle for control over the Laurent family's power now seemingly settled. Daniel's chest rose and fell with each shallow breath, his heart still racing from the intensity of it all.

And in that moment, with the darkness slowly receding, and the light of the artifact now gone, Daniel realized the truth: they had won. But the cost of it all—of everything they had fought for, of everything they had lost—was still settling in.

Kara was defeated, but the battle was far from over. And as Daniel turned to Emily, their hands still clasped tightly together, he knew that their future was still uncertain. But they had survived. And that was enough—for now.

Fifty-One

A Sacrifice Made

The dust in the safehouse hung thick in the air, a sharp contrast to the fragile stillness that had descended after the storm. Daniel stood at the center of the room, his chest still rising and falling with the remnants of adrenaline coursing through his veins. His gaze lingered on the spot where Kara had stood moments ago. She was gone now—vanished into the shadows as swiftly as she had come, defeated by the power of the artifact that had once been her prize. But despite the victory, despite the artifact's dimmed glow, Daniel couldn't shake the feeling that something was missing. That something—someone—was lost.

His father stood in the far corner of the room, his back to them, eyes fixed on the now-quiet artifact in his hands. The artifact that had once seemed like a curse, a dark, looming force, was now nothing more than a dull piece of forgotten history, its power muted. His father's posture, though still regal in its own way, felt heavier, as if the weight of what he had done was pressing down on him.

"Is it really over?" Emily's voice broke through the silence, soft yet firm, carrying the weight of her own uncertainty. She had been quiet for too long, standing just a few feet away from Daniel, watching him, watching his father. Her hand was still clasped tightly in his, her fingers trembling slightly, but her resolve was evident. They had won the battle, but at what cost? What now? The very questions that had been tormenting Daniel's mind since the moment his father had taken control of the artifact hung in the air between them, unresolved and aching.

Daniel turned to her, the weight of her gaze heavy on him. Her face was pale, still streaked with the remnants of the fear that had gripped her when the artifact had erupted in a blinding surge of energy. The fight had been long, and it had taken everything from them. But in her eyes now, despite the exhaustion, there was something else. A quiet defiance, a strength that had always been there, but had only come to the forefront in these darkest moments.

"I don't know," Daniel admitted, his voice thick with uncertainty. His grip on her hand tightened, a silent plea for reassurance, for something that could anchor him in this overwhelming storm. "I don't know if it's really over. Kara is gone, but…" He trailed off, his thoughts scattered. Kara had come so close, so close to having the artifact, to having the power. And yet, she had failed. But had she really failed, or had something even more dangerous been awakened in the process?

The room seemed to hold its breath as Daniel's gaze turned back to his father. The older man was still staring at the artifact, his hands clenched tightly around it as if it were both a source of power and a heavy burden. The artifact no longer glowed, but its presence still hung in the room like a lingering ghost, a reminder of everything that had come before.

His father spoke after a long pause, his voice low and distant. "It's not over yet." His eyes flickered toward Daniel, then back to the artifact, the weight of his words sinking deep into Daniel's chest. "We've only stopped one piece of a much larger plan."

Daniel's heart skipped a beat. "What do you mean? The artifact is useless now. Kara's gone. We've won."

His father turned toward him, his face impassive, unreadable. But there was something there—something hidden beneath the surface. The lines around his eyes were etched deep, the weight of his years and his choices pressing down on him in ways that Daniel could only begin to understand.

"You haven't won," his father said, his voice hardening. "We've only won this battle. The real war is far from over."

The words hit Daniel like a blow, and he felt his knees

weaken slightly. This was supposed to be the end. This was supposed to be their victory. But his father's words shattered that illusion, and the cold reality of what they were facing hit him all at once. The Laurent family had been a part of something far greater, far darker, than Daniel had ever imagined. They weren't just fighting for control of an artifact—they were fighting for the survival of a dynasty that had been built on power, corruption, and betrayal. And as much as Daniel had hoped that they had put an end to it all, his father's words confirmed his worst fear: there was no escaping it.

"Then what do we do?" Daniel asked, his voice barely a whisper. "What now?"

His father's eyes softened, but only for a moment. "We prepare," he said, his voice steady, but the burden in it was unmistakable. "There's more at play here than you realize. We've only scratched the surface."

Daniel's stomach churned as he absorbed his father's words. The implications of them were chilling, and he could feel the weight of them settling into his bones. What more was there? What else could there possibly be?

Before Daniel could ask another question, Emily spoke, her voice cutting through the tension. "What does that mean? What's coming? What are we facing?"

His father's gaze flickered to her, and for a moment, Daniel saw something in his eyes—something like regret. But it was gone too quickly for him to decipher. Instead, his father's face hardened once again, the mask of control slipping back into place.

"More than you know," he said quietly. "I've kept it hidden, kept you hidden from it. But it's coming. The forces that want control over this power—they're far from finished. And there are those who will stop at nothing to see it reignite. What I've done, what I've just begun, it won't be enough to stop them. We need to make sure it doesn't fall back into the wrong hands."

A heavy silence followed, the enormity of his words sinking in. Daniel's mind raced, trying to process everything his father had said. There was no easy path forward. No simple solution. They were caught in the middle of something far greater, something they couldn't control. And yet, as much as he wanted to escape it, he knew that he couldn't.

But then, it was Emily's words that shattered the quiet, her voice trembling but resolute.

"Then I'll help. We'll do this together," she said firmly, turning to Daniel. "We've already fought through so much. We're not stopping now."

Daniel turned to her, his heart aching with a mixture of admiration and fear. He wanted to believe her. Wanted to believe that they could face whatever was coming next together. But as much as he tried to reassure himself, the weight of everything that had happened—the betrayals, the manipulation, the lies—hung heavily between them. And with his father's admission, Daniel knew that the storm wasn't over. It had only just begun.

He opened his mouth to respond, but the words caught in his throat. Instead, he nodded slowly, knowing that she was right. They couldn't stop now. Not when everything they had worked for, everything they had fought for, was on the line.

Daniel's father turned away, taking a step back, the artifact still in his hands, its presence somehow both comforting and terrifying. "There's one more thing you need to understand," he said, his voice steady but filled with something darker. "The artifact—it wasn't just a tool of power. It was a seal. A seal that kept something locked away. And now, with it in our hands, we've unleashed more than we can control."

Daniel's chest tightened, his mind spinning as he processed the words. The artifact wasn't just a key to power—it was something else entirely. A barrier, perhaps. A barrier that had kept something imprisoned. Something even darker than the forces they had already seen.

"What are you saying?" Daniel asked, his voice barely audible.

His father paused, his face hardening once again. "We've opened a door that can't be closed. And now, we'll have to make the ultimate sacrifice to stop it from consuming everything."

Daniel's stomach dropped. The fear that had been gnawing at him suddenly crystallized into something sharper, more urgent. He had always known that the Laurent family's legacy was dangerous, but he had never imagined that it would lead to something like this. They were on the verge of something catastrophic, something that had been waiting for centuries to be unleashed.

And in that moment, Daniel knew the truth: there was no way out. No way to escape the darkness that had followed him his entire life. The only thing left was to fight, to make the sacrifice that would ensure their survival. And yet, as he looked at his father, at Emily, he understood that the true cost of this battle wouldn't just be their lives. It would be everything they had believed in.

"There's no choice," Daniel's father said, his voice filled with a quiet sadness. "The only way to stop this is to destroy it. To end the legacy once and for all."

The weight of his words sank into Daniel's chest like a stone. Destroy the legacy. End it. The thought was both a relief and a burden, but the path to doing so was one fraught with sacrifice. And he knew, with a certainty that chilled him to the core, that they would all have to pay the price.

"Then we'll do it," Daniel said, his voice steady. "Together."

But even as the words left his mouth, he felt the heavy

weight of the sacrifice they were about to make. It was no longer about the artifact. It was about everything they had lost, everything they would have to give up to make sure that the power didn't consume them all.

The storm had only just begun.

Fifty-Two

The Explosion

The safehouse was quieter than it had ever been before. The air had gone cold, heavy with the weight of the past hours, but Daniel couldn't shake the feeling that something was building in the silence. It wasn't just the artifact, now resting in his father's hands like some cursed relic. It wasn't just Kara's disappearance or the terror that had followed them for so long. No, it was something else—something more immediate, more dangerous.

Daniel could feel it in his bones, that deep, unshakable sense of impending doom, like a storm cloud gathering overhead, ready to strike at any moment. His father had said it was time to make the ultimate sacrifice, to end the Laurent legacy once and for all. The words still echoed in his mind, haunting him, even though they were said with an eerie

The Explosion

calm. He had known, deep down, that the price of stopping the power Kara had unleashed would come at a cost. But how high a price? How far would they have to go to destroy everything the Laurent family had built?

Emily stood at his side, her expression etched with the same uncertainty that gripped him. Her hand was still in his, her fingers trembling slightly, but her resolve was clear. They had come so far. They had survived the betrayals, the manipulation, and the terror. But now, in this quiet, foreboding space, with everything hanging in the balance, Daniel knew that they were on the verge of something far more catastrophic.

His father, standing across the room with the artifact still in his hands, looked as if the weight of the world was pressing down on him. His shoulders were tense, his posture rigid, and yet, there was something else in his eyes—something that Daniel couldn't quite place. Regret? Fear? Or perhaps it was the final acceptance of what had to be done.

"I never thought it would come to this," his father's voice broke the silence, sounding strained and distant. "But we've reached the point of no return."

Daniel swallowed hard, his mind racing. What had been set in motion couldn't be undone. They had opened the door, and now, there was no way to close it without facing the consequences. The family's dark legacy had always been a part of him, but now, it was more than that. It was a part of everything around him. The choices they made now would ripple through time, through their lives, through the world they thought they knew.

"It's not too late," Daniel said quietly, his voice filled with the weight of his own uncertainty. "We can find another way."

His father shook his head slowly, his face hardening, the lines etched deeply into his features. "There is no other way. The legacy has to be destroyed. The power we've awakened is too great to control. If we don't act now, it will consume us all."

Emily took a step closer to Daniel, her presence a comfort amidst the growing storm. "But what does that mean?" she asked, her voice barely above a whisper. "What will we have to do to end this?"

His father's gaze shifted from Emily to the artifact in his hands, and for a moment, Daniel thought he saw something flicker in his eyes—a glimmer of something like regret, but it was gone too quickly to be sure.

"It means we have to destroy it," his father replied, his voice unwavering. "The artifact is the key to everything—the power, the control, the curse. We've already seen what it can do. We can't let it fall into the wrong hands again."

Daniel's chest tightened, and his throat went dry. Destroy the artifact? Was that even possible? After everything they had fought for, was there really no other way to stop the legacy from consuming them all? The question echoed in his mind, but he already knew the answer. The artifact wasn't just a thing—it was a living entity, a force that had been bound for centuries, and now that it was unleashed, there was no going back.

"I don't want to do this," Daniel said softly, his voice thick with emotion. "But if it's the only way…"

His father's eyes softened, the weight of his gaze piercing through him. "We all have to make sacrifices, Daniel. You should know that by now. The only way to end this is to destroy the artifact, and everything it stands for."

The quiet hum of the artifact in his father's hands seemed to grow louder, as if it were alive, responding to the tension in the room. The power it radiated was undeniable, and Daniel could feel it, as if the very air around them was charged with an electric current. The room, once their refuge, now felt like a cage—a trap from which there was no escape.

"We can't just destroy it," Emily said suddenly, her voice rising with a mix of fear and determination. "There has to be another way. There has to be."

Daniel turned to her, his heart aching as he saw the fear in her eyes. She had always been his strength, his anchor, and now, in this moment, when the world felt like it was unraveling, she was still holding on to hope. But Daniel knew, deep down, that there was no escaping this. The world they had once known was gone. The choices they made now would shape everything to come.

"Emily…" Daniel began, his voice soft but filled with the weight of everything that had led them to this moment. "The only way to end this is to destroy it."

She shook her head, her hands clenched tightly in fists. "I won't let you do it. I won't let you destroy everything we've fought for."

Her words cut through Daniel like a knife, the raw emotion behind them pulling at him, twisting his heart. He wanted to believe that there was another way. He wanted to believe that they could walk away from this, free of the weight of the Laurent family's power. But the truth was too clear. They had opened the door, and now they had to face the consequences.

"It's the only way," Daniel said, his voice barely above a whisper. "If we don't destroy it, everything we've fought for will be lost. Everything."

Emily's eyes met his, her expression a mixture of pain and determination. "And what about you? What will you lose in the process? Will you sacrifice everything? Your life? Your soul?"

Daniel felt his heart skip a beat. He hadn't thought about it like that, hadn't allowed himself to consider the full weight of the cost. But Emily was right. The sacrifice wasn't just physical. It was everything—the very essence of who he was,

The Explosion

who they were. The Laurent legacy had already consumed so much of him, so much of them. Could he really destroy it? Could he destroy the one thing that had defined his family for centuries?

"I..." Daniel began, his voice faltering. "I don't know. I don't know if I can."

There was a long, pregnant pause, the silence hanging between them like a thick fog. The weight of their decision loomed over them, suffocating in its finality. Daniel felt the pressure of his father's gaze, the expectations that had been placed on him, the responsibility to end the legacy once and for all.

And then, without warning, the ground beneath them shook.

A low rumble vibrated through the room, sending a shudder through the floorboards. The walls seemed to tremble, and for a moment, it felt as though the very foundations of the safehouse were cracking under the weight of the explosion that was about to come.

"Get down!" Daniel shouted, instinctively pushing Emily to the floor, his body covering hers as debris rained down from above.

The force of the explosion rocked the room, sending everything spinning into chaos. The walls cracked and splintered, and the lights flickered as the power surged. Daniel's heart pounded in his chest as he heard the deafening roar of the explosion, the sound of the world crumbling around them. The room seemed to tilt as the blast sent shockwaves through the air, and in the chaos, Daniel couldn't tell where the blast had come from or how close it was. But one thing was clear: they were under attack.

"What the hell is happening?" Emily gasped, her voice muffled as she clung to him, her eyes wide with fear.

The floor beneath them buckled, sending them tumbling to the side as the walls around them buckled under the pressure. Daniel's body slammed into the ground, his head spinning as the room around him disintegrated. Dust and debris filled the air, choking him as he tried to push himself up. His limbs felt heavy, his vision blurry, but his heart still pounded as he looked around, trying to make sense of the destruction.

"Dad!" Daniel shouted, his voice hoarse, panic rising in his chest. "Dad, where are you?"

He struggled to his feet, ignoring the ringing in his ears as he searched the wreckage. The safehouse was crumbling, the structure buckling under the pressure of the blast, and everything felt like it was about to collapse. His eyes scanned the debris, but there was no sign of his father.

And then, through the smoke and dust, he saw him.

His father was on the other side of the room, lying motion-

The Explosion

less among the rubble, the artifact still in his hand, but there was something wrong. His father's face was pale, his body unnaturally still. Daniel's heart stopped as he ran to him, his legs unsteady beneath him. He reached his father's side, falling to his knees, and for a moment, the world seemed to slow.

"Dad?" Daniel whispered, his voice barely audible, the words filled with a deep, aching sorrow. "No. No, please. Not now."

His father's eyes fluttered open, just enough for Daniel to see the faintest glimmer of recognition before they closed again.

"It's... too late..." His father's voice was a rasp, weak but filled with a sense of finality. "It... it had to be done..."

Daniel felt his chest tighten, his throat constricting with emotion. "What are you saying?" he choked, tears threatening to spill as he reached out, trying to keep his father awake, trying to keep him from slipping away.

"It's the only way..." his father murmured, his voice trailing off as his hand gripped the artifact tightly, as if he were passing it on, passing the burden to Daniel.

And then, his hand went limp.

Daniel's breath hitched in his throat, his heart shattering as he realized what had just happened. His father had made the ultimate sacrifice. The one thing that would destroy the Laurent legacy for good—at the cost of his own life.

The explosion had been his father's final act.

And now, with the weight of that sacrifice, Daniel was left to carry on the fight, to finish what had been started. But in that moment, as the dust settled and the echoes of the explosion faded, Daniel knew that the true cost of their survival was only just beginning.

The battle for the future was far from over.

Fifty-Three

The Ultimate Betrayal

The room was in ruins. The walls were scarred, cracked from the explosion that had rocked the safehouse only moments ago. The air was thick with dust and the remnants of destruction. The once quiet and controlled space was now a chaotic battleground—shattered glass, broken furniture, and twisted metal were strewn across the floor. Daniel's breath came in sharp, shallow bursts as he knelt beside his father, his hands trembling as he tried to steady his father's lifeless body.

His mind spun, torn between grief, shock, and the overwhelming need to understand what had just happened. The artifact was still in his father's hand, its glow dimming with each passing second, as if it had drained the last of the life force from the man who had held it.

"No... no, please..." Daniel whispered, his voice cracking. His hands gripped his father's arm tighter, as though he could somehow will him to wake up, to move. "Dad, stay with me. Please. Not like this..."

But there was no response. His father's face was pale, his eyes closed, the finality of his sacrifice settling in like a suffocating weight. The safehouse, once a place of refuge, now felt like a tomb. His father had given everything, even his own life, to ensure that the Laurent legacy—the power they had all fought so desperately to end—would be destroyed.

Daniel's heart hammered in his chest as the magnitude of the sacrifice settled over him. The blast—the explosion—it had been his father's doing. He had detonated the safehouse to ensure the artifact's power wouldn't fall into the wrong hands. But now, as Daniel knelt beside him, the weight of his loss seemed unbearable. His father's final act had saved them, but at what cost?

Suddenly, a sound broke through the suffocating silence. A footstep. Then another. The sound of boots crunching on the rubble, heavy and deliberate. Daniel's head snapped up, his pulse spiking as he glanced toward the doorway. The figure that appeared through the smoke and dust was a silhouette, tall and imposing, a shadow among the destruction.

Daniel's heart stopped in his chest when he saw the person's face. It was someone he had never expected to see again—

The Ultimate Betrayal

someone he had thought was lost to the chaos forever.

Kara.

She stood in the doorway, her eyes gleaming with an eerie sense of satisfaction, her lips curled into a tight, knowing smile. She had survived. She had made it through the blast. But it wasn't her survival that caused the cold rush of dread to wash over Daniel. It was the way she stood there, untouched by the devastation, as if she had planned for this very moment.

Daniel's mind raced. She had been gone. She had disappeared after the last confrontation, vanishing into the shadows. But now, she was here, standing in the ruins of the safehouse, as though she had orchestrated everything. The explosion. The chaos. The death.

Kara's eyes scanned the room with cold, calculating precision, her gaze flickering briefly over Daniel's father's body before settling on Daniel. Her smile widened, but there was no warmth in it—only triumph.

"Quite the spectacle, wasn't it?" Kara said, her voice a smooth, venomous purr. "I must admit, I never thought it would come to this. But then again, I've always known the Laurent legacy would be a bit… explosive."

Daniel's pulse quickened, his fists clenching at his sides. The anger that had been smoldering within him since his father's death now erupted into a fierce blaze. "What the hell are you doing here, Kara?" he spat, his voice laced with venom. "You should have died with the rest of them. After everything—after all the chaos you've caused, you're still here?"

Kara's smile didn't waver. She took a step closer, the click of her heels on the broken floorboards echoing in the silence. "You've always been so quick to judge, Daniel. So quick to point fingers." She paused, letting the words sink in before continuing, her voice dripping with sarcasm. "But you're not wrong. I should've been dead. But I'm not, am I?"

Daniel took a step forward, his anger rising, his grief still raw. "You killed my father!" he shouted, the words burning like acid in his mouth. "You were behind all of this. You manipulated me, made me think I could escape, made me think there was a way out."

Kara's eyes glinted with a dangerous light as she tilted her head, considering his words. "Killed your father?" she repeated, her voice mocking. "That's one way to put it. But I prefer to think of it as… liberation."

She stepped closer, her heels clicking against the floor, the sound growing louder as she approached him. "The Laurent legacy isn't about what you want, Daniel. It's not about breaking free or pretending to be something you're not. It's about control. Power. Dominance. And your father—he knew that. He understood it better than you ever will."

Daniel's hands trembled with rage. "You don't know

The Ultimate Betrayal

anything about my father!" he shouted, stepping forward, fury rising in his chest. "You used him, just like you used me. You used all of us!"

Kara's smile faltered, just for a moment. Then, she laughed, a sharp, bitter sound that filled the room. "Used?" she repeated, her voice thick with disdain. "No, Daniel. You've always been the one being used. You were never in control. You never understood that the legacy—the power—it was always bigger than you. Bigger than your father. And now, I'll show you what that really means."

Daniel's stomach churned as her words hit him, the truth of them settling over him like a cold shroud. Everything he had fought for, everything he had believed in, had been a lie. His father had been a part of the same manipulation, caught in the same web of power and control that Kara had woven for years.

"But I don't think you fully grasp the situation, do you, Daniel?" Kara's voice dropped to a whisper, each word dripping with malicious intent. "You've been so focused on fighting the legacy, rejecting it. But you're just like the rest of them. You've always been a pawn, playing in my game."

The realization hit him like a punch to the gut, and for a moment, everything around him seemed to blur. "What are you talking about?" he asked, his voice hoarse, barely audible.

Kara's lips curled into a smile, and she took a final step

forward, closing the distance between them. "I never wanted to destroy the Laurent legacy, Daniel. I wanted to take it for myself."

Daniel froze, the blood draining from his face. His body went cold as the weight of her words sunk in. It was as if the ground beneath him had given way. "What?" he gasped, barely able to process what she had just said.

Kara nodded slowly, her smile widening. "Oh, yes. Your father and I… we were never enemies, Daniel. We were partners. We always were. He knew what had to be done. And in the end, he did what he had to do to give me control. You see, I didn't just want to end the legacy. I wanted to inherit it. And now, with the artifact in my hands, I'll do exactly that."

Daniel's heart pounded in his chest, his world spinning. The pain of his father's death, the confusion over everything he had believed about his family, the betrayal—it all came crashing down in that moment. His father hadn't just died to stop Kara. He had died to pass on the legacy. To give her what she wanted all along.

"You…" Daniel's voice faltered. "You're saying this was all part of your plan? From the beginning? My father's death? The artifact?"

Kara's eyes gleamed with an almost predatory delight. "Exactly. Your father was always part of the plan. He knew that to control the legacy, we had to take it back, to destroy the part of it that was fractured. And now, with the power in my hands, I'll reshape it. I'll reshape the Laurent family in my image. The power will be mine to control."

Daniel stumbled backward, his mind reeling. The air around him seemed to tighten, the walls pressing in on him as if they were closing in with the weight of the truth. His father had never really been the man he thought he was. The legacy—the power—had consumed him just as much as it had consumed Kara. And now, it was too late.

"You've been part of it all along," Daniel said, the words coming out in a barely audible whisper. "You... You've manipulated me, used me... killed my father."

Kara's smile was triumphant, but there was no warmth in it. "I didn't kill your father, Daniel. He sacrificed himself. But you've always been a pawn, and you always will be. You just didn't know it until now."

Daniel's heart shattered as the truth crashed over him. His father had known all along. He had known that his own death was part of Kara's plan. The ultimate betrayal—the one thing he had never seen coming.

And now, as Kara stood before him, the power of the Laurent legacy at her fingertips, Daniel realized that he had been caught in her web from the very beginning.

There was no escaping it. There was no way out.

The game was over. And Kara had won.

Fifty-Four

Love Confessed

The air was thick with tension, a heaviness that seemed to settle in the very walls of the ruined safe house. The remnants of the explosion still hung in the air, a constant reminder of the destruction that had already unfolded. Daniel's heart beat loudly in his chest, echoing in his ears as he stood frozen, staring at Kara. Her words, each one cutting deeper than the last, left him breathless, unable to move, unable to comprehend the full scope of what she had just revealed.

The room was a silent battlefield, the artifacts of the Laurent legacy scattered around them like remnants of a forgotten war. The light that had once gleamed from the artifact in Kara's hand now seemed distant, fading slowly into the darkness. Everything they had fought for—his father's sacrifice, the battle against the power that had nearly consumed them all—now seemed meaningless in the face of this ultimate betrayal.

But through the fog of betrayal and grief, one thing remained clear to Daniel: the love that had been burning inside him for so long was still there, flickering like a fragile flame in the storm. And it wasn't just for the legacy. It wasn't just for survival. It was for Emily.

As the dust settled around them, Daniel's gaze flickered to her, the one constant in the chaos. She was standing a few steps behind him, her eyes wide with confusion and pain. But in them, he could see something else. Something that was unmistakably familiar—hope. Even in the midst of everything that had happened, everything they had endured, Emily was the light in the darkness. And despite everything, he couldn't help but believe that she still held onto that same hope.

She was the one who had always been there, through all the battles, all the betrayals, all the lies. The thought of her standing by his side, of sharing whatever remained of the life they had fought so hard to protect, was the only thing keeping him from being swallowed whole by the anger and the despair that threatened to consume him.

His breath hitched as he turned to her, the weight of his heart too much to bear. He could see it in her eyes—her trust in him, her belief in him, even after everything that had happened. She had been the anchor when everything had spun out of control, and now, as the world seemed to crumble around them, it was time to hold on to her more tightly than ever before.

"Emily," Daniel's voice came out softer than he intended, hoarse with the emotion that had been building inside him. "I…"

He couldn't find the right words. The years of silence, the years of unspoken feelings, weighed on him. But now, in this moment—this moment where everything was falling apart—there was no more hiding. No more running. He had to say it, had to let her know before it was too late.

Emily looked at him, her face softening as she took a step closer, her eyes searching his. Her hand reached out to him, her fingers brushing against his, and the warmth of her touch sent a shock through his body. In that instant, everything else faded away. The destruction. The betrayal. Kara's victory. All of it seemed to melt away, leaving only the two of them standing in the wreckage.

"I've never been more afraid in my life," Daniel said, the words coming out more raw and vulnerable than he had intended. "But when I look at you… when I think of everything we've been through… I can't pretend anymore. I can't lie to myself. Not when everything feels so wrong. Not when I know what I feel for you."

Emily's expression softened further, and her hand gently cupped his cheek. Her touch was like a balm to his wounded soul, and he closed his eyes for a moment, trying to hold on to this fleeting moment of peace. But the chaos was still there—still looming over them, waiting to tear everything apart.

"Daniel…" Her voice was low, barely above a whisper. "You don't have to say it. You don't have to—"

But he cut her off, his eyes opening to meet hers, his heart pounding in his chest. "I do," he said firmly, his voice full of conviction. "I've spent so much time running from the truth. From what I feel for you. But I can't run anymore. I can't pretend like it doesn't matter. You matter. More than anything. You've always mattered."

The room seemed to hold its breath, as if even the walls were waiting for Emily's response. Her eyes were glistening, the hint of tears gathering there, but there was no fear in them. Only understanding. And something else—something that made Daniel's chest tighten. It was hope. Hope for something more. Something beyond the destruction and the chaos.

"You have no idea how much I've wanted to hear those words," Emily whispered, a tear slipping down her cheek. "But I thought… I thought it was too late. After everything we've been through. After everything we've lost…"

Daniel stepped closer to her, his hand gently wiping the tear from her cheek. "It's never too late," he said, his voice thick with emotion. "Not for us."

She looked up at him, her eyes full of pain and love, and in that moment, everything shifted. The weight of the world seemed to lift, and all that mattered was this moment—this moment where the truth was finally spoken, where the love they had both been hiding could no longer be denied.

"I love you, Emily," Daniel said, his voice filled with raw honesty, with the kind of certainty he had never felt before. "I always have."

The words hung between them, suspended in the air, and for a moment, neither of them moved. Neither of them spoke. But in that moment of silence, they both knew it was true. It had always been true.

Emily's lips parted, and a soft smile appeared on her face, the first real smile Daniel had seen from her in what felt like forever. It was gentle, full of warmth and tenderness. "I love you too, Daniel," she whispered, her voice trembling with emotion. "I always have."

The weight of their words seemed to settle over them like a blanket, wrapping them in something warm and comforting, even in the midst of the chaos that surrounded them. The world outside might have been crumbling, but for this one moment, in each other's arms, everything felt right. Everything felt like it could still be salvaged.

But as their lips met in a kiss—gentle at first, hesitant as if both of them were afraid of breaking the fragile moment—everything changed again. The room shifted. The silence was shattered by a low rumble, a tremor that seemed to shake the very foundations of the safehouse.

Daniel pulled away from Emily, his heart racing. The destruction was far from over. They could feel it now—an overwhelming sense of impending danger that seemed to rise like a tidal wave, threatening to crash down on them.

"What the hell was that?" Emily gasped, her eyes wide with alarm.

Daniel's gaze snapped toward the door, his body instinctively bracing for whatever was coming next. The rumble had come from deeper within the building, a sound that felt too much like an explosion. He could hear the crackling of something—metal scraping against metal—and the sound of footsteps. But these weren't the soft steps of someone trying to hide. These were purposeful, deliberate. And they were coming closer.

"We're not alone," Daniel muttered, his heart sinking. His hand instinctively reached for Emily's, and she grasped it tightly, her eyes filled with a mix of fear and determination.

And then, as if to confirm their worst fears, the door to the safehouse burst open with a deafening crash. Daniel's heart skipped a beat as the figure stepped into the room, a silhouette framed by the firelight and the smoke swirling in the air.

It was Raphael.

Love Confessed

His clothes were singed, his face bloodied, but his eyes were cold—unforgiving. His gun was gripped tightly in his hand, and there was no doubt in Daniel's mind that this was the man who had been pulling the strings all along. The man who had watched it all unfold, who had orchestrated the betrayal, the chaos.

And now, as he stepped into the room, Daniel could feel it: the final act of the Laurent family's legacy was about to unfold. And they were standing at the center of it.

"Surprised?" Raphael's voice was like ice, his tone mocking as he scanned the room, taking in the wreckage and the destruction. His gaze lingered briefly on Daniel and Emily before focusing on the artifact still in Daniel's father's lifeless hands. "I'd say I'm disappointed, but I didn't expect much else from you."

The world around them seemed to stop, time slowing as Daniel's blood ran cold. The ultimate betrayal was here. And Raphael was going to make sure that it would all come crashing down.

Daniel's heart pounded as the weight of everything settled on him. He had confessed his love to Emily, had let her into the deepest part of himself, but now, in the face of this final confrontation, he wasn't sure if there was any way out. The darkness had followed them this far. But there was one thing Daniel knew now, as the threat loomed before them.

He would fight for her. For the love they had, no matter the cost.

And this time, the fight would be different.

Fifty-Five

The Escape Plan

The room fell into a heavy silence after Raphael's entrance, and the air seemed to thicken with the weight of what had just unfolded. Daniel's pulse pounded in his ears, his body tense and rigid. The presence of Raphael, standing in the doorway with his gun aimed casually at the ground, was like a cold gust of wind sweeping through the room, extinguishing any warmth that had been left after the explosion. The look in Raphael's eyes—cold, calculating—told Daniel everything he needed to know. This was it. This was the moment when everything they had worked for, fought for, and sacrificed for would either come to a painful end or take a new direction.

The wreckage surrounding them was more than just the destruction of the safehouse. It felt like the ruins of their lives, everything they had known and hoped for, crumbling under the weight of betrayal, manipulation, and hidden agendas. Daniel's mind raced, trying to make sense of the situation. There had been so many twists and turns, so many betrayals, but Raphael's presence here, at this exact moment, brought everything into focus.

Raphael didn't seem to care about the devastation around him. He stood in the doorway, unscathed by the explosion, his posture relaxed, but there was an undeniable tension in the way he held himself. He was waiting. Waiting for something—maybe for them to speak, maybe for them to react. But Daniel couldn't give him the satisfaction. He had to keep his cool. He had to think.

Emily's hand was still firmly in his, her grip tight and trembling, but there was a fire in her eyes. She wasn't going to let this go without a fight. They had been through so much together, and Daniel could feel her resolve strengthening, despite the fear and uncertainty that surrounded them. She wasn't backing down. She couldn't. And neither could he.

"Raphael…" Daniel's voice was steady, though his heart was racing. He had to stay in control. He had to find a way out of this. "You've been behind all of this, haven't you? Everything. All the chaos, the manipulation, the deaths…"

Raphael's lips curled into a faint smile, but it wasn't a smile of amusement—it was one of victory. "You still don't understand, do you?" His voice was soft, almost mocking, as if he were explaining a simple truth to a child. "You were always a part of the plan, Daniel. You just didn't know it. I was never your enemy. You were just a pawn in a much bigger game."

Daniel's chest tightened, the words cutting through him like a blade. Everything—the pain, the struggle, the betrayals—had all been part of Raphael's plan. Daniel had been nothing but a puppet, a means to an end. The truth crashed over him, overwhelming and suffocating. His mind screamed in disbelief, but he couldn't afford to let it show. He couldn't afford to fall apart now. Not when everything was at stake.

"I never wanted any of this," Daniel said through clenched teeth, his voice low but firm. "I never wanted to be a part of your game, Raphael. You've destroyed everything. You've destroyed lives, families… and now you're standing here, expecting me to just roll over and accept it?"

Raphael's eyes flickered with something—maybe surprise, maybe irritation—but his smirk didn't falter. "You think I care about your little emotional outbursts, Daniel? You were never in control. None of us were. But now, you're finally seeing the truth. This has always been about power. Power that can't be stopped."

The coldness in Raphael's words sent a chill through Daniel's spine, but there was something else in his voice—something that Daniel couldn't ignore. This wasn't just about power. It wasn't just about controlling the Laurent legacy. No, there was something deeper. Something darker.

And that's when the realization hit him like a bolt of lightning.

"The artifact," Daniel whispered, his voice barely audible. "You're after the artifact. That's what this is all about. It's not just about the family. It's about the power the artifact holds. The power to control everything."

Raphael's eyes gleamed with approval, but there was no satisfaction in it. "Finally, you're starting to get it," he said, his voice dripping with disdain. "The artifact is the key to everything. It's the key to the Laurent legacy. The key to true power. And now that it's in my hands, nothing can stop me."

Daniel's stomach churned, his hands shaking with the fury of what he was hearing. The artifact wasn't just a symbol of the family's history—it was the key to something even more dangerous. And Raphael knew it. He had always known it.

But Daniel couldn't let that be the end. He couldn't let Raphael win. Not now. Not after everything they had been through.

"What now, Raphael?" Daniel said, his voice sharp, cutting through the tension in the room. "What do you want? What's your plan?"

Raphael's eyes narrowed, his posture shifting ever so slightly. "My plan?" he said, the mockery in his voice barely contained. "You really don't get it, do you? This has never been about me. It's always been about the legacy. About what comes next. You think your little fight against me has mattered? It hasn't. You're just a part of a much bigger picture. A picture I've been painting for years."

Daniel's mind raced as he tried to process the full weight of what Raphael was saying. There was a greater game at play—one that had been set in motion long before they had even known it. And now, they were standing at the center of it all, a storm that was about to tear everything apart.

"Everything you've done," Daniel said, his voice rising with frustration, "all the lies, the manipulation, the deaths—what's the point of it? What do you want from me?"

Raphael stepped closer, his gaze never leaving Daniel's. "You're not important, Daniel. Not anymore," he said coldly. "The power is. And when I have it, when I control the legacy, there will be no stopping me. No one will be able to touch me."

Daniel could feel the panic rising in his chest, but he couldn't afford to show it. He had to think—had to find a way out of this. They were running out of time, and with each passing second, the walls were closing in.

"We need to get out of here," Emily whispered, her voice filled with urgency. "There has to be a way."

Daniel turned to her, and the look in her eyes—full of fear, but also determination—was the spark that reignited the fire in him. They couldn't stay here. They couldn't let Raphael win. He couldn't let Emily be dragged into this madness any longer.

But how? How could they escape when it felt like the entire world was closing in on them?

"We need a plan," Daniel said, his voice low, filled with urgency. "There's no way we can just fight our way out of this. We have to get out, and we have to do it now."

Emily nodded quickly, her eyes scanning the room as if looking for some kind of escape. "The windows," she said suddenly. "They're reinforced, but they're not impenetrable. If we can get to the back, there's a chance we can break out."

Daniel's mind raced, the pieces of the puzzle coming together. If they could get out through the back, they could escape the safehouse before Raphael had a chance to stop them. But they couldn't waste time. They had to move now.

"Stay close," Daniel said to Emily, his voice firm but filled with the tension of the moment. "We get to the back, we break out, and we run. No looking back."

Emily gave him a small, determined nod. She was ready. They were both ready.

But just as they began to make a move, Raphael's voice stopped them in their tracks.

"You think you can just walk away?" Raphael sneered, his hand tightening around the gun. "You think you can just run from this?"

Daniel's eyes locked onto Raphael's, his heart hammering in his chest. This was it. They had to act fast. There was no more room for hesitation. They couldn't afford to wait any longer. They had to get to the back, and they had to do it now.

Without warning, Daniel grabbed Emily's hand and pulled her toward the door, his mind racing through the plan. But just as they reached the threshold, a shot rang out, echoing through the room.

The bullet missed them by inches, embedding itself into the doorframe. Daniel's heart stopped in his chest as he felt the rush of adrenaline flood through him.

They were running out of time.

"Move!" Daniel shouted, pulling Emily into the hallway, adrenaline pushing them forward. Every step felt like it could be their last, but there was no turning back now. They were almost there. They had to be.

As they rushed toward the back exit, Daniel's mind raced, the weight of what they had just uncovered weighing heavily on him. He couldn't let Raphael win. He couldn't let everything they had fought for be destroyed.

They were going to escape. They had to.

And this time, Daniel swore, they wouldn't stop until they were free.

Fifty-Six

The Public Revelation

The weight of the past few days hung heavily over Daniel as he navigated the chaotic streets of the city. He had thought he understood the power of the Laurent legacy, the twisted, poisonous roots it had sunk into the hearts of those who had once claimed it as their own. But what he had learned in the ruins of the safehouse—the truth about Raphael, about his father's role in all of it, and the deeper corruption that lay beneath everything he had believed—was something darker, something far more dangerous. And now, with Emily by his side, Daniel felt the full scope of what they were up against.

They had escaped the safehouse after the narrowest of moments, their bodies pressed against the cold walls of the alleyway as they ran. The sound of the shot that had nearly claimed them had been the last thing they heard before they made their escape. They had been fortunate. Just barely. But that didn't mean they were safe. Not by a long shot.

Raphael was still out there. His eyes, cold and calculating, would stop at nothing to ensure that the Laurent legacy lived on—no matter the cost. The artifact, the source of it all, had been his means to control everything, and now it was gone. But Daniel had no illusions. Raphael wouldn't let it go. The power was too great.

The tension in the air felt almost suffocating as Daniel and Emily navigated their way through the city's underground corridors, their footsteps echoing in the emptiness around them. They were running—not just from Raphael, but from a past that would never let them go.

"We need to do this carefully," Daniel said, his voice low and urgent as he checked over his shoulder, scanning the dark alleyways for any sign of pursuit. "We need to expose him. We need to expose everything."

Emily glanced at him, her face set with determination, though her eyes were filled with something else—something darker, a flicker of fear that Daniel couldn't ignore. She had always been the one who kept him grounded, the one who reminded him that there was more to life than the shadows of their past. But this was different. The stakes had changed.

"Are you sure you want to do this?" she asked, her voice

The Public Revelation

quiet, but edged with a seriousness that made Daniel pause. She knew the risk. The truth they were about to reveal would shake everything. It would expose secrets long buried, and the repercussions could be far-reaching. They were stepping into a storm, and once the truth was out, there would be no going back.

"I don't have a choice," Daniel replied. He gripped her hand tighter, the rush of adrenaline still coursing through his veins. "Raphael can't be allowed to manipulate the truth. He can't be allowed to rewrite everything. The Laurent legacy—it's too dangerous. We have to stop him."

Emily didn't argue. She didn't need to. They both knew what was at stake.

Daniel's mind was focused on one thing: the public revelation. The only way to put an end to Raphael's plans, to expose the corruption, was to make sure the world knew the truth. And he had the evidence. He had the recordings, the documents, the proof that Raphael had manipulated not just the Laurent family but countless others for his own gain. It had all been orchestrated for years, hidden behind layers of lies and deceit.

"Once this gets out, there's no turning back," Emily said, her voice steady but filled with apprehension. "What if... what if we can't stop him? What if he has something worse planned?"

Daniel met her gaze, his expression firm. "Then we'll stop

him together."

The weight of their plan pressed down on them both as they hurried through the streets, the city lights flickering faintly in the distance. Their goal was clear: to make the public aware, to expose Raphael for what he truly was—a dangerous manipulator who had used the Laurent family's name for his own gain. They had to make sure the world saw him for what he was before he had a chance to twist everything further in his favor.

And they had to do it quickly.

The underground network they were using to move through the city was a risky path to take, but it was their only option. Raphael had eyes everywhere, and the last thing they needed was to be cornered before they could make their next move. The tension between them was palpable, both of them knowing that every second counted.

As they reached the hidden door leading to a secure location, Daniel's phone buzzed in his pocket, snapping him from his thoughts. He pulled it out quickly, his fingers trembling slightly as he glanced at the message.

It was from an unknown number.

"You're too late."

Daniel's stomach dropped. His pulse quickened, and his mind raced. How could they be too late? What did it mean?

The Public Revelation

Was Raphael already moving ahead with his own plans?

He texted back, trying to keep his tone calm, even though his mind was spinning.

"What do you mean?"

The response was almost immediate.

"You can't stop it now. I've already won. You'll see soon enough."

Daniel felt a chill spread through him. His fingers hovered over the phone for a moment, but there was nothing more to say. Raphael had always been several steps ahead of them, manipulating everything from the shadows, pulling the strings, and now it seemed like they were playing right into his hands. But that didn't mean they were done. It didn't mean they could give up.

Daniel shoved the phone back into his pocket and motioned for Emily to follow him. They couldn't waste any more time.

Inside the secure location, Daniel quickly set up the equipment. The space was small and dimly lit, filled with monitors and old technology. They had to be careful—this was their last chance to get everything out into the world before Raphael could silence them for good.

He began uploading the files, his fingers moving quickly

over the keyboard. The evidence they had gathered wasn't just incriminating; it was damning. Raphael's role in the family's operations, the manipulation of the legacy, the cover-ups—everything was there. And it would be enough to bring him down.

As the files uploaded, Daniel's eyes flicked to Emily, who was standing at the far side of the room, watching him with a mix of concern and trust. He could see it in her eyes: the fear of what was coming, but also the unwavering belief that this was the only way forward.

"It's almost ready," Daniel said, his voice tight as he turned back to the computer. "Once this is live, it'll be out there for everyone to see. Raphael won't have a chance to deny it."

But Emily didn't answer. She was staring at the monitor, her face pale. Daniel turned toward her, his heart sinking when he saw the expression on her face.

"Emily?" he asked, his voice shaking with sudden dread. "What's wrong?"

Her eyes locked onto his, filled with something he hadn't expected to see. Something dark. Something terrifying.

"Look," she said, her voice barely above a whisper. "Look at this."

Daniel's breath caught in his throat as he turned toward the screen. What he saw made his stomach lurch.

The files they had just uploaded, the evidence of Raphael's machinations, had already been intercepted. Someone had deleted the entire folder. Someone had tampered with the system, wiping out everything they had worked for.

"No," Daniel whispered, his heart racing. "No, no, no—this can't be happening."

But it was happening. It had happened.

Before he could process it fully, Emily spoke again, her voice filled with quiet horror. "We're not just too late, Daniel. He knew we were coming. He's already exposed us."

Daniel's world seemed to tilt on its axis. His hands shook as he reached for the keyboard, desperate to retrieve the files, but it was useless. The moment had passed. The evidence was gone.

"Dammit," he muttered under his breath, his thoughts spiraling. "He's always been one step ahead."

Emily's gaze flickered to the door, and Daniel followed her eyes. There was a sudden chill in the air, an overwhelming sense of finality settling over them both. The trap had already been set. They had been played.

As if on cue, a loud noise erupted from the hallway—the unmistakable sound of footsteps. They were closing in.

"It's too late," Daniel whispered, the weight of everything crashing down on him.

They had lost. Or at least, that's how it felt. But even in the face of defeat, there was one thing that Daniel knew for certain: there was no way he could let it end like this. No way he would let Raphael destroy everything.

Not without a fight.

"We'll expose him," Daniel said, his voice low and firm. "Even if it's the last thing we do."

And with that, the final battle began—against Raphael, against everything that had been set in motion, and against the shadow of the Laurent legacy that threatened to swallow them whole.

But the truth would come to light. It had to.

Fifty-Seven

A Dangerous Backlash

The room seemed to close in around Daniel, the stale air thick with a tension that he could feel in his bones. His fingers hovered over the keys of the terminal, his heart pounding in his chest as he stared at the blank screen. The files were gone. The evidence that could have brought Raphael down, that could have exposed everything for what it truly was, had been wiped clean. There was no recovery. No way to get it back. His hope, the fragile thread that had held everything together for the last few hours, had just unraveled before his eyes.

Behind him, Emily was silent, her face pale, her eyes fixed on the screen with an expression that mirrored his own disbelief. He could feel the weight of her gaze on him, but he couldn't bring himself to look at her. Not yet. Not when the consequences of their failure were crashing down around them.

What were they going to do now? What hope did they have left?

"Daniel..." Emily's voice was soft but laced with an urgency that shook him out of his stupor. She didn't need to say anything more. Her words, heavy with the knowledge that they were running out of time, hung in the air between them. They had just reached the precipice of victory, only to watch it all slip away in an instant. "We have to think of something. We can't just... we can't let this be the end."

Daniel's eyes flicked to her, the raw fear in her gaze making his chest tighten. Her hair was disheveled, her face streaked with the dust of the explosion that had destroyed the safehouse just hours before. But there was something in the fire of her eyes—something unyielding—that brought him back to himself, that reminded him that they still had one option left. They still had a chance.

"I don't know how we're going to fix this, Emily," Daniel whispered, running a hand through his hair, frustration and panic swirling inside him. "This was our last shot. Raphael's already steps ahead of us. He's too powerful now. He's..."

But before Daniel could finish, the sound of rapid footsteps in the hallway interrupted him. His heart skipped a beat, and his eyes shot toward the door. The pounding grew louder, closer. There was no time left for indecision.

A Dangerous Backlash

"Hide," Daniel hissed to Emily, his voice urgent, harsh. "Now. Don't ask questions. Just do it."

Emily didn't argue. She moved quickly, slipping behind a pile of equipment in the far corner of the room. Daniel's eyes never left the door, his body tense and ready for whatever would come next. His hand hovered just above the desk drawer where he had hidden the last remnants of their back-up files. If they were going to escape with anything, it had to be those files, and they had to move fast.

The door swung open, and Daniel's breath caught as two figures stepped into the room. His pulse quickened as he recognized the first. The second was someone he hadn't expected—the figure clad in dark clothing, face partially obscured, standing confidently behind the first.

Raphael.

But the surprise wasn't just Raphael himself; it was the person standing beside him.

It was his father's old associate—someone Daniel hadn't seen since his childhood. Hector. Hector, the man who had always been around, lingering in the shadows, watching everything. He was the one who had helped shape the legacy, the one who had pushed his father in the direction that had ultimately cost him his life. And now, he was here.

"You should've known better, Daniel," Raphael's voice cut through the tension, smooth and predatory. "You thought you could outrun the legacy, thought you could play your little games. But you're a fool. You and your pathetic attempts to defy me. This was always going to end this way."

Daniel's grip tightened on the desk, his teeth grinding together as he fought the urge to shout, to confront them. But he couldn't—he had to remain calm. If he made one wrong move, if he acted out of desperation, it would be over. Everything they had fought for would be meaningless.

Hector stepped forward, his eyes scanning the room, his movements methodical and calculating. "I gave you the chance to do things the right way, Daniel," Hector's voice was low, tinged with something darker. "I warned your father. I warned him, but he was too proud. And now look at this mess. Everything's fallen apart. Everything's in jeopardy. And you, you think you can just fix it?"

Daniel's blood ran cold as Hector's words sank in. It wasn't just Raphael they had to deal with. It was Hector, too. The man who had been involved in the darkest parts of the Laurent family's history, the man who had stood by and watched it all unfold. And now, he was taking matters into his own hands.

"This ends today," Raphael said, his eyes glinting with malicious satisfaction. He took a step toward Daniel, his voice smooth as velvet, yet dripping with venom. "You don't have what it takes to stop me. You never did. The power I now control is something beyond your comprehension."

Daniel swallowed hard, trying to steady his breath. He had to think. He couldn't let them see how scared he was. He couldn't give them the satisfaction.

"And what do you think you're going to do with all that power, Raphael?" Daniel spat, his voice shaking but defiant. "What's the point of controlling the legacy if it's just going to destroy everything around you? You can't control something that's meant to be destroyed."

Raphael's lips twisted into a smile, the arrogance in his expression almost unbearable. "You're more naïve than I thought. It's not about destruction. It's about control. You see, Daniel, the world doesn't work the way you think it does. The people in power don't play by your rules. They never have. They only play by their own. And now that I'm in control of the Laurent legacy, the rules are mine to make."

Daniel's stomach churned as he realized the depth of Raphael's delusion. He didn't care about the world. He didn't care about the legacy. He cared only about power—about taking everything for himself, no matter who or what had to be destroyed in the process.

"I'll make sure the world knows about this," Daniel said, his voice hard with resolve. "I'll make sure they know what you've done. I'll expose you."

Hector's cold laughter filled the room, making Daniel flinch. "You think you have any leverage left?" Hector asked, his voice laced with contempt. "You have nothing, Daniel. Nothing."

Raphael stepped forward, his face a mask of calculated indifference. "You've already lost. It's over."

But Daniel's mind was racing, desperately trying to find an opening, some way out. His eyes flickered toward Emily, hidden behind the corner. She had been so quiet, so still, but he could feel her presence. He knew she was watching. Waiting for the moment when they could make their move.

Then, a thought hit him.

He had no proof left. The files were gone. The last of the evidence was erased. But there was one last chance. One way to turn this all around. The truth. The truth about Raphael. About everything.

Daniel reached into his pocket, pulling out his phone, his fingers shaking as he unlocked it and began to type. The connection wasn't great, but it would be enough. His fingers moved faster, a plan forming in his mind. He had to expose Raphael. He had to get the truth out there, before it was too late.

"You think you can stop me with a few meaningless clicks on a screen?" Raphael sneered, taking another step closer, his eyes narrowed. "You've already lost. You've failed."

Daniel didn't respond. His mind was focused on one thing:

getting the message sent. He needed to upload the evidence he had—he needed to make sure the world knew who Raphael truly was. The public revelation had to happen. It had to.

His thumb hit 'send' just as Raphael moved toward him, too late to stop him. The message was on its way.

And then, with a sudden force, Daniel lunged at Raphael, his hand reaching for the gun that was now in his grasp. The world seemed to freeze in that moment, the tension so thick it was suffocating.

"Now," Daniel whispered, his voice firm and low.

The room exploded into chaos.

Raphael's expression morphed from disbelief to fury as the force of Daniel's move caught him off guard. The gun clattered to the floor, the sudden action shattering the brief calm. Daniel reached for Emily, pulling her from behind the corner as the first gunshot rang out.

The force of the blast rocked the walls, sending Daniel stumbling backward, but he didn't stop. Not this time. Not when they were so close. With one last desperate push, they ran—together, against everything Raphael and Hector stood for, against the crushing weight of the past, toward the one thing they still had left.

Hope.

Fifty-Eight

The Rescue Mission

The world around Daniel seemed to blur in slow motion as he dragged Emily through the chaos. The gunfire that had erupted only moments before still echoed in his ears, and the tremor in his hands betrayed the adrenaline coursing through his veins. His heart pounded against his ribs, the urgency of the situation sinking in with each step they took. Time had become a blur of motion and panic, and they had no time to stop, no time to think. They had to keep moving.

The explosion of chaos in the room where they had just confronted Raphael and Hector seemed distant now, replaced by the deafening sound of their footsteps reverberating through the halls of the underground complex. Daniel's mind raced, calculations running like a clock in his head. They had triggered something far more dangerous than

The Rescue Mission

they had anticipated. Raphael wouldn't stop until he was in control of the entire Laurent legacy, and now, with their plan exposed and everything unraveling, Daniel couldn't shake the feeling that they were already too late.

But he couldn't let that stop him. Not now.

His grip on Emily's hand tightened, pulling her with him as they dashed down the dimly lit corridor. Their breaths were sharp, labored, but Daniel couldn't afford to slow down, not when every second mattered. They had to find a way out. They had to escape.

And in the distance, he could hear the unmistakable sound of approaching footsteps—heavily booted and deliberate. Raphael's men were closing in.

"Keep moving," Daniel hissed through clenched teeth, his voice harsh but filled with urgency. "We're not safe yet."

Emily's face was pale, the color drained from her skin, but there was something else in her eyes now—resolve. She wasn't panicking, not like Daniel had expected. She was steady, her mind focused, her gaze forward, as they continued running through the underground labyrinth. They had been through so much together already, and Daniel could see it now: Emily wasn't about to let fear control them.

They rounded a corner, and Daniel skidded to a stop, nearly pulling Emily off balance as he tugged her into a side alcove.

The last thing they needed was to be seen. The tightness in his chest increased, and his pulse quickened as he realized just how much trouble they were in. They had no backup. No weapons. No real plan. It had all been a gamble—a desperate hope that exposing Raphael's truth would be enough to turn the tides in their favor.

But it wasn't enough. Not anymore.

"Daniel…" Emily whispered, her voice barely audible. She was looking at him, her eyes wide with concern. "We can't keep running forever. We need to figure out a way out of here."

He didn't want to admit it, but she was right. They couldn't keep running. There were too many threats closing in. They couldn't outrun them forever. They needed a way out. A way to outsmart Raphael and his men.

"I know," Daniel said, his voice hoarse. He took a deep breath, trying to think. "We need a plan. A real plan. We can't just escape blindly. We need leverage."

He glanced back toward the hallway they had just come from, hearing the muffled sounds of voices approaching. Raphael's men. They were getting closer. Every moment they spent standing still, hiding in the shadows, brought them closer to being discovered.

The escape had to be now.

The Rescue Mission

His eyes locked onto the narrow ventilation shaft at the top of the alcove. It wasn't much, but it was their only chance. He took a step toward it, feeling the faintest stir of hope. They couldn't go through the main exit. There were too many guards. They couldn't fight their way out. But they could get out of sight, get out of the building, and maybe—just maybe—buy themselves enough time to plan their next move.

"Up there," Daniel said, nodding toward the shaft. "We can crawl through and get to the outer building. The vents should lead us outside, away from the guards. It's our only chance."

Emily's eyes followed his gaze. Her jaw clenched, and despite the urgency of the moment, she nodded. "Let's do it."

They had no time to waste. They both scrambled toward the vent, Daniel's fingers working quickly as he pulled open the grate, the sound of metal scraping against metal harsh in the silence of the corridor. They had to be quick, quiet. Every sound could bring them closer to discovery.

As soon as the vent was open, Daniel motioned for Emily to climb in first. He followed her in immediately, pulling the grate back into place behind them with a soft but deliberate sound. The tight crawl space felt claustrophobic, the air thick with the smell of dust and age. Their bodies pressed together as they moved, trying to remain as quiet as possible, their breath shallow and fast.

The air was cool and musty, the metal walls of the vent echoing their every movement. The sound of footsteps grew more distant, but Daniel's nerves stayed on edge. He couldn't let his guard down. He couldn't afford to think they were safe. Not yet. Not until they were far enough away from Raphael's reach.

They crawled through the ventilation shaft for what felt like an eternity, the dark, enclosed space disorienting and oppressive. Daniel kept his hand on Emily's back, guiding her forward, trying to stay focused despite the fear gnawing at him. Every turn, every bend in the shaft, felt like they were being led deeper into the unknown. He had no idea where the vent system would take them. All he knew was that they couldn't stop. They couldn't afford to hesitate.

"Just a little farther," he murmured, trying to offer reassurance, though his own voice felt thin in the oppressive silence.

Emily didn't reply, but he felt her nod against his hand. She was with him. They were in this together, and that gave him the strength to keep going. No matter how hopeless it seemed, they had to keep moving forward.

After what seemed like hours, they reached the end of the shaft. It opened into a small storage room, one of the back entrances of the building that connected to the outside world. Daniel's heart leapt at the sight of freedom, but he couldn't let his relief show. They weren't out of danger yet. Raphael would be looking for them, and they had to be quick. They couldn't afford to linger.

Daniel eased the vent grate open, careful not to make a sound. The storage room was dark, the only light coming from the faint glow of the streetlights outside filtering through the narrow window. He peered through the gap in the grate, scanning the area for any signs of movement. The streets outside were empty, but he knew better than to think they were alone.

"We need to move, now," Daniel whispered, his voice low. He helped Emily through the opening, his hands steady despite the rush of adrenaline pumping through his veins.

Once they were both out of the vent, Daniel grabbed Emily's hand, pulling her toward the back door of the storage room. He turned the handle slowly, his heart racing, and slipped through the door into the alley outside.

They were in the clear—at least for the moment. The alley was dark, and the street beyond seemed quiet, but Daniel couldn't let his guard down. They had to move fast, find a way to get out of the city before Raphael's men had a chance to track them down.

"Where do we go?" Emily asked, her voice barely audible in the silence between them.

"We need to get to the docks," Daniel replied, his mind working quickly. "It's the only place we can get off the grid. If we can get there, we can disappear. But we need to move fast."

They moved swiftly through the alley, trying to stay out of sight as they made their way to the street. Every sound, every movement felt amplified as they passed through the shadows, the fear of being caught dogging their every step. They had no backup, no plan, no way of knowing what Raphael had already set in motion. They had to assume the worst—that Raphael would stop at nothing to find them.

The tension in the air was suffocating as they rounded a corner, and then, just as they thought they were in the clear, a loud crash broke the silence behind them.

Daniel's heart skipped a beat.

"They found us," he muttered, his voice tight with fear.

"We need to run. Now," Emily said urgently, her grip on Daniel's hand tightening.

Without thinking, they took off down the street, their footsteps pounding on the pavement as they raced toward the docks. The sounds of pursuit grew louder behind them—shouting, footsteps growing closer. Daniel's mind raced. They couldn't outrun them on foot. But the docks—there was a boat. The last thing Raphael would expect would be for them to escape by water.

They had to make it there. They had to make it in time.

The Rescue Mission

"Come on!" Daniel shouted, his voice hoarse, as they sprinted toward the docks, the world around them fading into a blur of motion. The sound of pursuit grew louder, but Daniel refused to stop, refusing to let Emily down.

They had one chance.

And they were going to take it.

Fifty-Nine

The Legal Victory

The courtroom was eerily silent as the judge's gavel echoed through the chamber, signaling the beginning of the final leg of this tumultuous trial. Daniel sat in the front row, his fingers white from gripping the edge of the chair, his eyes fixed on the man who had orchestrated the destruction of so many lives. Raphael, sitting just a few feet away, appeared calm—too calm. His expression was carefully neutral, as if he were an observer, not the man whose empire was crumbling around him. But Daniel knew the truth. The truth was about to come to light, and there was nothing Raphael could do to stop it now.

He glanced briefly at Emily beside him. Her hand was steady in his, though he could feel the tension vibrating through her. She had been with him from the very beginning of this

The Legal Victory

fight, standing by him through the chaos and the danger, and now, in this moment, their resolve was as unshakeable as the walls surrounding them. But they both knew this was the final battle—the battle for justice, for the truth, and for the future.

Their legal team had worked tirelessly, piecing together the evidence Daniel had managed to salvage. The back-up files, the recordings, the documents—everything that had been erased, recovered. Raphael had underestimated their determination, and now, the story of the Laurent family's corruption and manipulation was about to be broadcast for the world to see. It had taken time, strategy, and careful planning, but Daniel had not come this far just to watch it all slip away.

"Ladies and gentlemen of the jury," the judge's voice broke through the stillness, firm and commanding, "we will now proceed with the closing statements. I remind you that the matter at hand is serious and that the decisions you make will have far-reaching consequences. Counsel for the defense, you may proceed."

Raphael's lawyer, a tall man with an air of authority, stood and adjusted his tie. He was composed, confident, and well-practiced, but there was an undeniable tension in the air. Raphael, though he appeared unmoved, had to be feeling the pressure. The case against him was stronger than anyone had anticipated. The documents Daniel's team had presented, the testimonies, the undeniable connections between Raphael and the illegal activities that had come to light—everything pointed to one inevitable conclusion: Raphael was guilty.

The defense attorney began his closing argument with practiced ease, his words smooth and calculated. He spoke of Raphael's innocence, his leadership of the Laurent family, the good he had done for the community, and the way in which the evidence against him had been, in his words, "misinterpreted" or "manipulated" by a smear campaign. The lawyer even attempted to discredit some of the witnesses who had bravely stepped forward, painting them as disgruntled former employees or individuals with grudges. It was the usual tactic: discredit the messenger when you can't disprove the message.

Daniel's jaw clenched as he listened, the anger rising in him like a tide. He knew Raphael. He knew the lies that had been spun, the lives that had been destroyed. He knew what Raphael was capable of. And hearing the defense lawyer try to whitewash the crimes, try to present a picture of a man who had done no wrong, filled Daniel with a cold fury.

But then, the defense lawyer's argument faltered, the cracks in his case becoming more and more evident as Daniel's team had slowly and methodically dismantled every lie, every manipulation. The jury had been listening, absorbing every word, and Daniel could see that they weren't buying it. The lies were no longer enough to hold up.

The defense finished their argument, sitting down with a smug, knowing look, but Daniel didn't let that intimidate him. He knew the truth. And now, it was time to make sure the jury knew it too.

The prosecution team, led by an experienced and relentless attorney, stood to deliver their closing remarks. The energy in the room shifted. There was no more doubt. They had everything they needed to bring Raphael to justice.

The prosecutor, a woman in her mid-forties with a no-nonsense attitude, wasted no time. She began by outlining the evidence they had presented— the documents detailing the illegal activities orchestrated by Raphael, the witnesses who had risked their lives to come forward, the recordings of phone conversations where Raphael had orchestrated bribes, blackmail, and intimidation.

She spoke clearly and with purpose, her words cutting through the air like a blade. "We are here today not just because of one man's greed, but because of the destruction he has caused. The lives he has ruined. The families he has broken apart. The future he has stolen. The defendant, Raphael Laurent, has shown time and time again that he believes he is above the law. But today, that will no longer be tolerated."

Daniel's chest swelled with a mixture of pride and apprehension. They had come so far, and yet, there was still a part of him that couldn't quite shake the fear that Raphael would find a way out of this. He was a master manipulator, and his wealth and influence had always shielded him from consequences. But now, with the weight of the law behind them, and the truth finally in the open, there was no escaping it.

The prosecutor's voice grew firmer, more impassioned as she continued. "The evidence is irrefutable. The testimony is clear. The defendant has used his position of power to exploit others for his own gain, to further the interests of the Laurent family at any cost. This is not a man who should be allowed to walk free. This is a man who must be held accountable for his actions."

Daniel's eyes flicked to Raphael, who had been sitting motionless, but now his face seemed to harden. The calm exterior was cracking, the façade of the untouchable billionaire starting to slip. Raphael's cold gaze met Daniel's across the courtroom, and for a moment, their eyes locked, both of them knowing that this was the endgame. The trial that had seemed like it would drag on forever was coming to a head, and neither of them was going to walk away unchanged.

The prosecutor turned to the jury, her voice steady and unwavering. "The Laurent family legacy has been built on lies, deceit, and manipulation. But today, we stand at the precipice of a new beginning. A beginning where justice is restored. Where the truth prevails. Where the law is no longer an instrument of oppression but a beacon of hope for those who have been silenced."

Daniel felt the weight of her words settle over him. This wasn't just a victory for him, for Emily, for their team. It

The Legal Victory

was a victory for everyone who had ever been manipulated, lied to, or betrayed by Raphael's machinations. This was the moment where everything came crashing down, where the world would finally see Raphael for who he truly was.

The prosecutor's closing argument ended with a clear call to action: "We ask that you deliver the only verdict that fits the crimes committed here today. Guilty. For the sake of justice. For the sake of the victims. For the future of this community."

The courtroom remained silent as the prosecutor returned to her seat, her eyes never leaving the jury. The weight of the moment hung in the air, and Daniel felt the tension in the room build with each passing second. His eyes flickered to Emily, who had been watching him closely throughout the trial. She gave him a small, reassuring nod, and for the first time in what felt like forever, Daniel allowed himself to breathe.

The jury was deliberating. The final decision was now in their hands.

And yet, as Daniel sat there, waiting for the verdict, something else lingered in the back of his mind. Raphael. He was still dangerous. The fight wasn't over yet. No matter how much the evidence stacked against him, Daniel knew that Raphael would never stop. He would fight, claw, and do whatever it took to regain control.

But in that moment, sitting in the courtroom, with the

future hanging in the balance, Daniel knew one thing for certain: whatever happened next, they had done it. They had exposed the truth. They had fought for justice, and they had won.

The jury returned after what felt like an eternity. Daniel's breath caught in his chest as they filed back into the room. The foreperson stood, and the judge called for silence.

"Have you reached a verdict?" the judge asked.

The foreperson nodded, their voice steady as they spoke the words Daniel had been waiting for.

"We, the jury, find the defendant, Raphael Laurent, guilty on all counts."

Daniel's heart soared in his chest, the weight of the last few months finally lifting. The room seemed to buzz with energy as the realization settled over everyone present. Raphael was guilty. The truth had prevailed.

And in that moment, with Emily's hand still tightly in his, Daniel knew that justice had finally been served. The Laurent legacy had been brought to its knees, and the world would never be the same again.

Sixty

A New Beginning

The city sprawled beneath Daniel as he stood on the rooftop of the building, the wind whipping through his hair, and the faint hum of life below him a stark contrast to the chaos that had just unfolded. The final verdict in the courtroom had been delivered, and Raphael was now facing the consequences of his years of manipulation and deceit. It had been a victory for justice, for truth, and for the countless lives that had been affected by the Laurent family's reign of terror. But for Daniel, the fight had only just begun.

The sun was setting behind him, casting long shadows across the skyline. It had been a long road to get here, filled with danger, betrayal, and the constant threat of failure. But now, as he stood there, watching the orange and purple hues of the sky fade into night, Daniel could finally allow himself to feel something else—something he hadn't allowed himself to feel in a long time: hope.

Behind him, the door to the rooftop opened, and Daniel didn't need to turn around to know who it was. Emily's presence was like a steady anchor in the storm that had defined their lives for so long. She approached quietly, her footsteps soft against the concrete, until she was standing beside him, her shoulder just barely touching his.

"Beautiful, isn't it?" she said, her voice low but filled with wonder as she gazed out at the cityscape.

Daniel nodded, his gaze fixed on the horizon. "It is," he agreed, his voice thick with emotion. "It's hard to believe everything that's happened. It feels like we've been living in a storm, and now, it's finally starting to clear."

Emily's eyes turned to him, a soft smile curling on her lips. "It is, isn't it? But I think we've earned the right to breathe, don't you?"

Daniel let out a breath he didn't realize he had been holding, the tension that had built up in him over the past few months slowly ebbing away. He turned to look at her, his heart swelling with something he couldn't quite name. It wasn't just relief—it was something deeper. Something that had been buried inside him for far too long.

"Do you ever think about what comes next?" he asked, his voice quieter now. "About what we're going to do with all this... freedom?"

Emily's smile faded just slightly, and she met his gaze with a level of understanding that sent a chill down his spine. She knew. She knew what this victory meant for them, and for the world they had been a part of. It wasn't just the fall of Raphael and his empire. It was the end of a chapter in their lives that had been defined by darkness, by manipulation, and by the shadows of the past.

"I do," she replied softly. "I think about it all the time. And, to be honest, I'm not sure. I don't know what the future holds for us. But I know that I don't want to live in the shadows anymore, Daniel. I want to build something. Something that's ours. Something that's real."

Her words struck him deeply, and for a moment, he didn't know what to say. The truth was, he didn't know what came next either. They had been so focused on surviving, on bringing Raphael to justice, that they hadn't allowed themselves the luxury of thinking beyond the fight. But now that it was over, now that they had won, the world seemed suddenly... wide open. And with that freedom came the overwhelming question: What now?

Daniel swallowed hard, trying to make sense of the emotions that were swirling within him. He thought back to everything they had been through—the betrayals, the near-death encounters, the constant threat of losing everything. He thought about his father, the man he had once admired, and the legacy that had poisoned his family. And he thought about Emily—the one constant in all of it. The one person who had stood by his side, who had never wavered, even when everything seemed lost.

"I don't want to live in the shadows either," Daniel said, his voice steady now, filled with conviction. "I want something better for us. For both of us. A life where we can finally be free. Free from the past. Free from everything Raphael and my family have done."

Emily's hand found his, and for a moment, they just stood there, looking out over the city together. The noise of the world below them felt distant, almost irrelevant, as they stood in the stillness of the night. It was a rare moment of peace, one they hadn't been afforded in a long time. And in that silence, Daniel realized something profound—something he hadn't let himself fully grasp until now.

They had won. They had fought, and they had survived. But survival was only the first step. The real victory, the true victory, would be in what they built together. What they chose to make of the life they had earned.

"It's not going to be easy," Emily said, her voice breaking the silence again, but this time with a quiet certainty. "Building a life, starting over… It's not going to be easy. But I think we can do it. Together."

Daniel turned to face her fully now, his eyes searching hers, looking for the truth in her words. The hope, the faith, the belief that they could really do it—that they could make a new beginning, together, from the ashes of everything they had been through.

He pulled her toward him, wrapping his arms around her, holding her close. She rested her head against his chest, and for the first time in what felt like forever, Daniel felt the weight of everything lift from his shoulders. There was still so much to do. There was still so much they didn't know. But in this moment, standing together on the rooftop, they had everything they needed.

"I'm scared," Daniel admitted, his voice barely a whisper, though it felt like a confession. "Scared of what comes next. Scared of... what's waiting for us."

Emily looked up at him, her eyes soft, full of understanding. "I'm scared too. But I think that's okay. It's okay to be scared. We've survived the worst of it, Daniel. And now, we get to choose what happens next. And that's more than either of us ever thought we'd have."

For a moment, neither of them spoke, and the only sound was the distant hum of the city below. They stood together in the night, their hearts beating in unison, both of them caught in the quiet certainty that whatever came next, they would face it together. Whatever challenges lay ahead, they would tackle them side by side.

But even as the peace of that moment settled over them, Daniel couldn't shake the gnawing feeling in the back of his mind. The world they had left behind—the world of power struggles, of manipulation, of betrayals—wasn't going to disappear overnight. Raphael's fall had been significant, but it hadn't wiped away everything. The Laurent legacy, the corruption that had built it, would linger. There would be others who sought the same power. And there would be people who would try to fill the vacuum left by Raphael's defeat.

But they didn't have to fight it alone anymore. They didn't have to live in the shadows of the past.

"Let's build something new," Daniel said, pulling back slightly to look into her eyes, the conviction in his voice unwavering. "Let's leave behind everything we've known and start fresh. Together."

Emily smiled, a soft, radiant smile that lit up her face. "Together," she agreed, her voice filled with a quiet strength.

And in that moment, Daniel knew that no matter what came next, they would face it as partners—united in their resolve to make a new beginning. The past had been written, and they couldn't change it. But the future? That was theirs to shape.

The night was still and quiet, the weight of the world finally lifting. The road ahead would be difficult. There would be obstacles, challenges, and moments of doubt. But for the first time, Daniel felt ready to face it all. Because, with Emily by his side, anything was possible.

A New Beginning

And so, as the sun dipped below the horizon, they turned away from the rooftop and walked into the unknown together—hand in hand, hearts full of hope, ready for the new beginning they had earned.

Sixty-One

The Café Revival

The first time Daniel stepped into the old café, the musty scent of wood and coffee beans filled his nostrils, a nostalgia so deep it almost knocked the breath from his lungs. The café had been a part of his childhood, a quiet place in the heart of the city where he had spent countless afternoons with his father. It was here, in the worn booths and flickering candlelight, that he had first learned the art of business, the delicate balance of risk and reward. It had been a place of refuge, a place where he had once thought the world could be at peace.

But that was before everything had fallen apart.

Now, as Daniel pushed open the door and stepped inside, it was hard to believe that this was the same place. The shelves were dusty, the tables empty. The walls, once

The Café Revival

adorned with pictures and quotes, were now bare, save for the peeling wallpaper. The small, family-run café had fallen into disrepair, abandoned by those who had once believed in its potential. The scent of stale coffee hung in the air, mingling with the dust of neglect.

Daniel could feel the weight of the past pressing on him as he walked across the creaky wooden floor, his boots echoing in the silence. The old barista counter was still there, though the once-polished espresso machine now sat in a corner, covered in grime. The soft glow of the afternoon sun filtered through the half-closed blinds, casting long shadows across the room. It felt like a ghost of its former self—a place that had once been full of life, now a hushed echo of a time gone by.

"Are you sure about this?" Emily's voice broke through the silence, her hand resting lightly on his arm. She had been quiet since they arrived, her eyes scanning the room with a mix of curiosity and apprehension. It wasn't just the café's physical state that made her uneasy—it was the weight of everything that had led them here.

Daniel turned to face her, his expression softening as he met her gaze. She had been with him through every step of this journey—from the courtrooms to the escape plans, from the fall of Raphael to the uncertain future they now faced. And yet, even now, as they stood at the threshold of something new, Daniel could sense the quiet fear in her eyes. The fear of what came next.

"I'm sure," Daniel said, his voice steady. He reached out, taking her hand in his and giving it a reassuring squeeze. "We need this. We need a place to start fresh. A place that's ours. Something that reminds us of what we're fighting for."

Emily's eyes softened, and she gave a small nod, though the uncertainty still lingered in the air. They had both been through so much, and the idea of starting something new after everything that had happened felt like an impossible challenge. But Daniel couldn't ignore the pull of this place, the sense that it could be the beginning of something better. The café was more than just a building—it was a symbol of resilience, of hope, of the possibility of a fresh start.

"We can fix this," Daniel said quietly, more to himself than to Emily. "We can bring it back to life. Together."

He stepped behind the counter, his fingers trailing along the old wood as memories flooded back. This had been his father's dream—a small business, a safe space where people could gather, connect, and share moments over coffee. But somewhere along the way, that dream had faded, buried under the weight of ambition, greed, and betrayal. Now, standing in the heart of the café, Daniel knew that it was time to revive that dream. It was time to make it his own.

The next few days were a blur of work. Daniel and Emily spent long hours cleaning, scrubbing away the grime that had built up over the years. They stripped the walls of their peeling wallpaper and replaced the worn-out furniture with new pieces—simple, modern, but still true to the café's original spirit. It was a labor of love, and as they worked, Daniel couldn't help but feel the weight of the past slowly lifting. With each brushstroke, each new coat of paint, the café began to take shape again. It was a slow, exhausting process, but it felt right.

By the time the renovations were complete, the café had been transformed. The walls, once bare and tired, were now adorned with local artwork. The floors gleamed with a fresh coat of polish. The shelves, now stocked with fresh ingredients, were filled with jars of coffee beans, tea leaves, and sweet syrups. The espresso machine, polished and gleaming, was once again perched behind the counter, ready for use. The small stage in the corner was cleared, ready for local musicians to play and for the community to gather.

Daniel stood in the doorway, looking out at the newly revived café. The space was brighter, warmer, full of life and energy. There was a buzz in the air, a sense that this place was more than just a business—it was a gathering place. A place where people could find solace, comfort, and a sense of community.

"It's perfect," Emily said softly, stepping up beside him. She was smiling now, her earlier hesitation replaced by a quiet sense of accomplishment. "You really did it, Daniel. You brought it back."

Daniel smiled, his heart swelling with pride. "We did it," he corrected, turning to her. "Together."

They had done it. They had built something from the ground up, something that was not defined by the ghosts of the past but by the hope of the future. The café was no longer a symbol of lost dreams—it was a place of new beginnings. And with it, they had created something that could stand on its own, separate from the shadows that had once haunted them.

But just as Daniel was about to turn away from the doorway and step inside, a voice broke through the noise of the café, calling out from the street.

"Hey! Is this the new place?"

Daniel's heart skipped a beat, his body tensing as he turned to see who was approaching. Standing in front of the café was a woman, her face familiar but not quite. She was holding a small notebook in her hand, a pen tucked behind her ear. Her expression was one of curiosity, but there was also something else in her eyes—a recognition, a sense of familiarity that Daniel couldn't quite place.

Before he could speak, Emily had already stepped forward, her smile wide and genuine. "Yes, we just reopened. Welcome!"

The woman's eyes scanned the café, her gaze lingering on the new décor, the vibrant atmosphere, before settling back on Daniel. There was something about her—a confidence, a spark of recognition—that caught him off guard.

"You don't remember me, do you?" she asked, her smile widening just slightly.

Daniel's brow furrowed as he studied her. And then, it clicked. His heart raced, and a rush of memories flooded back. The woman standing before him was none other than Mia, the journalist who had helped expose Raphael's crimes, the one who had given him the push he needed to take the first steps toward bringing down the Laurent empire. She had been a key player in the legal battle, providing critical evidence that had helped secure Raphael's conviction.

"Mia?" Daniel said, his voice tinged with disbelief.

Mia smiled, the warmth in her eyes making her all the more familiar. "Yes, it's me. I didn't know you were opening a café, Daniel. I've been following your journey since the trial. You know, I never thought I'd see the day when Raphael was brought to justice. But here you are, standing in front of your own café. I have to admit, I'm impressed."

Daniel's heart lifted as he stepped toward her. "It's a long story. But yes, here we are. A new beginning."

Mia's eyes twinkled with curiosity. "And what's the story behind this place? Why a café?"

Daniel paused, considering her question for a moment. "It's simple, really. My father built this café. It was his dream. And after everything we've been through, I realized that the best way to honor that dream, to honor everything we've fought for, is to start fresh. To build something that's ours. Something real."

Mia's expression softened, and she nodded. "I get it. And it's good to see that you've found your own path. Starting over after everything you've been through... It's not easy. But from what I see here, it looks like you've done it. And that's something worth celebrating."

Daniel smiled, the weight of everything they had endured slowly lifting as Mia spoke. He could see it now. The café wasn't just about coffee or pastries or the simple comforts of life—it was about resilience. About starting again, no matter how impossible it seemed. It was a place for people to gather, to find a little bit of hope, even in the darkest times.

"We're having a grand reopening event next week," Emily said, stepping forward with a bright smile. "You should come by. It's going to be a celebration of everything we've been through and everything we're moving toward."

Mia's smile widened. "I wouldn't miss it for the world."

And with that, the café felt complete. It wasn't just the walls, the décor, the coffee—it was the people who would fill it, the community that would come together, the new beginnings that would take root in this small, quiet corner of the city. For the first time in a long time, Daniel felt at peace. The fight was over. The war had been won. And now, the real work could begin.

The Café Revival

Together.

Sixty-Two

A Charitable Gesture

The sun hung low in the sky, casting a warm, golden glow over the café as Daniel watched the last few customers of the day filter out onto the streets. The café, a place that had once seemed so foreign and empty, now felt like home—a place of refuge, not just for him and Emily, but for the community that had embraced them since they reopened the doors. It had been a few months since they'd revived the space, and the transformation had been nothing short of remarkable. The once-neglected establishment now thrived, bustling with life. The coffee was rich and inviting, the air filled with the hum of conversation, the clink of mugs, and the soft strains of jazz playing in the background.

It was the middle of the afternoon, the usual lull between the lunch and dinner rush, and Daniel leaned against the counter, his gaze drifting to the small stage in the corner where local musicians had begun to gather for the evening's performance. The café had become a hub for creativity and connection—a space for artists, musicians, and writers to come together, sharing their passions and finding common ground. But as much as he appreciated the growth and success of the café, Daniel couldn't shake the feeling that something was missing. It wasn't the café itself, but the deeper sense of purpose that had driven him to open it in the first place. The fight for justice had been a crucial chapter in his life, but now, as the café stood as a testament to resilience, Daniel knew that there was more he needed to do. More he could do.

His thoughts were interrupted by the sound of the door chime, and he turned to see an older woman walk in, her presence calm and composed. She was dressed in a simple, but elegant, navy-blue dress and carried a small handbag, her silver hair neatly pulled back into a bun. Her eyes, sharp and clear, scanned the café as if she were looking for something—or perhaps someone. When she spotted Daniel behind the counter, she smiled warmly and made her way over to him.

"Good afternoon, young man," she greeted him with a soft, yet confident, voice. "I've heard a great deal about your café, and I must say, I've been quite curious to see it for myself."

Daniel straightened, surprised by her approach. "Good afternoon. I'm glad you stopped by. We've been working hard to make this place a community gathering spot."

The woman nodded approvingly as she took a seat at one of the empty tables near the window, her eyes never leaving Daniel. "I can see that. The atmosphere is warm and inviting, much like the stories I've heard. You've built something truly special here, and I've come to see if there might be a way I can help you build something even greater."

Daniel raised an eyebrow, intrigued by her words. She was clearly well-spoken and confident, and there was something in her demeanor that suggested she wasn't someone who made empty promises. "I'm not sure I understand," he said cautiously. "What do you mean by helping build something greater?"

The woman smiled knowingly, as if she had been expecting his response. "I'm Margaret Hartwell," she began, introducing herself with a graceful tilt of her head. "And I represent a charitable foundation that focuses on supporting young entrepreneurs like yourself—people who are trying to make a positive impact on their communities, but who might need a little extra support to take things to the next level."

Daniel's mind raced as he processed her words. A charitable foundation? Supporting young entrepreneurs? It was an offer he had never expected, but something about it intrigued him. The idea of taking the café—and his life—further into a space of positive influence, of reaching beyond the small circle of loyal customers they had gathered, seemed almost too good to be true.

"I'm listening," Daniel said, his voice steady but filled with curiosity. He walked over to the table, where Margaret was now settled, taking a seat across from her.

Margaret smiled again, her eyes twinkling with a quiet intensity. "I've been following your story, Daniel. The café's revival, your journey through the legal battles, and the personal transformation you've gone through. You've turned this place around, and that's no small feat. But I believe you have the potential to do even more. Your café can be a beacon of hope for so many others—especially young people who are looking for a way to break free of the limitations life has placed on them. A space for mentorship, for learning, for growth."

Daniel felt a spark of excitement, but there was something still nagging at him—something that kept him from diving headfirst into this new opportunity. "And what does that have to do with your foundation? What exactly are you offering?"

Margaret placed her hands on the table, leaning forward slightly, her expression earnest. "Our foundation is interested in funding projects that have the potential to create real change. But more than that, we aim to support people who have vision, people who want to lift others up and help them build a better future. If you're open to it, we could help you expand the café into something even more impactful—something that serves not just coffee, but also as a space for education, for empowerment. We could help you establish programs, provide scholarships for young people interested in the food industry, the arts, or even business management.

We could turn this café into a place where people come not just to sip coffee but to learn, grow, and change their lives."

The words hit Daniel like a wave, and for the first time in what felt like ages, he felt a sense of clarity. He had been so focused on simply surviving, on getting the café up and running again, that he had never truly allowed himself to imagine how much more it could be. The possibilities were vast—mentorship programs for young people, training for aspiring baristas and chefs, workshops for artists and musicians looking to hone their craft. The café could become a community resource, a hub of transformation, a beacon of hope for those looking to start anew.

"You're talking about something bigger than just a café," Daniel said, his voice low with awe. "You're talking about building a space that can change lives. Help people build their futures."

Margaret nodded, her smile widening. "Exactly. You've already shown that you have the heart and the drive to make a difference. All you need now is the support to take it to the next level. And that's where we come in."

Daniel's mind raced as the vision of the café's future began to take shape in his mind. The impact it could have—on young people, on the community—was immense. But there was still a part of him that hesitated. The weight of responsibility, of taking on something this large, felt overwhelming.

A Charitable Gesture

"I'm honored by the offer, Margaret," Daniel said, taking a deep breath. "But I'm not sure I can do something this big. This kind of responsibility, this level of commitment… it's a lot."

Margaret's expression softened, and she leaned back in her chair, her eyes thoughtful. "I understand your hesitation, Daniel. But I'm not suggesting you do this alone. Our foundation would be here to guide you, to help you every step of the way. This is about building a team—a group of people who share your vision and are willing to work together to make it happen. I believe in you, Daniel. I believe in this café, and I believe in what you can do with the right support."

The words hung in the air between them, and Daniel felt the weight of them settle into his chest. He had spent so much of his life fighting for something better, for a future free from the shadows of his past. He had fought for justice, for truth, and for the opportunity to create something meaningful. But now, he had the chance to build something even bigger—to create a legacy that wasn't just about him, but about the people he could help along the way.

Emily had been listening quietly, her eyes wide as she processed the conversation. When Daniel turned to her, she gave him a gentle nod, her expression calm but filled with warmth and encouragement. She believed in him, in them, in this new chapter they were about to begin.

"You've always wanted to make a difference, Daniel," Emily

said softly, her voice filled with conviction. "I think this is your chance. Our chance."

Daniel felt his heart surge with a mixture of excitement and fear. This was it. This was the moment when everything could change. He had come this far, and now, with the opportunity to create something that could change lives, he knew that this was the right path forward.

"I'll do it," Daniel said, his voice firm with resolve. "I'll take the support. I'll take the chance. Let's build something that matters."

Margaret's eyes shone with approval, and she extended her hand across the table. "I knew you'd make the right choice. Together, we'll create something that will impact lives for years to come."

Daniel took her hand, shaking it firmly, a sense of purpose settling over him. This was the beginning of something new—something bigger than the café, something that could reach out and touch the lives of so many others.

And as the door to the café opened and the evening light poured in, Daniel felt a quiet sense of certainty fill him. This was just the beginning of their journey. Together, they were going to make a difference.

And that difference would start here.

Sixty-Three

Rebuilding Trust

The café hummed with life as the evening crowd settled in, the clinking of coffee mugs and the soft murmur of conversations blending into a familiar rhythm. It was a sound that Daniel had grown accustomed to in the months since the grand reopening, a sound that had come to symbolize the new life that had taken root here. But tonight, the usual comfort of the café felt like a backdrop to something heavier, something that had been weighing on his mind for days.

Daniel sat at a small table by the window, the soft light of the streetlamps casting shadows across his face. The café was busier than usual—more people were coming in, eager to enjoy the food, the music, the sense of community that had been restored. But despite the warmth and energy around him, Daniel's thoughts were elsewhere. They were on the conversation he had been avoiding, the one he could no longer put off. The conversation that had been building ever since he had made the decision to accept Margaret's offer to expand the café into something bigger—a mentorship program, a charitable initiative, a hub for the community to learn and grow.

But as ambitious as the vision was, there was a darker side to it—a side that Daniel had tried to ignore. The foundation's support, the trust that had been extended to him, came with a price. And the price was not just financial—it was personal.

For days, Daniel had been wrestling with his feelings of guilt and unease. The café was thriving, yes, but there was something that still felt broken. Something that had been shattered long before the café's doors were even reopened. The weight of past mistakes, the betrayals, the lies—everything that had happened with Raphael, his family, the legacy that had defined so much of his life—still lingered like a shadow, creeping into the corners of his thoughts. And it wasn't just his own actions that he was questioning. It was the people he had hurt along the way, the people who had stood by him, trusted him, only for him to push them away.

And then there was Emily.

Emily had been his constant. She had been there from the very beginning, standing by him through the darkest moments, through the twists of fate and the betrayals that had defined their lives. She had seen him at his lowest, and she had never once wavered. But as much as he wanted to believe that they could move forward, that they could create something new and beautiful together, there was still a crack in their foundation—a crack that had formed long before the café's revival.

Daniel knew that he couldn't continue building this future without addressing the past. He had to rebuild the trust that had been damaged, the trust that he had taken for granted. He had to find a way to heal what had been broken.

The door to the café opened with a soft chime, and Daniel looked up, his breath catching in his throat when he saw Emily standing in the doorway. She was wearing her usual calm expression, her eyes soft but guarded. She glanced around the room, spotting Daniel immediately, and then made her way toward him.

"Hey," she said softly as she approached the table, her voice warm but tinged with something else—something he couldn't quite place. "It's getting busy tonight."

Daniel nodded, his heart thudding in his chest. "Yeah. It's been a good day. People seem to really be enjoying the new space."

Emily smiled faintly and took a seat across from him, her gaze settling on him with a quiet intensity. There was something in the way she looked at him—a vulnerability, a question that lingered between them, unspoken but present.

She had always been able to read him like an open book, and tonight, Daniel could feel the weight of her gaze as if she were waiting for him to say the words that had been hanging in the air for days.

"I've been thinking," Daniel began, his voice quiet, his hands restless on the table. "About everything. About the café, about the future, about what we're doing here. But also about… us. About you and me."

Emily's expression softened, and she leaned forward slightly, her elbows resting on the table. "What do you mean?" she asked, her voice steady but gentle, as if she already knew where this conversation was going.

Daniel swallowed hard, trying to gather the words that felt trapped in his throat. "I've spent so much time focused on building this place—on fixing everything around me—that I didn't take the time to fix what was inside. What was broken. And I… I realize now that I hurt you, Emily. I didn't always see what you needed. I didn't always trust you the way I should have. And I'm sorry. I've been trying to rebuild everything, but I need to rebuild the trust we had first."

There it was. The thing he had been avoiding for so long. The words that he had been too afraid to say, even though he knew they were the only way forward.

Emily was silent for a long moment, her gaze dropping to her hands on the table, fingers tracing the rim of her coffee cup. Daniel held his breath, waiting for her to speak, unsure of what she would say. He had never been good at admitting his mistakes, at facing the truth of his own failings. But this time, there was no running from it. He had to face it. And he had to face her.

When Emily finally spoke, her voice was low and calm, but there was a hint of something deeper in her words—something that made Daniel's heart ache. "I've been waiting for you to say that," she said quietly. "For you to admit it. For you to see what you did. Because, Daniel, I'm not sure I can keep going if we don't rebuild that first."

Her words struck him like a punch to the gut, and he felt the weight of them settle heavily in his chest. She had been waiting. Waiting for him to finally see the truth. Waiting for him to understand what had been broken all along. It was a humbling realization, one that made him feel small, but it was also the moment that he knew they could move forward. If they were willing to face the past and rebuild what had been lost.

"I know," Daniel whispered, his voice thick with emotion. "And I know it's going to take time. I know I can't just fix it all overnight. But I'm willing to try. I'm willing to do whatever it takes to rebuild that trust. To prove to you that I'm here for you. That I see you, that I trust you, and that I'm not going to run away from this anymore."

Emily's gaze softened, and she exhaled slowly, the tension in her shoulders easing. "I'm not going anywhere, Daniel," she said, her voice steady. "But I need to know that you're in this with me. That you're willing to rebuild, not just the café, but everything between us."

"I am," Daniel said, his voice full of conviction now. "I promise you, I am."

There was a long pause as they sat in the quiet of the café, the hum of conversation and the soft clinking of coffee cups filling the space around them. Daniel could feel the weight of the moment—the weight of their shared history, the weight of the trust that had been broken, but also the weight of the possibility that lay ahead. Rebuilding trust wouldn't be easy. It would take time, effort, and vulnerability. But in that moment, Daniel knew that it was worth it. That she was worth it.

Emily leaned back in her chair, her eyes meeting his with a softness that made his heart flutter. "Then we start over," she said, her voice filled with a quiet hope. "One step at a time."

Daniel nodded, his chest tight with emotion. "One step at a time."

And in that moment, as they sat across from each other in the warmth of the café, surrounded by the laughter and chatter of the people they had come to care about, Daniel knew that this was the beginning of something new. Something real. Something that would take time, effort, and patience. But it was worth it. Because this time, they would rebuild. Together.

Sixty-Four

The Final Threat

The café was quiet in the early hours of the morning, a stark contrast to the bustling energy of the previous evening. The first light of dawn filtered through the tall windows, casting long shadows across the hardwood floors. Daniel sat alone at the counter, a cup of coffee in hand, staring into the depths of his mug as his mind raced. The café had become everything he had hoped for—a place of refuge, a sanctuary for the community—but something still gnawed at him. There was a darkness lurking in the periphery, something he couldn't shake. And the closer he got to peace, the closer that darkness seemed to get to him.

He wasn't alone in his thoughts for long.

The bell above the door chimed softly, and Daniel looked

up. Emily stood in the doorway, her silhouette framed by the morning light. She was dressed in a simple jacket, her eyes tired but determined. She had been with him through every twist and turn, every trial and victory, but this new unease that seemed to have gripped him was something she, too, had begun to sense.

"Morning," Emily said, her voice soft but carrying an edge of concern. She walked over to him, her footsteps light on the wooden floors.

"Morning," Daniel replied, forcing a smile but not quite masking the tension in his eyes. "Did you sleep?"

Emily raised an eyebrow, her lips curling slightly. "Not much. But I think we're both well-acquainted with sleepless nights, aren't we?"

Daniel chuckled softly, but the humor didn't reach his eyes. "Yeah. I guess we are."

She sat down next to him, her gaze flickering to the mug in his hands. "What's on your mind?"

Daniel hesitated, his fingers tightening around the mug. The weight of the conversation that had been building for days, weeks, seemed to hang in the air between them. He knew that whatever was coming—whatever danger still loomed—would be more than just a threat to the café. It would be a threat to everything they had fought for, everything they had rebuilt. And that thought sent a chill through him.

"I don't know how to explain it," Daniel finally said, his voice low and tense. "It's like we're being watched. Like someone's waiting for the right moment to strike. I can feel it, Emily. I know we're not out of the woods yet."

Emily's expression softened, and she placed her hand gently over his. "Daniel, we've been through so much already. We've fought for this place, for everything we have. I know you're scared, but whatever happens, we'll face it together. You don't have to carry this alone."

Daniel met her gaze, her words offering some comfort, but they weren't enough to erase the feeling in his gut. He had been through a lot—more than anyone should ever have to endure—and he had learned something during those dark days: that the shadows of the past had a way of catching up with you, no matter how far you ran. He had fought to escape the grip of his family's legacy, to distance himself from the horrors Raphael had unleashed, but now, as his life had finally begun to settle, the whispers of danger were returning. And this time, he couldn't ignore them.

Just then, the sound of footsteps echoed from the back of the café, and both Daniel and Emily turned toward the door leading to the kitchen. It was too early for anyone else to be here. The staff wouldn't arrive for hours, and the only person who could have been back there was—

"Margaret," Daniel said, rising from his seat, his tone sharp with suspicion.

Margaret Hartwell, the woman who had offered her foundation's support, had been a major part of the café's expansion. She had been a mentor of sorts, a guiding hand for the future of the café. But recently, something about her—about the way she seemed to be pushing them—had felt off. It was as though there was an agenda Daniel couldn't quite pin down, and though she was offering support, he couldn't shake the feeling that there was something she was hiding. Something bigger than he was ready to confront.

Margaret entered the room, her footsteps measured and deliberate. She was dressed in a sharp suit, as always, but today her expression was more serious than usual, her eyes darkened with an emotion that Daniel couldn't place.

"Good morning, Daniel," Margaret said, her tone polite but lacking warmth. "Emily." She nodded at both of them before taking a seat at the table closest to the counter.

"Margaret," Emily said, her voice cautious. "What brings you here so early?"

Margaret paused for a moment, studying them both. She didn't immediately answer, instead reaching into her handbag and pulling out a manila envelope. "I wanted to talk," she said, her voice calm but with a quiet intensity that set Daniel on edge. "There are some things that need to be addressed before we can move forward with the next steps of the project."

Daniel felt his throat tighten. "What kind of things?"

Margaret's eyes flicked to the envelope, and she slid it across the counter toward Daniel. He hesitated for a moment before reaching for it, his fingers brushing the edge of the envelope. He opened it slowly, pulling out several sheets of paper. As he scanned the contents, his stomach dropped.

The documents were filled with names, dates, and figures—figures that were far too familiar. They were contracts—contracts that had been signed under the table, agreements that were tied to the very heart of the café's expansion. But what stood out most were the names of people he had never agreed to work with—people from Raphael's network, individuals who had been involved in his shady dealings, and some whose connections reached deep into the underbelly of the city's criminal world.

"This is a joke, right?" Daniel asked, his voice rising, his anger bubbling just beneath the surface. "You've been keeping these deals from me?"

Margaret didn't flinch. She didn't even look apologetic. "These are the people who can make your café grow, Daniel," she said, her voice cold. "People with the resources, the influence, the ability to elevate this place to a level you can't even imagine. You've been so focused on your 'clean slate,' but you can't grow without compromise. And compromise requires alliances."

Daniel felt a cold fury rise inside him. He looked up from

The Final Threat

the documents and met Margaret's eyes, his heart racing in his chest. "You've been playing me all along, haven't you? Using me to get to this point. You knew exactly who I was, who I used to be. And now you're bringing in people connected to Raphael? You think I'm going to let you do this?"

Margaret's lips curled into a thin smile, her eyes sharp and calculating. "You're not in a position to make demands, Daniel. You've been given a rare opportunity. Your café could be the crown jewel of this city. But you're too blinded by your moral high ground to see what's right in front of you. There's no place for the naive in this business."

Emily stood up, stepping in between Daniel and Margaret, her voice steady but firm. "No. We didn't fight this hard, we didn't rebuild everything, only to have you destroy it with your shady dealings. This café is ours, and we won't let you turn it into something we never intended."

Margaret's smile faded, and for the first time, Daniel saw a flicker of annoyance in her eyes. "This is bigger than you, Emily. This is about power. About legacy. You think you can operate outside of the system, but the system will always catch up with you. You're both out of your depth."

Daniel's heart raced as he felt the weight of her words. Margaret wasn't just offering help. She was trying to take control of everything they had built, to turn the café into something it was never meant to be. And she wasn't going to stop.

Margaret stood up, her eyes never leaving Daniel. "You've been warned. The foundation has its interests, and if you want to keep going, you'll play by their rules. If you don't…" She didn't finish her sentence. Instead, she turned and walked toward the door, her heels clicking against the floor.

As the door swung closed behind her, Daniel stood frozen, his fists clenched. The documents lay in front of him like a weight he couldn't lift. Emily placed a hand on his arm, her voice soft but full of resolve. "We can't let her do this. We've worked too hard."

Daniel turned to face her, his eyes filled with determination. "No, we can't. But this isn't just about the café anymore. This is about stopping her—stopping everything Raphael set in motion. We have to fight back."

The storm that had been brewing in Daniel's chest was now a raging tempest. Margaret had thrown down the gauntlet, and it was clear that this wasn't just a business deal—it was a final play for control. But Daniel knew one thing: He wouldn't back down. Not now. Not when everything they had fought for was on the line.

"Let's finish this," Daniel said, his voice resolute. "We're not going to let her destroy everything we've built. This ends now."

And with that, the battle for the future of the café, for the future of their lives, had begun.

Sixty-Five

A Test of Faith

The morning fog clung to the streets like a heavy, suffocating blanket, dimming the city's usual buzz as Daniel stood outside the café, his hands shoved deep into the pockets of his jacket. The weight of everything that had transpired over the past few weeks pressed down on him, suffocating in its intensity. Margaret's visit yesterday had confirmed all of his suspicions—she hadn't been here to help; she had been here to take control. To manipulate him into doing things he wasn't ready for, things that threatened to undo everything he had fought so hard to build. The café was more than a business to him now. It was a lifeline, a place of healing, of redemption, and he would be damned if he allowed someone like Margaret to corrupt it.

But the truth was, Daniel didn't know where to turn. He

couldn't fight Margaret and her foundation alone. The resources at her disposal were too vast, too overwhelming. He had spent so many years running from his past, running from the legacy that had been forced on him, and now, it felt like his past had found a way back to haunt him, threatening to undo everything he had rebuilt.

He took a deep breath, inhaling the cold, crisp air, trying to steady his racing heart. The fog began to lift, the faint light of the morning sun breaking through the haze, but the unease gnawing at his gut wouldn't fade. Today was going to be different. It had to be. He couldn't keep running from the storm, not when it was barreling down on him.

The sound of footsteps broke his reverie, and Daniel turned to see Emily approaching. Her eyes were filled with that same quiet determination that had been present since the beginning, since their first conversation about the café, about building something that was their own. But today, that look in her eyes felt heavier, more burdened.

"Morning," she said softly, her voice steady but there was a hint of concern in her tone. "I brought coffee. You look like you could use it."

Daniel gave her a tired smile, grateful for the gesture, but the weight of the situation was still heavy on his shoulders. "Thanks," he said, taking the cup from her hand. He took a sip, the warm liquid a small comfort in the cold morning.

"You're still thinking about it, aren't you?" Emily asked, her voice barely above a whisper as she leaned against the café's entrance. "Margaret's offer. What she's asking of you."

Daniel's gaze lingered on the horizon, the cityscape slowly coming into view as the fog began to dissipate. The question hung in the air between them, a silent acknowledgement of the tension that had been building ever since Margaret had laid out her plan for the café. He couldn't deny it; the temptation was there. Margaret's offer had been enticing—resources, connections, a way to elevate the café into something that could change the community in ways they had never imagined. But at what cost? What price was he willing to pay for that kind of success?

"I'm not sure what to do, Emily," Daniel admitted, his voice heavy. "The café… this place means everything to me. It's everything I've fought for. But Margaret's offer, the foundation's backing… it's too much. I don't know if I can trust them. I don't know if I can trust her."

Emily stepped closer, her hand gently resting on his arm, grounding him in the present. "I don't think you have to do this alone," she said, her voice filled with quiet strength. "We've been through so much, Daniel. Together. And we've built something beautiful here. We can keep it that way. You don't have to sell your soul to make this place succeed."

Daniel's heart clenched at her words. He had come so far, but now, at the crossroads of his future, he found himself questioning everything. Could he trust himself to make the right decision? Could he trust anyone? His past had been full of betrayal, manipulation, and lies—things he had spent years trying to escape. And now, here he was again, standing on the edge of something new, unsure of whether the right choice would pull him toward something greater or drag him back into the darkness.

"I don't want to let you down," he murmured, his eyes meeting hers. "I don't want to let anyone down. I promised you, I promised myself, that this café would be different. But I don't know if I'm strong enough to keep it that way. The foundation is powerful. They have resources, connections—everything we need to grow. But it's not just about the money, Emily. It's about what we lose in the process."

Emily's hand tightened around his arm, her touch warm, steady. "We don't have to lose ourselves, Daniel. Not if we stay true to what this place was meant to be. We've always talked about building something for the community—something that gives back, something real. You can't let that vision die just because it's hard. You've fought for this, and I believe in you."

Daniel felt a wave of emotion wash over him. It wasn't just her belief in him—it was the realization that he wasn't alone in this. Emily had been there for him, stood by him, through every dark moment of his life, and she was still standing beside him now. Maybe, just maybe, he didn't have to face this alone. Maybe they could rebuild, not just the café, but everything they had lost along the way.

A Test of Faith

But as much as he wanted to believe it, something in the pit of his stomach told him that the threat was far from over. Margaret was playing a dangerous game, and she wasn't going to stop until she had everything she wanted.

Before Daniel could speak, a shadow fell over them. He turned to see a figure approaching, walking briskly down the street toward the café. The figure was tall, dressed in a dark coat, their face obscured by the brim of a hat. But there was something unmistakable about the way they moved, the air of authority they carried with them. Daniel's stomach dropped as recognition struck him.

It was Hector.

The man who had once been a part of his father's inner circle, the man who had helped shape the Laurent legacy. The man who had been behind so many of the lies, so many of the schemes. Daniel's pulse quickened as the realization sank in. Hector was here. And if he was here, it could only mean one thing: the final move in the game was about to be made.

Emily noticed his shift in posture and turned, following his gaze. She stiffened as she recognized the figure, her hand instinctively reaching for Daniel's.

"What does he want?" Emily asked, her voice low with suspicion.

Daniel didn't answer immediately. He stood frozen, watching Hector approach with slow, deliberate steps. The man's face was impassive, his eyes sharp and calculating. He stopped just in front of them, his gaze flicking from Daniel to Emily, his lips curling into a thin smile.

"I see you've been busy," Hector said, his voice smooth, almost casual. "I must admit, I wasn't sure you'd still be here after all this time. But it seems you've managed to make something of yourself. A café, a community, all on your own. Impressive."

Daniel's chest tightened at Hector's words. He had never trusted the man, never felt safe in his presence. Hector had always been a part of the darker side of the Laurent family, the side that thrived on manipulation, intimidation, and power.

"What do you want, Hector?" Daniel asked, his voice sharp.

Hector chuckled, a low, almost amused sound. "You've been avoiding me, Daniel. You've been avoiding what you know is coming. But you can't hide forever. You've made a lot of noise with this little café of yours, and I'm afraid that's going to draw attention. People in power don't like being ignored. People like Margaret, for example. She's already made her move, and now it's time for you to make yours."

Daniel's mind raced, the pieces of the puzzle starting to fit together in a way he hadn't anticipated. Hector was here to finish what Raphael had started—whether through brute force or manipulation, Daniel didn't know, but one thing was clear: the final threat was upon them.

"Margaret's been using you," Daniel said, his voice low with anger. "You've been pulling the strings behind the scenes. I won't let you take this from me. I won't let you destroy everything we've worked for."

Hector's smile faded, and his eyes turned cold. "You don't have a choice, Daniel. This is bigger than you. Bigger than your little café. You've made the mistake of thinking you can fight against something this powerful. You're just a small player in a much larger game."

Daniel's grip on Emily's hand tightened as his heart raced. This wasn't just a threat to the café—it was a threat to everything he had built, everything he had worked for. The storm was finally here, and this time, he couldn't run from it.

But as Hector's words sank in, something inside Daniel clicked. He had been running his entire life—from his family's legacy, from Raphael, from the shadows that loomed behind him. But now, standing on the edge of everything he had fought for, Daniel knew one thing for certain: he wasn't going to run anymore.

He wasn't going to let Hector, or Margaret, or anyone else tear this down.

"This ends now," Daniel said, his voice firm with resolve. "I've already lost enough. But I won't lose this."

The tension in the air was thick, charged with the weight of the threat that hung over them. And for the first time in a long time, Daniel knew what he had to do. This wasn't just a test of faith in the café. It was a test of faith in himself. He had to trust that everything he had worked for—everything he had rebuilt—was worth fighting for.

And with that, the final battle began.

Sixty-Six

The Letter of Closure

The sky had turned a deep shade of purple by the time Daniel sat in the dimly lit office of the café. The usual hum of activity from the evening rush had died down, leaving behind an eerie silence that wrapped around him like a shroud. His hands rested on the desk before him, fingers curled around a letter he had found earlier that day. The envelope, yellowed with age, was unassuming at first glance, but Daniel knew what it was. He had felt its weight, the burden of the past it carried.

The letter was from his father.

His heart thudded heavily in his chest as he slowly slid his finger along the edge of the envelope, carefully opening it. He had been avoiding this moment for weeks, knowing the inevitable confrontation with his past was looming.

But now, in the quiet of the café, with everything that had transpired with Margaret and Hector still fresh in his mind, he couldn't delay it any longer. The final piece of his father's legacy was in his hands, and there was no more running.

With a deep breath, Daniel pulled out the neatly folded piece of paper inside. He glanced at it for a moment, the familiar handwriting on the page reminding him of a time long gone—of a time when his father had been more than just a name, more than just a shadow haunting his every step. Daniel had always admired his father, had looked up to him for guidance and wisdom. But now, all those memories were tainted. His father had been complicit in the very empire that had torn their lives apart, the empire that had brought pain, betrayal, and darkness into their home.

But this letter… it was his father's final attempt to explain himself, to offer some kind of resolution. It was a letter of closure—if that was even possible.

He unfolded the paper, and as his eyes scanned the words, his pulse quickened. The words were written clearly, each sentence carefully chosen, but there was something heavy in them, a weight that seemed to press down on his chest as he read.

—-

Daniel,

The Letter of Closure

I know that by the time you read this, the world will have changed. The decisions I made, the choices I took, have left us both in a place where redemption may no longer be possible. I am not writing this letter in an attempt to absolve myself of my actions, nor to offer excuses for the path I chose. What I did, I did out of a misguided sense of responsibility, a belief that the legacy of the Laurent family could be preserved—no matter the cost.

The truth is, I failed you. I failed you in more ways than I can count. You were always meant for more than what I gave you. I pushed you toward a future that wasn't your own, a future that was shaped by the weight of power and money, rather than by your heart and your own vision.

But in this moment, as I sit here alone, knowing that time is running out, I see clearly now. The choices I made—those decisions to bind you to this legacy—have only served to destroy everything I hoped to protect. I wanted you to inherit something great, something strong, but all I gave you was a burden, a curse.

I have no right to ask for your forgiveness. I have no right to expect you to understand. But I need you to know this: I did what I thought was best, in the only way I knew how. I thought I could keep you safe, that I could keep our family's name alive without realizing the cost. I thought you would carry the torch without understanding what was inside it. But I was wrong, Daniel. So very wrong.

There's no easy way to say this, but you must understand.

Margaret is the only one who can finish what I started. She has the vision, the means, and the connections that I didn't have. I know you don't trust her. I know you think she's a threat, but if there's any chance of saving the Laurent legacy from total ruin, she's the one who can do it. It was always her. She was always the key. She's the one who will turn the tide, even if it means sacrificing everything.

I'm sorry, Daniel. For everything. For the secrets, the lies, the pain. But in the end, it was never about you or me—it was always about power.

You have a choice now, my son. You can turn away from everything, walk away from the past, and start fresh. Or you can take what's left of this legacy, take what Margaret offers, and rebuild it from the ashes. The decision is yours.

I love you. I always have.

—Your Father

—-

Daniel's hands trembled as he finished reading the letter. The weight of his father's words, the raw emotion behind them, slammed into him like a freight train. His father's confession was a devastating blow. For years, Daniel had carried the burden of their family's history, the shadow of a legacy he had never asked for but had been forced to carry. And now, here was the final piece of that legacy—the truth.

The Letter of Closure

His father had always been a man of ambition, a man who believed that power and control were the only ways to ensure survival. But the truth, the brutal truth, was that all of it had come at the expense of his family, at the expense of Daniel's future. His father's admission—that everything had been done for power—rang through Daniel's mind like a bell tolling in the distance. The man he had once looked up to, the man he had thought he would become, had been consumed by his own greed, his own need to protect something that had long since lost its value.

Daniel sat in silence for a long time, the letter still in his hands. His mind was spinning, the words echoing through him in waves, threatening to drown him. He had spent so many years blaming himself, blaming his father for the distance between them, for the things he had lost. But now, for the first time, Daniel saw the truth for what it was. His father hadn't failed him because of who he was; he had failed him because of the path he had chosen—the path of power, of control, of manipulation. His father had been a prisoner of that world, just as Daniel had been. But now, it was clear: the only way forward was to break free from that world once and for all.

Daniel's heart pounded in his chest as he set the letter down, his mind made up. He could feel the weight of it, the finality of it, the weight of what was at stake. He had to stop Margaret. He had to stop the foundation from taking everything he had worked for, from turning the café into just another piece of the Laurent legacy.

But it wasn't just about the café anymore. It was about everything that had been lost—the trust, the love, the hope. It was about the chance to break free, to build something new, something that wasn't weighed down by the past.

Daniel stood up from the desk, the letter still lying on the surface in front of him. His hands were steady now, the decision clear in his mind. He walked over to the window and looked out at the city, the morning light now fully breaking through the darkness, casting everything in a soft, golden glow. He could see the future unfolding before him, a future where he didn't have to be bound by the legacy of his father, a future where he could finally live for himself.

The letter had given him the closure he needed, but it had also given him something else: a choice.

And as Daniel took one last look at the café, at the community he had worked so hard to build, he knew that this was the moment when everything would change. He would face Margaret, face whatever came next, but he would do it on his terms. He would not allow the past to define him any longer.

It was time to move forward. It was time to reclaim his future.

Sixty-Seven

The Return of an Heir

The heavy rain beat against the windows of the café, its relentless rhythm echoing in the otherwise still room. The soft hum of the kitchen in the back and the occasional clink of cups from the tables did little to distract Daniel from the gnawing feeling deep in his gut. The decision had been made, but it felt as though everything was about to slip from his grasp. He could feel the tension in the air—thick, suffocating, like a storm building in the distance, waiting for the right moment to strike.

The café, once his refuge, now felt like a battleground. A place where he would either win everything or lose it all. The foundation's shadow loomed large, and Margaret's cold gaze was never far from his mind. He had tried to ignore it, to focus on what was good, what they had built together, but something told him that the game wasn't over. Not yet.

Daniel's hand rested on the edge of the counter, his fingers tracing the outline of the worn wood. The door to the café opened, and the familiar jingle of the bell caused him to glance up. He saw Emily enter, her eyes scanning the room before locking onto him. She was alone, her usual calm demeanor replaced by an urgency he hadn't seen before.

"Daniel," she said, her voice tense, laced with concern as she crossed the room toward him. "I just got off the phone with the lawyer. There's been an unexpected development. We need to talk."

Daniel's heart skipped a beat, the unease that had been building in him for days now flaring up into full-blown panic. He stood up straight, trying to steady himself, but the weight of her words already had him reeling.

"Tell me," he said, his voice hoarse, barely able to keep the edge of desperation from creeping in. "What's happened?"

Emily hesitated for a moment, her gaze shifting as though she were weighing how much to say. Finally, she met his eyes, and there was a flicker of something—an acknowledgment of the gravity of the situation.

"It's about your family," she said slowly, carefully. "There's been a claim. A man named Adrian Laurent. He's the son of your father's brother. He's back in the picture."

Daniel felt the blood drain from his face. Adrian Laurent? The name struck him like a slap. Adrian had been a distant relative, one that Daniel hadn't thought about in years—part of the family he had distanced himself from after the fallout with his father. He had heard whispers over the years, stories about Adrian's disappearance and the chaotic circumstances surrounding it. But Daniel had thought he was long gone, lost in the shadows of the Laurent family's twisted legacy.

"Adrian?" Daniel repeated, his mind racing. "What do you mean, he's back?"

Emily leaned in closer, her voice lowering. "He claims to be the rightful heir to the Laurent estate. He says that your father's will was manipulated—that it was never meant for you to inherit the family's holdings. According to him, your father changed his will just before he died, naming him as the sole heir."

Daniel's world tilted on its axis. He had always believed that he was the rightful heir to everything—the legacy of his family, the café, everything that had come before. But now, this new player, this mysterious Adrian, was casting a long shadow over it all.

"This doesn't make sense," Daniel muttered, more to himself than to Emily. "I'm the one who fought for this. I'm the one who rebuilt everything. My father was clear. I was the heir. What does this man want?"

Emily's expression darkened. "He wants everything, Daniel. He's not just looking to reclaim what's his. He wants to take everything from you. The café, the legacy, the power. And he's not going to stop until he has it."

Daniel's chest tightened. The weight of it all was beginning to crush him. The café was his life now, but if Adrian was truly the heir, if his claims were legitimate, everything he had worked for could slip through his fingers like sand. He couldn't lose it. Not now. Not when he had fought so hard to build something real, something free from the past.

"How do we stop him?" Daniel's voice was firm now, the resolve slowly returning to his bones. "I'm not going to let him take it from me."

Emily's face softened, and she placed a hand on his arm. "We need to be smart, Daniel. If Adrian is back, then he's got his own allies, his own network. We can't just rush into this headfirst. We need to find out everything we can about him, about his intentions. And we need to know what his claim really means. Is it legally binding? Is there any way we can prove it's false?"

Daniel nodded, taking in her words, but the unease never left his chest. There was no doubt in his mind that Adrian would stop at nothing to claim what he believed was rightfully his. And if Adrian was as ruthless as Daniel feared, the fight would be far more dangerous than anything he had dealt with before.

As the door to the café opened again, Daniel's gaze snapped to the entrance. His breath caught in his throat. The figure that walked in was tall, with sharp features, a cold gaze, and an air of authority that made the hairs on the back of his neck stand up. It was Adrian Laurent.

The man's eyes scanned the room before locking onto Daniel, and a slow, calculating smile spread across his face.

"Well," Adrian's voice was smooth, almost mocking. "It's been a long time, cousin."

Daniel's heart raced as Adrian slowly approached the counter, each step measured, deliberate. There was no sign of hesitation in his movements, no doubt in his expression. Adrian was here for one thing: to claim what he believed was his. And Daniel knew that whatever had been left in his father's will, it wouldn't be enough to stop this man.

"I'm sure you've heard by now," Adrian continued, his voice low, but carrying. "I'm the heir to the Laurent legacy. My father's death wasn't an accident. It was the end of a chapter, but not the end of the story. And now, it's time to claim what's mine."

Daniel stood still, his mind working quickly. The café had always been his escape, his sanctuary, but now it was being threatened by the very blood running through his veins. He could feel the weight of the Laurent family's history on his shoulders, the legacy that had nearly destroyed him, now staring him in the face.

"You don't know what you're talking about," Daniel said,

his voice steady, though his heart raced in his chest. "You can't just waltz in here and take what you think you're owed. This café, this legacy, this place—it's mine. And I won't let you take it."

Adrian's eyes glinted with amusement as he stepped closer, his voice growing colder. "You think it's yours, Daniel? You've been playing the hero, rebuilding what was broken, but you've always known the truth. Your father made sure of it. The will was clear. I was always meant to take over. You were just a placeholder—a convenient tool to keep things running smoothly until I returned."

The words hit Daniel like a slap, and for a moment, the room seemed to close in around him. He had always believed he was the one who had earned the right to lead the Laurent name, to restore the legacy. But now, Adrian's words made him question everything. Had his father truly left it all to him? Or had it all been part of some twisted plan? Was Daniel just a pawn in his father's game, an afterthought in the bigger picture?

"You're wrong," Daniel said, his voice low, filled with defiance. "You don't get to walk in here and take it all from me. I won't let you."

Adrian's smile faltered for a fraction of a second, but he quickly regained his composure. "We'll see about that. You can fight all you want, Daniel, but in the end, you'll find that there are forces far stronger than you at play. Your little café, your vision—it's nothing compared to what's coming."

The Return of an Heir

As Adrian turned and made his way back toward the door, Daniel's heart pounded in his chest. He was alone. Alone in the face of a powerful legacy, a family's bloodline that he couldn't escape. The storm had arrived, and it wasn't going to pass quietly.

"Emily…" Daniel began, his voice barely a whisper as he turned to face her. "I'm not going to let him win."

She stepped forward, her hand resting gently on his shoulder, her eyes filled with determination. "We're in this together, Daniel. We've always been. And we'll fight this, every step of the way."

And with that, the battle began—not just for the café, but for the future of everything they had worked for. A battle not just against Adrian, but against the darkness of a past that refused to stay buried.

The fight for the Laurent legacy was far from over. And this time, Daniel would make sure it ended on his terms.

Sixty-Eight

A Proposal Under the Stars

The night had fallen gently over the city, the kind of still, quiet night that seemed to stretch endlessly into the horizon. The café was closed for the night, its warm glow now muted, and the streets outside were bathed in the soft, golden light from the streetlamps. Daniel stood at the edge of the rooftop, staring out over the city, his mind swirling with the events of the past few days. The fight for the future of the café, the return of Adrian Laurent, and the relentless pressure from Margaret had left him feeling like he was standing at the edge of a precipice. He was uncertain of what lay ahead, but one thing was clear: the world was changing around him, and he had to decide what role he would play in it.

The city sprawled before him, a maze of streets and buildings, but up here, on the rooftop of the café, it felt like everything was at peace. The gentle breeze ruffled his hair, and the cool night air seemed to carry away some of the heaviness in his chest. It was the kind of evening where the world seemed to slow down, where time stood still just long enough to give you a moment of clarity. He hadn't had a moment like this in a long time, and it was exactly what he needed.

Emily had been with him through it all. Through the rebuilding of the café, the relentless battles with Margaret and Hector, and the overwhelming sense that something more was at stake. She had stood by him, never wavering, and now, standing on this rooftop, he felt a sense of gratitude that was almost overwhelming. She had been his constant, the one person who had never judged him, never turned away, no matter how dark things had gotten.

Daniel glanced over his shoulder and saw her standing in the doorway of the rooftop, her silhouette framed by the soft light from inside. She was watching him with that quiet intensity, her eyes filled with warmth and understanding, but also something else—a curiosity, an expectation. She knew something was coming. He could feel it, the unspoken question between them, the weight of everything that had built up to this moment.

"Hey," she said softly, her voice carrying across the distance. She stepped closer, the heels of her boots clicking against the rooftop as she approached him. "I've been looking for you."

Daniel turned to face her, his heart giving a small, nervous leap as their eyes met. "I needed some time to think," he said, his voice quiet but firm. "Just… needed a moment to breathe."

She smiled, the gentle curve of her lips making the weight of the moment feel a little lighter. "I understand," she said, reaching out to take his hand. "It's been a crazy few weeks. I think we've both been carrying a lot."

Daniel nodded, squeezing her hand gently as they stood there for a moment, the city stretching out beneath them, the hum of life distant but comforting. There was something about being with her that made everything feel right, like the world was falling into place, even if just for a moment.

"I've been thinking about that, too," Daniel said after a beat, his voice soft but filled with an urgency that caught Emily's attention. "About how we've gotten through all of this—everything that's happened, all the twists, all the battles—and how, through it all, you've been by my side. You've been my rock, Emily. My constant."

She tilted her head slightly, her expression tender, but there was a glimmer of something else in her eyes, something that suggested she knew where this was going. "You've been mine too, Daniel," she replied, her voice steady but laced with emotion. "We've been through so much together, and I wouldn't change any of it. I believe in what we've built here. In the café, in our future. In us."

Daniel's heart beat faster as he felt the weight of her words settle into him. This wasn't just about the café. This was about them—about everything they had fought for, everything they had overcome. And as the night stretched out before him, the stars overhead offering a soft, guiding light, Daniel knew that this was the moment. The moment he had been waiting for, the moment that would change everything.

He took a deep breath, the cool night air filling his lungs, and then he let it out slowly. This wasn't easy. It wasn't simple. But it was necessary.

"I can't imagine my life without you, Emily," Daniel said, his voice strong now, clear. "I never thought I'd find someone who understood me the way you do. Someone who sees me, who sees everything I've been through, and still believes in me. Still believes in us."

Emily's eyes softened as she stepped closer, her breath catching in her throat. There was something vulnerable in her gaze, something that mirrored the way Daniel felt in this moment. "Daniel, what are you saying?"

He turned fully to face her, the weight of the question in his chest now palpable. His hand reached into his pocket, fingers brushing against the cool metal of the small box that had been there for weeks, waiting for this very moment. The moment when he would have the courage to ask the question that had been burning in his heart for so long.

"Emily..." he began, his voice cracking slightly as he pulled the box from his pocket and opened it. The soft glint of the diamond ring inside caught the moonlight, its beauty a stark contrast to the heavy emotions that flooded him. "I've been thinking about this, about what's next for us, for the café. I know we've been through so much. And I don't know what the future holds, but I do know this: I want you in it. I want you by my side, every step of the way. I want to build something together, something that's ours. Something that can't be torn apart by the past."

Emily's hand flew to her mouth in surprise, her eyes wide as she looked at him, at the ring, at the sincerity in his eyes. She didn't say anything at first, the words caught in her throat as she stood frozen, the weight of the moment seeming to suspend time itself.

"Emily..." Daniel repeated, his voice full of warmth and certainty now, "Will you marry me?"

There was a long pause, a beat where it felt like the world itself held its breath, waiting for her answer. And then, slowly, Emily reached out, her hand trembling slightly as she took the ring from the box, her fingers brushing against his. Her eyes never left his as she spoke, her voice thick with emotion.

"Yes," she whispered, her voice barely above a breath. "Yes, Daniel. I'll marry you."

The words were a balm to Daniel's soul, the weight he had

been carrying for so long finally lifting. A flood of relief washed over him, but it was more than that. It was joy. It was hope. It was the future he had longed for, the one that had felt so out of reach just weeks ago. The future where he wasn't just fighting for survival, but for something real, something beautiful, something that was worth every sacrifice they had made to get here.

Daniel pulled her into his arms, holding her tightly as the weight of the moment settled in. The stars above seemed to shine a little brighter, the night a little softer as they stood there together, the world stretching out before them.

"I love you," Daniel whispered into her hair, his voice filled with a depth of emotion that he had never known he was capable of.

"I love you too," Emily replied, her voice muffled against his chest. "Always."

And in that moment, under the stars, Daniel knew that everything was possible. The fight, the struggles, the uncertainty—all of it had led to this. To this moment where they could finally take a breath and step forward together. No more fear. No more doubts. They had each other. They had the café. And now, they had a future.

As they stood there, wrapped in each other's arms, the storm that had raged in Daniel's heart for so long began to fade. The future was theirs to shape, to build, to create. And as the city lights flickered below them, a quiet promise settled in the air—a promise that no matter what the world threw their way, they would face it together.

And for the first time in a long time, Daniel knew that the battle for their future was not just about surviving—it was about living. And with Emily by his side, he was ready to live. Ready to build something new. Something that was theirs.

Sixty-Nine

The Wedding Sabotage

The sun was setting, casting a warm golden hue across the horizon as the guests gathered in the open courtyard of the café. It was the day Daniel had been waiting for, the day he would marry Emily—the woman who had stood by him through everything, the woman who had helped him build something new from the ashes of his past. The wedding was to be small, intimate, just a handful of close friends and family, but it was perfect. Everything had been carefully planned, from the simple decorations to the soft music that played in the background. The air was filled with anticipation, with joy, with hope.

But amidst the joy, there was a tension in the air that Daniel couldn't shake. As he stood at the front of the courtyard, waiting for Emily to make her entrance, his thoughts kept drifting back to the threats they had faced. Adrian's return,

Margaret's manipulations, the constant sense of unease that had clung to him like a shadow. He had hoped that this day would mark the end of it all—that with this union, with Emily by his side, they would finally be free of the past. But something deep in his gut told him that today wouldn't be as simple as he hoped. The peace they had worked so hard for had always seemed fragile, and it was that fragility that made his heart race with every passing second.

Emily had gone to change into her wedding dress a short while ago, and he hadn't seen her since. He had been pacing, his mind swirling with thoughts of what they had built, but also what still lingered in the darkness—the past, Adrian, Margaret. Everything he had tried to outrun was still there, lurking, waiting for the right moment to strike.

"Daniel," Emily's voice broke through his thoughts, and he turned to see her walking down the steps from the café, the soft rustle of her dress making his heart leap in his chest. She looked radiant—more beautiful than he had ever imagined. The simple gown she wore was elegant, flattering, and it clung to her form in a way that made her look like something out of a dream. Her hair was loosely pinned back, soft tendrils framing her face, and her eyes were bright with a mixture of love and nervousness.

But it wasn't just her beauty that made Daniel's heart swell. It was the way she looked at him—the way her gaze met his, full of trust, full of faith. She had always believed in him, even when he hadn't believed in himself. And now, as she stood there in front of him, he couldn't help but feel a profound sense of gratitude.

"You look stunning," Daniel said, his voice thick with emotion as he walked toward her, his heart pounding. "I'm the luckiest man alive."

Emily smiled softly, but there was something in her eyes—something that wasn't quite right. A flicker of hesitation, a slight tightness around her eyes. Daniel caught it, but before he could ask, the moment was interrupted by the sound of the door opening.

A figure emerged from the shadows of the café's interior—tall, imposing, his dark suit immaculate. Daniel's blood ran cold. It was Adrian.

"What is he doing here?" Emily muttered under her breath, her hand instinctively reaching for Daniel's. But Adrian was already making his way toward them, his presence commanding the space in a way that sent a chill through the air.

Daniel's eyes narrowed as Adrian stopped just a few feet from them, his lips curled into that same cold, calculating smile. He hadn't been invited, hadn't been welcome, yet here he was, showing up as though he owned the place.

"I see the festivities have started," Adrian said, his voice smooth, his eyes flicking between Daniel and Emily, his gaze lingering a moment too long on Emily. "I trust you haven't forgotten that family should always be included in such important events. Or did you think you could just move on from everything that's been done?"

Daniel stepped forward, putting himself between Adrian and Emily, his posture tense. "This is not your business, Adrian. You weren't invited here. You need to leave."

Adrian chuckled, the sound low and dark, like a snake's hiss. "Ah, but I am part of your business, aren't I? Your father's business. Your legacy. Your future." His gaze shifted, and his eyes narrowed. "But perhaps you're not as interested in that anymore, are you?"

Before Daniel could respond, a strange sound pierced the air—a loud, sudden crash from inside the café. Emily flinched, her body stiffening, and Daniel spun around, his instincts kicking in. He didn't know what had happened, but the sound had been unmistakable—a deliberate noise, a distraction.

Adrian, however, didn't flinch. His smile only deepened as he turned his gaze back to Daniel, as though everything was going according to plan.

"What's happening in there?" Emily asked, her voice trembling.

Daniel hesitated for a second before rushing toward the door of the café, his heart racing. Something was wrong. He could feel it in the pit of his stomach. His eyes locked with Emily's for a moment—her gaze filled with worry and fear—and without another word, he pushed through the door.

Inside, chaos reigned.

The tables had been overturned, chairs scattered across the floor. The soft music that had been playing was abruptly cut off. At the center of the room, a figure stood, a man Daniel recognized instantly—one of Adrian's associates, someone who had been part of the shady dealings surrounding the Laurent family in the past. The man was holding a large, heavy-looking object in his hand, and a quick glance around the room revealed more figures, all of them positioned strategically, their eyes cold and calculating.

"What is this?" Daniel demanded, his voice trembling with a mixture of anger and fear as he stepped forward, his gaze sweeping over the room.

"You didn't think we'd let you have a wedding without a little excitement, did you?" Adrian's voice echoed from the doorway. He had followed Daniel inside, his presence looming behind him like a shadow. "You and Emily seem to think you can just leave the past behind, but the past is never truly gone, Daniel. It always comes back."

The figure in the center of the room lifted the object he was holding, revealing a large detonator, its red button glowing ominously. Daniel's breath caught in his throat. His eyes locked onto the device, then quickly flicked to Emily, who was standing just outside the doorway, frozen in shock.

"You—" Daniel began, his voice shaking, "—you've rigged the café?"

Adrian's lips curled into a smile. "Not the café. Just the back room. The foundation, the legacy—it's all worth more than you can imagine, Daniel. You should've listened to me. You should've taken the deal when you had the chance. Now, it's too late."

Daniel's pulse raced, his mind spinning with the realization of what was happening. He had made the decision to fight back, to resist Adrian's claims, to protect the café. But now, Adrian had taken it to another level. A life-and-death game.

"We can stop this," Daniel said, his voice steady despite the panic threatening to rise in his chest. He could feel Emily's presence at his back, but he didn't dare look away from Adrian and his associate. "We can fix this. There's still time. I won't let you destroy everything."

Adrian's smile widened, his eyes glittering with malice. "You think you can just fix this with your words? Your little café won't survive. Not when the Laurent legacy has been stolen from me. This is the only way."

Daniel's mind raced, the pieces of the puzzle slowly falling into place. The sabotage, the distraction, everything had been carefully orchestrated. But what Adrian didn't know was that Daniel wasn't alone in this fight. He had Emily. And he had a plan.

The Wedding Sabotage

With a quick motion, Daniel reached for his phone in his pocket, his fingers trembling as he sent a message to his team. There was no time to explain everything, but he trusted them. They had prepared for something like this. They had to.

Then, in one swift motion, Daniel lunged toward the man holding the detonator. He had no choice but to act now. The future he had built, the life he was about to begin with Emily, depended on him taking this risk.

The café was about to explode—but not in the way Adrian thought.

Seventy

The Last Obstacle

The air was thick with tension as Daniel surged forward, his heart pounding in his chest. The detonator in the hands of Adrian's associate loomed like a ticking clock, its red button glowing ominously in the dim light of the café. Time was running out, but Daniel wasn't about to let it slip away. Not now, not after everything they had fought for. He had to act quickly, and he had to act decisively.

In a flash, Daniel grabbed the edge of a nearby chair, lifting it off the ground and hurling it across the room. It collided with one of the thugs closest to the detonator, sending him stumbling back in surprise. The room erupted into chaos as the other men scrambled to react, their eyes wide with panic as they realized Daniel wasn't going to back down.

The Last Obstacle

But Daniel wasn't focused on them. His only goal was the man holding the detonator. He had to get to it before Adrian's plan was set into motion. His body moved on pure instinct, the training he had picked up over the years kicking in as he charged forward, dodging the men who tried to block his path.

"Get him!" Adrian barked, his voice cold and commanding, but there was an edge of uncertainty in it now. The tables had turned. Adrian's control was slipping, and Daniel could feel it. He was gaining ground.

With a swift movement, Daniel tackled one of the men in his way, knocking him to the floor. He didn't hesitate. He sprang to his feet and moved toward the detonator, his eyes never leaving it. The associate holding it was still disoriented from the chair's impact, but the moment Daniel got close enough, the man recovered and lunged at him, trying to push him back.

Daniel wasn't going to let him. With a roar, he shoved the man aside, sending him crashing into the counter. For a second, everything was still. The only sound in the room was the rapid beat of Daniel's own heart. His eyes locked onto the red button of the detonator.

But before he could reach it, Adrian stepped forward, blocking his path. The cold smile on Adrian's face sent a chill down Daniel's spine.

"You're too late," Adrian said, his voice dripping with

satisfaction. "You really thought you could escape this legacy? You thought you could outrun what's always been yours? What's always been destined for me? This is bigger than you, Daniel. Bigger than your little café and your new life. This is about power. And you're standing in the way."

Daniel's breath came in short bursts, his mind racing. Every part of him screamed to fight, to keep going. But Adrian's words—his cold, calculated words—stung. They were a reminder of the weight of what Daniel was fighting against. A reminder that the Laurent legacy had never been simple. It had always been about control, about power, and about blood. But Daniel wasn't just fighting for control anymore. He was fighting for Emily. For their future. And he wasn't going to let Adrian take that from him.

Without thinking, Daniel lunged at Adrian, knocking him off balance. The two of them crashed to the floor, the sound of their bodies hitting the ground drowned by the chaos unfolding around them. The men who had been working for Adrian scrambled to intervene, but Daniel's focus was entirely on Adrian, on ending this fight once and for all.

Adrian's grip tightened around Daniel's neck, his face twisted in a mask of fury. "You're not going to win," Adrian hissed, his words barely audible over the pounding in Daniel's ears. "This is my family's legacy. It's always been mine."

Daniel could feel the pressure of Adrian's hands closing in, but he wasn't ready to give up. He couldn't. He had too much to lose.

With every ounce of strength he had left, Daniel shifted his body, breaking free of Adrian's hold. He grabbed a nearby metal object and swung it at Adrian with all his might. The sound of metal hitting flesh echoed in the room as Adrian cried out, his grip loosening for just a moment. That was all Daniel needed.

With one final push, Daniel threw Adrian off him, sending him crashing into the nearby wall. The man crumpled to the ground, his body barely moving. Daniel's heart still hammered in his chest, but the adrenaline was fading. He could feel his hands shaking as he scrambled to his feet, his eyes locked on the detonator that was still within reach.

Before he could reach it, another figure emerged from the shadows—someone Daniel hadn't seen in the chaos, someone who had been waiting for the right moment. It was Margaret.

"Daniel," she called, her voice smooth and mocking, as though she were watching a scene unfold in slow motion. "You've done well. You've made it this far. But you still don't understand. You can't escape this. You can't escape the Laurent legacy. It's in your blood."

Daniel froze, his mind reeling. Margaret had been playing him from the start, hadn't she? She had used him to get what she wanted, manipulating him and his dreams for her own gain. And now, here she was, standing between him and everything he had fought for.

"Margaret," Daniel said, his voice low, the tension in his body palpable. "This is over. You can't have it. You can't control this anymore."

Margaret's lips curled into a smile, but there was no warmth in it. "You think you can just walk away, Daniel? After everything? After all that I've done for you, for your little café? You think I'll just let you ruin everything I've worked for?"

Daniel's pulse quickened, the realization sinking in. He hadn't just been fighting for the café—he had been fighting for his own freedom. Margaret had tried to control him, tried to drag him back into the world of power and legacy that had nearly destroyed him. But now, Daniel knew what he had to do. He had to end it.

"Listen to me," Daniel said, his voice steady now, filled with resolve. "You don't get to dictate this anymore. I'm not your pawn. And I'm not the man I used to be. You're done. This is over."

Margaret's eyes flashed with anger, her lips twisting into a snarl. "You think you can just walk away from all of this? You think you can just take the café and pretend it was all yours? You don't get to have everything, Daniel. Not after what you've done."

Before Daniel could respond, Margaret made a swift move,

The Last Obstacle

her hand reaching for the detonator. Daniel's heart lurched in his chest. She was going to destroy everything. She was going to end it all, right here, right now.

In that instant, Daniel's body acted before his mind could catch up. He lunged at Margaret, knocking her hand away from the device. The two of them tumbled to the floor, the detonator slipping from her grip. Daniel reached for it, his fingers barely grazing the cold metal, but then—

The loud, deafening sound of a door crashing open filled the room. The sound of heavy footsteps followed. It was his team—his allies. They had arrived.

"Get back!" one of them shouted as they rushed into the room, disarming the remaining thugs with precision. In seconds, the chaos in the room began to subside, the tension lifting as Daniel grabbed the detonator and threw it to the side.

Margaret, now surrounded by the men Daniel had trusted, glared at him. "You think this is over, Daniel? You think you've won?" she spat. "You've only just begun to understand what you've set in motion. You can't stop this. It's too big."

Daniel stood over her, his chest rising and falling with the intensity of the moment. His team had the situation under control, and Margaret was now disarmed, her control slipping away.

"Maybe it's too big for you," Daniel said, his voice low and resolute. "But it's not too big for me. Not anymore. I'm done running from my past. And I'm done letting people like you tear down everything I've worked for."

Margaret said nothing in response, her eyes burning with fury, but Daniel knew one thing: the battle was finally over. She had lost.

With the room now quiet, Daniel looked around at the destruction—the overturned chairs, the broken glass, the tension that had filled the space just moments before. But now, it was just noise. The storm had passed.

He turned to Emily, who had entered the room just in time to see everything fall apart. Their eyes met, and for the first time in what felt like forever, Daniel allowed himself to relax. She was safe. He was safe. And everything they had worked for, everything they had fought for, was still standing.

"We did it," Daniel whispered, his voice thick with relief.

Emily nodded, her eyes soft. "We did it, Daniel."

As the last of Adrian's men were led out of the café, and the police arrived to take Margaret away, Daniel felt a wave of exhaustion wash over him. But beneath it all, there was something else—a sense of peace. The final obstacle had been removed. And now, they could finally begin their future together.

The Last Obstacle

And this time, it was theirs.

Seventy-One

Chapter 71

Chapter 71: The Last Obstacle

The air was thick with tension as Daniel surged forward, his heart pounding in his chest. The detonator in the hands of Adrian's associate loomed like a ticking clock, its red button glowing ominously in the dim light of the café. Time was running out, but Daniel wasn't about to let it slip away. Not now, not after everything they had fought for. He had to act quickly, and he had to act decisively.

In a flash, Daniel grabbed the edge of a nearby chair, lifting it off the ground and hurling it across the room. It collided with one of the thugs closest to the detonator, sending him stumbling back in surprise. The room erupted into chaos as the other men scrambled to react, their eyes wide with

Chapter 71

panic as they realized Daniel wasn't going to back down.

But Daniel wasn't focused on them. His only goal was the man holding the detonator. He had to get to it before Adrian's plan was set into motion. His body moved on pure instinct, the training he had picked up over the years kicking in as he charged forward, dodging the men who tried to block his path.

"Get him!" Adrian barked, his voice cold and commanding, but there was an edge of uncertainty in it now. The tables had turned. Adrian's control was slipping, and Daniel could feel it. He was gaining ground.

With a swift movement, Daniel tackled one of the men in his way, knocking him to the floor. He didn't hesitate. He sprang to his feet and moved toward the detonator, his eyes never leaving it. The associate holding it was still disoriented from the chair's impact, but the moment Daniel got close enough, the man recovered and lunged at him, trying to push him back.

Daniel wasn't going to let him. With a roar, he shoved the man aside, sending him crashing into the counter. For a second, everything was still. The only sound in the room was the rapid beat of Daniel's own heart. His eyes locked onto the red button of the detonator.

But before he could reach it, Adrian stepped forward, blocking his path. The cold smile on Adrian's face sent a chill down Daniel's spine.

"You're too late," Adrian said, his voice dripping with satisfaction. "You really thought you could escape this legacy? You thought you could outrun what's always been yours? What's always been destined for me? This is bigger than you, Daniel. Bigger than your little café and your new life. This is about power. And you're standing in the way."

Daniel's breath came in short bursts, his mind racing. Every part of him screamed to fight, to keep going. But Adrian's words—his cold, calculated words—stung. They were a reminder of the weight of what Daniel was fighting against. A reminder that the Laurent legacy had never been simple. It had always been about control, about power, and about blood. But Daniel wasn't just fighting for control anymore. He was fighting for Emily. For their future. And he wasn't going to let Adrian take that from him.

Without thinking, Daniel lunged at Adrian, knocking him off balance. The two of them crashed to the floor, the sound of their bodies hitting the ground drowned by the chaos unfolding around them. The men who had been working for Adrian scrambled to intervene, but Daniel's focus was entirely on Adrian, on ending this fight once and for all.

Adrian's grip tightened around Daniel's neck, his face twisted in a mask of fury. "You're not going to win," Adrian hissed, his words barely audible over the pounding in Daniel's ears. "This is my family's legacy. It's always been mine."

Daniel could feel the pressure of Adrian's hands closing in,

Chapter 71

but he wasn't ready to give up. He couldn't. He had too much to lose.

With every ounce of strength he had left, Daniel shifted his body, breaking free of Adrian's hold. He grabbed a nearby metal object and swung it at Adrian with all his might. The sound of metal hitting flesh echoed in the room as Adrian cried out, his grip loosening for just a moment. That was all Daniel needed.

With one final push, Daniel threw Adrian off him, sending him crashing into the nearby wall. The man crumpled to the ground, his body barely moving. Daniel's heart still hammered in his chest, but the adrenaline was fading. He could feel his hands shaking as he scrambled to his feet, his eyes locked on the detonator that was still within reach.

Before he could reach it, another figure emerged from the shadows—someone Daniel hadn't seen in the chaos, someone who had been waiting for the right moment. It was Margaret.

"Daniel," she called, her voice smooth and mocking, as though she were watching a scene unfold in slow motion. "You've done well. You've made it this far. But you still don't understand. You can't escape this. You can't escape the Laurent legacy. It's in your blood."

Daniel froze, his mind reeling. Margaret had been playing him from the start, hadn't she? She had used him to get what she wanted, manipulating him and his dreams for her own gain. And now, here she was, standing between him and everything he had fought for.

"Margaret," Daniel said, his voice low, the tension in his body palpable. "This is over. You can't have it. You can't control this anymore."

Margaret's lips curled into a smile, but there was no warmth in it. "You think you can just walk away, Daniel? After everything? After all that I've done for you, for your little café? You think I'll just let you ruin everything I've worked for?"

Daniel's pulse quickened, the realization sinking in. He hadn't just been fighting for the café—he had been fighting for his own freedom. Margaret had tried to control him, tried to drag him back into the world of power and legacy that had nearly destroyed him. But now, Daniel knew what he had to do. He had to end it.

"Listen to me," Daniel said, his voice steady now, filled with resolve. "You don't get to dictate this anymore. I'm not your pawn. And I'm not the man I used to be. You're done. This is over."

Margaret's eyes flashed with anger, her lips twisting into a snarl. "You think you can just walk away from all of this? You think you can just take the café and pretend it was all yours? You don't get to have everything, Daniel. Not after what you've done."

Chapter 71

Before Daniel could respond, Margaret made a swift move, her hand reaching for the detonator. Daniel's heart lurched in his chest. She was going to destroy everything. She was going to end it all, right here, right now.

In that instant, Daniel's body acted before his mind could catch up. He lunged at Margaret, knocking her hand away from the device. The two of them tumbled to the floor, the detonator slipping from her grip. Daniel reached for it, his fingers barely grazing the cold metal, but then—

The loud, deafening sound of a door crashing open filled the room. The sound of heavy footsteps followed. It was his team—his allies. They had arrived.

"Get back!" one of them shouted as they rushed into the room, disarming the remaining thugs with precision. In seconds, the chaos in the room began to subside, the tension lifting as Daniel grabbed the detonator and threw it to the side.

Margaret, now surrounded by the men Daniel had trusted, glared at him. "You think this is over, Daniel? You think you've won?" she spat. "You've only just begun to understand what you've set in motion. You can't stop this. It's too big."

Daniel stood over her, his chest rising and falling with the intensity of the moment. His team had the situation under control, and Margaret was now disarmed, her control slipping away.

"Maybe it's too big for you," Daniel said, his voice low and resolute. "But it's not too big for me. Not anymore. I'm done running from my past. And I'm done letting people like you tear down everything I've worked for."

Margaret said nothing in response, her eyes burning with fury, but Daniel knew one thing: the battle was finally over. She had lost.

With the room now quiet, Daniel looked around at the destruction—the overturned chairs, the broken glass, the tension that had filled the space just moments before. But now, it was just noise. The storm had passed.

He turned to Emily, who had entered the room just in time to see everything fall apart. Their eyes met, and for the first time in what felt like forever, Daniel allowed himself to relax. She was safe. He was safe. And everything they had worked for, everything they had fought for, was still standing.

"We did it," Daniel whispered, his voice thick with relief.

Emily nodded, her eyes soft. "We did it, Daniel."

As the last of Adrian's men were led out of the café, and the police arrived to take Margaret away, Daniel felt a wave of exhaustion wash over him. But beneath it all, there was something else—a sense of peace. The final obstacle had been removed. And now, they could finally begin their future together.

Chapter 71

And this time, it was theirs.

Seventy-Two

Chapter 72

Chapter 72: A New Family

The sun had barely begun to rise, casting long shadows across the empty streets as Daniel stood on the balcony of the café, the cool morning air biting at his skin. The storm of the past few weeks—the chaos, the threats, the betrayal—had passed, and yet the silence that followed felt almost deafening. It was a calm unlike anything he had known before, a stillness that seemed to settle deep within him, allowing him to breathe for the first time in what felt like ages.

The café had reopened just a day ago, but even as the lights flickered on and the first of the morning customers trickled in, Daniel could still feel the weight of everything that had happened. He had spent so much time running from the

Chapter 72

past, so much time protecting himself from the world that had always felt like a cage, that he had never stopped to really see what he was building. But now, as the early morning light bathed the café's wooden floors and reflected off the glass tables, he realized it wasn't just a business. It wasn't just a place of refuge for himself or Emily. It was home.

The soft sound of footsteps behind him broke his reverie, and Daniel turned to find Emily approaching, her smile faint but genuine, as if she, too, was trying to absorb the calm that surrounded them. Her hair was pulled back loosely, strands framing her face, and she was dressed casually, in the way she always did on early mornings when she came to help open up the café. There was a look of quiet contentment on her face that told him she, too, had finally accepted the reality of what they had built.

"I didn't expect to find you out here so early," Emily said, her voice filled with warmth. She leaned against the doorframe, her arms folded across her chest. "You're usually the last to wake up these days."

Daniel chuckled softly, the sound still carrying a note of tension, of exhaustion, but also relief. "I couldn't sleep. I was thinking... about everything. About what we've been through, what we've lost and what we've gained. It's hard to believe it's really over."

Emily stepped outside, standing beside him, her gaze following his as it drifted over the city below them. The view from the café was one of the best in the city, perched high on the rooftop where the morning sun painted the world in shades of amber. For a brief moment, the weight of it all—of their struggles, their victories—seemed to dissipate into the calm of the morning.

"We made it," Emily said softly, her voice almost a whisper. "And we did it together. Everything we've been through, every obstacle, it's all led us here. To this moment. To this place."

Daniel turned to face her, his gaze searching her face for some sign of doubt, some crack in the façade she had so carefully constructed in the midst of the storm. But there was none. She was here, with him, and for the first time in a long time, he could feel the steadiness of her presence—her belief in them, in what they had built.

"You're right," Daniel said, his voice low, filled with a depth of emotion that he hadn't been able to express until now. "We've come so far. And I couldn't have done any of this without you."

Emily smiled, her eyes softening. "And you wouldn't have needed to," she said, stepping closer to him, "because we've always been in this together. Every step, every decision. We made this café what it is. It's ours."

The weight of her words settled over him, filling the quiet space between them with meaning. It wasn't just a café they had built—it was a family. And that realization struck

Chapter 72

him with the same intensity as the events of the past few weeks. Through everything—the betrayals, the threats, the uncertainty—there was one constant: Emily.

Daniel's heart skipped a beat as he watched her, his emotions swirling within him. There had been so much loss in his life. So much pain. And yet, here she was, standing beside him, offering something he had never known he needed. A future. A family. A life that was his—one that was real, that couldn't be taken from him. Not by Margaret. Not by Adrian.

He reached for her hand, his fingers brushing against hers in the quiet of the morning. She didn't pull away; instead, she grasped it, her touch steady and warm. For a moment, they just stood there, hand in hand, looking out over the world they had carved out for themselves. The noise of the city was distant now, drowned out by the peace that surrounded them. It felt as though everything was in its right place for the first time in years.

"I was thinking about the future," Daniel said, his voice steady now, filled with the kind of certainty that had eluded him for so long. "About what we want. What we want to build. And I realized something." He paused, looking into her eyes, searching for the right words. "I want it all. I want to build a future with you, Emily. I want to share everything with you. And I want us to create a family—a real family. One that's ours, from the ground up."

Emily's eyes widened slightly, and Daniel could see the

surprise and emotion flicker across her face before she quickly masked it with a smile. She stepped closer to him, her breath steady and even, her hand still firmly holding his.

"I want that too, Daniel," she whispered. "I want us to build something lasting. Something that lasts beyond this café. Something that's rooted in love, trust, and the future we can create together."

Daniel felt the weight of her words in his chest, and for a moment, it was as if the world had paused, leaving just the two of them on the rooftop, standing together in the quiet morning light. The uncertainty of the past had melted away, replaced by a vision of what could be.

Before he could respond, the sound of the door creaking open behind them startled both of them, and they turned to see a familiar figure stepping out onto the rooftop—Sophie, one of the café's long-time employees and close friend. Her smile was wide, and her eyes sparkled with excitement.

"Morning!" Sophie called, her voice cheerful, and she waved at both of them. "You two better hurry up! The ceremony's starting soon. Everyone's already here, and I'm not sure how much longer the guests are going to wait."

Daniel and Emily exchanged a brief glance, both of them smiling. It had taken some time to get here, to the day of their wedding, but now that it was finally happening, there was a sense of joy in the air—joy that had been missing for

Chapter 72

far too long.

"You're right," Daniel said with a grin, his hand still holding Emily's. "We should get inside. But first—"

Before Sophie could ask what was going on, Daniel turned back to Emily, his expression softening. He stepped close to her, his hands gently cupping her face, his thumb brushing the side of her cheek.

"Emily," he said, his voice low and earnest. "There's something I need to ask you."

Her brow furrowed in confusion, and she opened her mouth to ask him what was going on, but Daniel gently placed his finger against her lips.

"Before we go in there," he continued, "I want to ask you one last thing. Will you be the mother of our children? Will you create this family with me?"

Emily blinked, clearly surprised, her eyes wide with emotion. She took a step back, her fingers tracing his jawline, as though trying to make sense of what he had just said. The room was still for a moment, and then, a slow, soft smile spread across her face.

"Yes," she whispered, her voice thick with emotion. "Yes, Daniel. I will. I will create this family with you."

And in that moment, everything clicked into place. Everything that had brought them here, everything they had fought for, every moment of fear and doubt—all of it faded into the background. There was only the two of them, together, standing on the edge of something new, something beautiful.

The storm had passed, and the sun was shining.

As they turned toward the door, Sophie's voice rang out behind them. "You two lovebirds coming or what? Everyone's waiting!"

Daniel laughed, pulling Emily with him toward the door, the weight of the past finally slipping away. They walked hand-in-hand, the promise of a new family—a real family—stretching out before them, ready to be built from the ground up, starting now.

And as they stepped inside, ready to begin the next chapter of their lives, Daniel knew that this was just the beginning of something extraordinary. Something that would last. Something that couldn't be torn apart by the past, by legacy, or by anyone else.

Together, they were ready to build their future. And nothing would stand in their way.

Seventy-Three

Chapter 73

Chapter 73: Reclaiming the Legacy

The sun hung low in the sky, casting a warm orange glow over the city. It was early evening, and the streets buzzed with the usual life, but inside the café, there was an unfamiliar stillness. It wasn't quiet—no, the café had never been quiet, not with the soft hum of conversations and the clink of cups and plates—but the stillness was there, in the air, like a momentary pause before a storm. The kind of pause that came just before everything changed.

Daniel sat at the counter, his hands wrapped around a cup of coffee he hadn't taken a sip of. His eyes were fixed on the door, waiting for something—or someone. His mind raced with a thousand thoughts, each one more pressing than the last. They had fought for this. The café, the life he and Emily had built, the future they were starting to carve together—it was all on the line. And tonight, they were going to face the final piece of the puzzle. The one thing that had haunted Daniel for years: the Laurent legacy.

The past few days had been a whirlwind. The wedding, the promises of a new future, and then… everything that had come after. Adrian's return, the sabotage, Margaret's manipulations. But now, everything was coming to a head. Adrian was back, and with him, the legacy he believed was his by birthright. Margaret had played her hand, but Daniel had seen through it. It was time to reclaim what was his— not just the café, but the entire legacy. This wasn't just about bloodlines; it was about control, about ownership, about defining the future on his own terms.

Daniel glanced up as the door opened, a bell chiming softly, and he saw Emily step inside. She was a vision in a simple black dress, her eyes as determined as ever, but there was a quiet tension in her expression. The past few days had been as hard on her as they had been on him, but here they were, standing on the brink of everything they had ever wanted. Emily had been his anchor through all of this, her presence a steady reminder that no matter what happened, they would face it together.

"Ready?" Emily asked, her voice steady, though there was an edge to it that told Daniel she was just as anxious as he was.

Chapter 73

Daniel nodded, his heart racing. "Ready as I'll ever be."

Together, they walked toward the back of the café, where the small office had been transformed into a war room of sorts. Papers, legal documents, and files were scattered across the desk, some of them marked with the familiar insignia of the Laurent estate. Daniel had spent the better part of the day going through them, connecting the dots, figuring out what had been left behind in his father's wake. But what he had discovered, what he was about to confront, was far more than just legal papers. It was the key to everything: the final document, the one that would cement his place in the Laurent legacy and break Adrian's hold on it once and for all.

The door to the office creaked open, and standing in the doorway was Hector. The man who had been both an ally and an enemy, who had been lurking in the shadows of the Laurent empire for years, now found himself at the crossroads of the family's fate. Daniel's eyes narrowed as he stepped into the room, his posture tense, but Hector's expression was unreadable.

"I assume you're here for the same thing," Daniel said, his voice steady but laced with an edge of suspicion. He hadn't trusted Hector for years, and even though they had worked together to expose Adrian's true intentions, Daniel knew better than to let his guard down.

Hector's lips curled into a tight smile, but there was something dark behind it, something Daniel couldn't quite place.

"I'm here for what's mine," Hector replied, his voice smooth, his gaze never leaving Daniel's. "And I'm sure we both know what that is."

Emily's hand subtly gripped Daniel's arm, a silent reminder that they were in this together. She didn't trust Hector either, but she was a fighter, just like him, and there was no way she was going to let anyone take what they had built. Together, they had fought too hard for this.

"Let's get this over with," Daniel muttered, turning his attention to the stack of papers on the desk. He was looking for one thing, one document that would settle everything—the will, the final testament of his father, the one that would prove once and for all that the Laurent legacy was his.

The tension in the room thickened as Daniel flipped through the pages. It wasn't the first time he had seen his father's will, but he had never had the full picture, never seen everything his father had left behind. Now, as his fingers skimmed the document, his eyes widened with realization. There, in the fine print, was the one thing he had been searching for. His father had left a provision that ensured the Laurent empire would pass to him—under one condition: he had to prove himself by reclaiming the legacy. And that meant confronting Adrian.

Daniel's heart raced as he read the words aloud, his voice cold and steady. "'The rightful heir to the Laurent legacy will be determined not by birthright, but by strength, by vision, and by the ability to shape the future of this empire.

Chapter 73

The one who can prove their worth will take control. And this legacy will pass to them.'"

Emily's breath caught in her throat as she turned to look at Daniel, her eyes wide with understanding. "So it's true. Your father wasn't leaving it to Adrian by default. He left it to you, on your terms. You just have to prove you can take it."

Daniel's mind was already racing, connecting the dots. The legacy wasn't about who was born into the Laurent name—it was about what they could make of it. And now, Daniel knew what he had to do. This wasn't just about reclaiming a name. It was about proving he could do more with it than anyone else ever had. He could reshape the future, build a legacy that wasn't defined by power and manipulation, but by hard work, integrity, and the belief that things could be different.

"I'll show them," Daniel said, his voice low and filled with resolve. "I'll show Adrian. I'll show Margaret. I'll show them all what this legacy can truly be. And I won't let anyone stop me."

Suddenly, the door to the office slammed open with force, and Adrian strode into the room, his presence like a dark cloud descending. He was flanked by a few of his remaining allies, their eyes cold and calculating, but Adrian's gaze was locked on Daniel, his smirk never wavering.

"I see you've found what you were looking for," Adrian

said, his voice smooth and condescending. "But it's too late. The empire was never meant to be yours, Daniel. My father's will made that clear. And now, it's time to take what's rightfully mine."

Daniel stepped forward, his hand clenching into a fist. "It's not your empire, Adrian. It was never yours to begin with. And this family, this legacy—it's not something you can control with threats and intimidation. I'm going to prove it."

Adrian's eyes flicked to the papers on the desk, then back to Daniel, his lips curling into a smile. "You think you can beat me at my own game? You think you can step into the world I've spent years building and just take it from me? You're a fool, Daniel."

Daniel's voice dropped to a dangerous whisper. "Maybe I'm a fool. But at least I'm not the one hiding behind lies and manipulation. This isn't just about power, Adrian. It's about doing what's right. Something you'll never understand."

Adrian's smirk faltered, his eyes darkening as his jaw clenched. "You're making a mistake," he said, his voice laced with venom. "And when you fail, you'll see just how much of a mistake you've made."

The tension between them was palpable, crackling in the air like an impending storm. But Daniel wasn't afraid. He wasn't intimidated by Adrian's threats or his cold words. He had come too far, had fought too hard, to let anyone

Chapter 73

take this from him now.

"I've already won," Daniel said, his voice firm, unwavering. "And I'm going to take what's mine. You're done."

As Adrian's face twisted with anger, his allies shifting nervously behind him, Daniel knew the moment had arrived. This was the moment he had been waiting for—the moment he would reclaim the legacy that had been his all along. Not by birthright, not by force, but by his own strength, his own vision.

And as Adrian turned to leave, his footsteps heavy and defeated, Daniel knew this battle was over. The legacy was his. And this time, he was going to build something that would last. Something better. Something that couldn't be taken from him.

Seventy-Four

Chapter 74

Chapter 74: Emily's Triumph

The café was nearly empty now, the last of the evening crowd slowly filtering out as the sun set beyond the horizon. The warm orange glow of twilight seeped through the windows, casting long shadows across the floor. The air was still and quiet, save for the soft hum of the lights overhead. For the first time in what felt like months, Emily could breathe without the heavy weight of impending danger pressing down on her. Tonight was different.

She walked through the café, her footsteps echoing against the wooden floors. The place she and Daniel had built from the ground up now felt more like home than ever. It wasn't just the physical space—the décor, the coffee, the food—

Chapter 74

it was the atmosphere they had created here, the sense of belonging, the spirit of resilience that had become the café's lifeblood. And that was something neither Margaret nor Adrian, nor anyone else, could take from them.

Tonight had been a victory. A hard-fought victory. Adrian had been driven out. The documents that proved Daniel's rightful place in the Laurent legacy had been signed. The café was safe. They were safe. Emily had stood by Daniel through everything—the betrayal, the manipulations, the impossible odds—and now, at last, they had emerged victorious.

But even as she walked through the café, a small part of her couldn't shake the lingering tension. A part of her was still waiting for the other shoe to drop. For the next twist in the story, the next person to threaten everything they had worked so hard to build. It was in her nature to prepare for the worst. But tonight… tonight, she was trying to allow herself to truly enjoy the peace they had fought for.

She stepped into the back room, the space where Daniel was already waiting for her, standing by the desk, his face lit by the soft glow of the desk lamp. His silhouette was framed by the faint light filtering in through the windows. There was a calmness in the way he stood, a certain quiet satisfaction in the air. But Emily knew, as always, that beneath the calm exterior, Daniel was still processing everything—the fight, the victory, the unexpected turns in the road that had brought them here.

"I thought I'd find you here," Emily said, leaning against the doorframe and crossing her arms over her chest. Her voice was soft, but it carried the weight of everything she had been holding inside for weeks.

Daniel turned to face her, his eyes meeting hers with a flicker of something that softened the hardness of his features. His face was tired, but there was a quiet pride there, too—pride not just in the victory they had achieved, but in the woman who had stood beside him through it all.

"Didn't want to keep you waiting," he said, his voice light, but there was an edge of something deeper—something that suggested more had been going on in his mind than he was letting on.

Emily pushed herself off the doorframe and walked toward him. She stood for a moment, just looking at him, her gaze searching, trying to read him in the way she always did. They had been through so much together, and she knew him better than anyone else. The weight of the past few months—everything they had fought for, everything they had lost—was still there, but there was something else in his eyes tonight. Something that told her he was finally beginning to let go of the past.

"I'm glad it's over," Emily said softly, her voice barely above a whisper. "All the fighting. The uncertainty. We've come so far, Daniel. We've won."

Daniel gave a small nod, but his gaze didn't leave hers.

Chapter 74

There was something unspoken in the air between them—something that had been brewing for weeks, maybe even months. Something that had built itself slowly, quietly, as they had fought together, side by side, to reclaim their lives, their future. And tonight, it felt like everything was coming to a head.

"I couldn't have done any of it without you," Daniel said, his voice rough with emotion. "You've been the one constant through everything. When I couldn't see a way out, when I was drowning in the mess of my own past, you were there. You've believed in me even when I couldn't believe in myself."

Emily felt a lump form in her throat, her heart swelling with emotion as Daniel's words washed over her. She had always known he was capable of so much more than he believed. But to hear him say it—hear him acknowledge everything she had done, everything they had fought for—it made her feel like all of the pain, the uncertainty, the sleepless nights, had been worth it.

"I believe in us," Emily replied, her voice steady but thick with emotion. She reached out, gently cupping his face in her hands, feeling the roughness of his skin, the warmth of his breath. "I always have."

Daniel closed his eyes for a moment, leaning into her touch, and when he opened them again, there was something different in his gaze. Something vulnerable, something real, that hadn't been there before. The weight of the past—

of his father's legacy, of the battles they had fought—seemed to lift from him. And in that moment, Emily understood that it wasn't just the café that they had built. They had built something more—a future together, a partnership that was unshakeable.

"I want to thank you, Emily," Daniel said, his voice quiet but filled with sincerity. "You've done more for me than anyone could ever understand. And I want you to know that I will spend the rest of my life proving that. I don't know what the future holds, but I know that with you, I can face anything."

Her heart skipped a beat as she felt the intensity in his words. It wasn't just a declaration of love—it was a promise. A promise that, no matter what came next, they would face it together.

"And I'll be right there with you," Emily said softly, her voice full of quiet strength. "Through whatever comes. We've made it this far, and we'll keep going. Together."

For a moment, they simply stood there, the world outside fading into the background as they were lost in the quiet connection between them. The weight of everything that had come before had finally lifted, replaced by something stronger, something more enduring. They had fought the battles, faced the darkness, and now they were ready to step into the future, hand in hand.

But just as the silence between them felt as though it was

Chapter 74

about to settle into something peaceful, the door to the back room creaked open, and Sophie stepped in, her eyes wide with excitement. She was carrying a small envelope, one of the many they had been sorting through in the office earlier. Her face was lit with a look of anticipation, and she didn't even wait for Daniel or Emily to speak before she thrust the envelope into their hands.

"This just came for you," Sophie said, breathless. "It's from the lawyer's office. They said it's urgent."

Daniel exchanged a look with Emily, his brows furrowing slightly as he tore open the envelope. The contents were few—just a single sheet of paper, its edges crisp and white, stamped with the official seal of the Laurent estate.

As he read through the document, his grip tightened, and a quiet gasp escaped his lips. Emily's heart skipped a beat as she leaned in closer, her gaze fixing on the page as Daniel's voice broke the silence.

"Emily..." Daniel's voice was thick with disbelief, his eyes wide. "It's... it's a final settlement. Everything's been cleared up. The legacy—it's officially ours. The café. Everything."

Emily blinked, not fully understanding what she was reading at first. But as the words settled into her mind, a rush of emotions swept over her. This was it. This was the final confirmation that they had won. They were free of the legacy that had haunted Daniel for so long. The future they had fought for was finally within their grasp.

"I can't believe it," Emily whispered, her voice thick with emotion. "It's really ours. We did it."

Daniel wrapped his arm around her, pulling her close, as if he needed the physical reminder that this moment was real. That all of their sacrifices had led to this.

"We did it," he repeated, his voice filled with wonder. "Together."

Sophie stood at the door, her eyes soft with admiration for the two of them. "I'm so happy for you both," she said quietly, her voice full of sincerity. "You've been through so much, and you deserve this. All of it."

Emily smiled, her heart full, but her gaze remained fixed on Daniel. This was their moment. The culmination of everything they had worked for, everything they had built. They had fought the odds, faced the shadows of their past, and emerged victorious.

Tonight, the café was not just a business. It was their home. Their future. A legacy of their own.

And as Daniel held her close, Emily knew that this was just the beginning. Together, they would reclaim everything that was theirs, build a future on their own terms, and create the family they had always dreamed of.

The night was theirs. And with each step they took forward, the world outside seemed to bend to their will. It was their

Chapter 74

time now.

Seventy-Five

Chapter 75

Chapter 75: The Final Farewell

The café stood quietly in the early morning light, its windows still fogged from the night before, reflecting the first rays of dawn. It was a time of transition. The world outside was just beginning to stir, and yet, inside the walls of the small business Daniel and Emily had fought so hard to protect, there was a heavy, suffocating silence. It wasn't just the end of the night shift, nor the usual quiet that enveloped the space when the day was still young—it was something deeper. Something permanent.

Today marked the end of the chapter. The last obstacle was gone. Adrian had been swept away, Margaret had been neutralized, and the final legal papers had been signed. The Laurent legacy was no longer a weight, but a stepping stone

Chapter 75

to something new, something better. Yet, as Daniel stood at the counter, gazing out into the world that had once seemed so daunting and now appeared strangely calm, there was a palpable emptiness in his chest. His fingers gripped the edge of the counter as he stared at the empty chairs, the stillness surrounding him an unexpected feeling of loss.

Everything was set to change. Everything had already changed. It was time for him to move forward, but the past still lingered, heavy in the air. The ghosts of what had been—the legacy, the family, the promises broken—remained, and despite the victories they had fought for, Daniel could feel the weight of it all.

"Daniel?"

The soft sound of Emily's voice snapped him out of his thoughts, and he turned to see her standing at the entrance of the back room, her eyes searching his face, concern etched in her expression. She was dressed simply, her hair loose around her shoulders, but the look in her eyes told him she knew something was off. Emily always knew when something wasn't quite right.

"You okay?" she asked, taking a few slow steps toward him, her hand reaching out to touch his arm gently. The warmth of her touch grounded him, but the knot in his chest remained.

Daniel sighed deeply, running a hand through his hair as he looked back at her. "I don't know. I thought I'd feel different.

I thought that after everything we've been through, I'd feel… free, but there's still this emptiness. This… sense of finality."

Emily's face softened, her gaze never leaving his. "I understand," she said quietly, her voice filled with empathy. "You've fought for so long, and even though everything is finally falling into place, it's hard to know what comes next. But you're not alone in this. We've built something real here, Daniel. Together. And whatever the future holds, I'm with you."

Daniel smiled faintly at her words, but the uncertainty in his chest didn't fade. They had built something, yes. The café, their future, the life they'd carved out of the rubble of his past. But there was still a part of him—an aching, raw part—that couldn't let go. The past had been so deeply woven into his identity that he wasn't sure how to move forward without it. His father's legacy, Adrian's claims, everything he had struggled to escape—it still haunted him.

"You're right," Daniel said finally, his voice tinged with a quiet frustration. "But it's hard to just forget it. To let it go completely."

Emily stepped closer, her presence a quiet strength. "You don't have to forget, Daniel. You just have to let it rest. Let the past be what it was, and allow yourself the space to embrace what's ahead. The past doesn't have to define your future, not anymore."

Daniel nodded slowly, the weight of her words settling

Chapter 75

in, but he still couldn't shake the feeling of something unfinished. The café, their victory, it all felt like a bridge to a future he had not yet fully understood. And there was something else, something lingering at the back of his mind—something that had been quietly haunting him.

"I think I need to do something," Daniel said, his voice distant as he looked at the café around him. "There's something I haven't faced. Something I've been running from. And I can't move forward without it."

Emily tilted her head, her brows furrowing slightly. "What do you mean?"

Daniel took a deep breath, his chest tight as he met her gaze. "I think I need to say goodbye."

Emily was silent for a moment, her expression unreadable as she processed his words. "Goodbye to what?" she finally asked, her voice soft.

"To my father," Daniel replied, his voice strained with the weight of the truth. "I've been holding on to this... this anger, this resentment. I've let it shape me for so long, and it's not helping me anymore. I've let the legacy define my life, but I can't let it control me anymore. I need to let it go, Emily. I need to say goodbye to him—for good."

The room seemed to fall silent at his words, the air thick with the weight of what he was saying. Emily stepped closer, her hand resting on his, grounding him in that moment. "I think that's the only way you'll truly be free, Daniel," she said quietly. "But you don't have to do it alone. I'll be with you. Every step of the way."

Daniel met her gaze, his heart swelling with gratitude. She had always been there, hadn't she? Through every twist, every turn, every moment of darkness. She had stood by him, supported him when he thought there was nothing left to fight for. And now, in this final moment, as he faced the past that had defined so much of him, he knew she would be there. She would always be there.

"I know," Daniel whispered, his voice thick with emotion. "I just don't know how to say goodbye. How do I let go of everything I've been carrying for so long?"

Emily's eyes softened, and she stepped even closer, wrapping her arms around him. The warmth of her embrace was like a balm to his soul, a safe harbor in the storm. "You don't have to have all the answers right now," she murmured. "You don't have to have it all figured out. But you're not alone anymore. And together, we can face it. You can face it."

Daniel closed his eyes, resting his forehead against hers as the emotions that had been building inside him threatened to break free. He had fought so hard to bury the past, to outrun it. But now, for the first time, he realized that the only way to truly move forward was to face it head-on. To let it go, to give it the closure it deserved. And that meant letting go of his father. Letting go of the legacy that had

Chapter 75

been a burden for so long.

"I'm ready," Daniel said softly, his voice breaking slightly as he pulled away from Emily, wiping his eyes. "I'm ready to say goodbye."

As he turned to walk toward the door, Emily followed closely behind him, her hand resting on the small of his back, a silent show of support. They walked out of the café together, the world outside just beginning to come alive as the early morning sun cast long shadows on the street. The city felt different now, quieter somehow, as if the weight of the past was lifting with each step they took.

They arrived at a small, secluded spot at the edge of the city—a park that Daniel had visited many times before. It was here, amidst the quiet of the trees and the birdsong, that he had last seen his father. A place where his memories and his anger had been allowed to fester, where the unresolved pain of his past had been left to haunt him.

The bench where his father had sat was empty now, as it had been for years. Daniel stood there for a moment, his gaze fixed on the empty space, before he slowly sank onto the bench, his hands resting on his knees.

Emily stood beside him, her presence comforting but silent. She didn't push him. She didn't speak. She simply waited, knowing that this moment was his.

Daniel closed his eyes, taking a slow, steady breath as he

gathered his thoughts. The words he needed to say were finally clear in his mind, the things he had kept locked away for so long beginning to spill out.

"I spent so many years resenting you, Dad," he whispered into the quiet air. "I hated what you did to me. To this family. I hated the way you made me feel like I was never enough. Like I had to live up to something I never wanted. I've carried that for so long. But I don't want to carry it anymore. I don't want to be defined by what you left behind. I want to build something different. Something better. And for that… I need to say goodbye. I need to let go of the anger. Of the hurt. I can't do it anymore. I'm done."

The silence that followed was heavy, but for the first time, Daniel felt like he could breathe. He wasn't burdened by the past anymore. The anger, the resentment—it was gone. And as he sat there, letting the words sink in, he realized something. It wasn't just about saying goodbye to his father. It was about saying goodbye to everything that had held him back. The legacy. The expectations. The lies. It was time to start fresh.

Emily sat beside him, her hand resting on his as they both looked out over the park, the light of the morning sun spilling over them. There was no grand declaration. No fireworks. Just the quiet understanding between them. The promise that, no matter what came next, they would face it together.

"I'm proud of you, Daniel," Emily said quietly, her voice

Chapter 75

filled with warmth.

Daniel smiled, a true, genuine smile, and squeezed her hand. "I couldn't have done it without you."

And as they sat together in the soft light of the morning, Daniel knew that this was the true farewell. The final goodbye to the past that had haunted him for so long. The legacy was no longer his to bear. And now, for the first time, he could walk forward into the future—free, and at peace.

Together, they had reclaimed the future. And nothing would stand in their way.

Seventy-Six

Chapter 76

Chapter 76: A Global Impact

The café was buzzing with activity, the clinking of coffee cups, the soft hum of conversation, and the scent of freshly brewed espresso filling the air. Yet, despite the usual comfort of the space, Daniel could feel a tightness in his chest. The room seemed smaller, the weight of the world pressing down on him. He wasn't sure when it had started, this feeling that something larger was unfolding, but now that he felt it, it was almost suffocating. The café had grown to something far beyond what he had ever imagined—something that wasn't just local, wasn't just about rebuilding his life or his family's legacy. It had become a symbol. And now, it was about to go global.

The recent months had been a whirlwind of legal battles,

Chapter 76

personal triumphs, and newfound responsibilities, but this… this was different. The small café that Daniel had rebuilt from the ground up had caught the attention of some powerful individuals, and not just in their city or their country, but across continents. The plan had always been simple: grow the café, turn it into a safe space for the community, and prove that things could be different. But now, it seemed their mission had expanded beyond what Daniel had ever expected.

A knock on the back door broke him out of his thoughts. His pulse quickened. He had been waiting for this moment.

"Come in," Daniel called, his voice steady but his mind racing. The door opened, and Emily stepped in, her usual calm demeanor slightly strained, the lines of concern etched on her face.

"You've been quiet today," she said, her eyes searching his face as she closed the door behind her. "Is everything okay?"

Daniel forced a smile, but it didn't quite reach his eyes. "Yeah, I'm fine. Just… thinking."

Emily narrowed her eyes, sensing the tension in the air. She stepped closer, her gaze softening as she placed a hand on his shoulder. "What are you thinking about? This doesn't feel like just 'thinking,' Daniel."

Daniel sighed, his fingers running through his hair as he met her eyes. "It's this whole thing, Emily. What's happening with the café. It's growing faster than I ever expected, and it's starting to feel… bigger than us. The foundation, the support we've gotten—it's all escalating. I thought we could keep it small, local, build it at our own pace. But now…" His voice trailed off as he shook his head. "I don't know how to keep up with it."

Emily paused, her hand still resting on his shoulder. She had always been his grounding force, but now, she seemed to sense the enormity of the situation. "It's okay to feel overwhelmed," she said softly. "You've done more than most people ever dream of. This is a huge step, but you're not alone in this. We're in this together, Daniel. You don't have to carry it all by yourself."

Daniel looked at her, the weight of her words settling over him. She was right. They had always been a team, and no matter how big the challenge, they had faced it together. This was just another obstacle. But it wasn't the obstacle that worried him—it was the scale of everything they had created. The café had become a beacon, and now, the world was watching.

"We need to talk," Daniel said, his voice suddenly more resolute. "About the next step. We've built something, and now it's time to decide how to use it. What kind of impact do we want to have? It's not just about keeping the café alive anymore—it's about what we do with the platform we've created."

Emily's brow furrowed slightly, her concern now mixing

Chapter 76

with curiosity. "What do you mean by 'platform'?"

Before Daniel could answer, the door opened again, and Sophie entered, her expression unusually serious. She carried a file in her hands, and when she stepped into the room, she didn't waste time with pleasantries.

"We've got a situation," Sophie said, setting the file down on the desk. "I've been reviewing the latest reports. The café's success has been nothing short of explosive. The press coverage, the social media buzz—it's reaching beyond anything we could've anticipated. We're not just a local business anymore. International investors have taken notice."

Daniel's stomach tightened at the words. "International investors?" he repeated, disbelief creeping into his voice. "What are you talking about? I thought we were keeping this small, focused on the community."

Sophie nodded, her expression serious. "I know that's what we planned, Daniel, but the interest is undeniable. We're being contacted by groups from Europe, Asia, and even the Middle East. There's a global movement starting around what we're doing here. It's about more than just coffee. It's about community-building, about redefining what business can be in this new world. And the investors see that. They want in."

Daniel stood there, silent for a moment, his mind racing. This wasn't what he had envisioned. They had worked so hard to build something pure, something for their community. But now it felt like they were teetering on the edge of something much larger—something he wasn't sure he was ready for.

"What do they want from us?" Emily asked, her voice cutting through the tension.

Sophie looked at them both, her expression serious. "They want to take the café global. They want to scale it. Take the concept to major cities around the world. They see the potential to build something bigger—a brand, a movement. They believe we can create a network of cafés that aren't just about serving coffee, but about making a global impact. They want to help us expand, bring our message of change and community to a larger audience."

Daniel felt his pulse quicken. The words "global impact" echoed in his mind. This wasn't just about their small corner of the world anymore. It was about something far bigger. The possibilities were dizzying, but so was the weight of the responsibility.

"I don't know," Daniel muttered under his breath. "This wasn't the plan. I didn't want to sell out, to turn this into some big corporate machine. This is supposed to be about people, not profits."

Emily stepped forward, her hand gently resting on his arm. "Daniel," she said softly, "this is your choice. It always has been. But we can't ignore the fact that what we've

Chapter 76

created here is special. It's more than just a business. It's a movement. And if we can take that movement global—if we can reach more people, do more good—then we need to think about what that means for us."

Daniel's mind whirled. The thought of scaling the café, turning it into something that reached people across the globe, felt both exhilarating and terrifying. He wasn't sure he was ready for that kind of responsibility, but then he remembered why they had started this journey in the first place. It wasn't just about the café. It was about changing lives, about building something that mattered. They had already done so much in their community. Could they really ignore the chance to have that impact on a global scale?

"Are we ready for this?" Daniel asked, looking up at Emily, his voice uncertain.

Emily met his gaze and smiled softly. "You've always been ready. And I believe in us. We've built this together, and we can take it as far as we want. But it's your decision. I'm with you, no matter what."

Daniel exhaled slowly, his thoughts still racing. The decision he was facing felt impossibly big. They could stay small, keep the café a community staple, or they could seize this opportunity, grow, and share their message with the world. The thought of turning down global recognition was overwhelming, but so was the idea of losing what they had built—the intimate, personal connection they shared with every customer, every individual who walked through their doors.

"I didn't ask for any of this," Daniel said quietly, the weight of it all pressing on him. "I just wanted to create something real. Something honest. Something that wasn't tied to my family's legacy or any of the things that have haunted me."

Sophie took a step closer, her tone changing to one of quiet understanding. "I know, Daniel. But you've already created something real. And now, you have a chance to take that to the world. You have the power to influence change on a much larger scale, to spread this message of community and integrity far beyond what we could have imagined. You've been given a gift. And it's up to you to decide how to use it."

For a long moment, Daniel stood in silence, his eyes fixed on the papers in front of him. The opportunity to expand, to reach more people, was right there in front of him. He could feel the weight of the decision pressing on him, but it wasn't just about the café anymore. It was about a message, a vision, a future.

"I'm not going to let this become something I don't believe in," Daniel said finally, his voice filled with determination. "But I'm also not going to stand in the way of something that could make a difference. If we can do this right, if we can scale it without losing what makes this place special, then I'm in. But we're doing it on our terms. We won't compromise on what matters. We can make a global impact, but it has to stay true to what we started."

Chapter 76

Emily smiled, her eyes shining with pride. "That's what I love about you, Daniel. You'll never lose sight of what's important."

Sophie's expression softened as she nodded. "That's the spirit. This is just the beginning."

The weight of the decision still hung heavily in the air, but for the first time, Daniel felt a spark of excitement. The future wasn't as daunting as it had once seemed. It was full of possibility. They were going to take this global. They were going to change the world. And together, they would ensure that the café—and everything it represented—would remain grounded in the values that had made it a success

Seventy-Seven

Chapter 77

Chapter 77: The Diamond Beneath the Dust

The sun dipped low behind the hills, casting long, deep shadows across the worn streets of the city. The once-vibrant neighborhood was now tinged with a quiet, haunting desolation. This was where it all began—the place that had shaped Daniel's life for so long, the heart of everything that had come to define his existence. The café, now a thriving beacon of hope, had roots buried deep in this soil. But the road ahead was not as simple as it seemed, and tonight, the ghosts of the past were about to resurface in ways Daniel wasn't prepared for.

Daniel stood at the entrance of the alleyway, the once-familiar street corner now feeling like a distant memory. The air smelled of dust and decay, the familiar scent of his

Chapter 77

youth. His hands clenched into fists, the old anger rising up in his chest. It had taken him years to escape this place—the neighborhood, the people, the memories—and yet, here he was again. Not by choice, but because there was something he had to confront.

The café had become more than just a business. It had become his legacy, his future. And as much as he had tried to move beyond the shadows of his father's empire, he couldn't escape the ties that bound him to the past. There were still whispers—rumors—that the Laurent name would never be free of its past sins. And as the days passed, those whispers grew louder, creeping closer to the life he had built with Emily.

Tonight, it wasn't just about the café anymore. It was about reclaiming the final piece of the legacy—the diamond that had been buried beneath the dust of his father's mistakes. It was time for him to face the truth, to uncover what had been hidden for so long.

Daniel's heart pounded in his chest as he walked deeper into the alley, each step echoing in the stillness. He had come here to confront the past, but he had never imagined it would feel like this—like walking into the lion's den, knowing that the danger was closing in, ready to swallow him whole.

He had told Emily he was going to handle this on his own, that he needed to confront the ghosts of his past without dragging her into the mess. She had protested, of course—

she had always been by his side, a steady force that grounded him. But he had insisted. Tonight, he had to face the one thing he had avoided for years: the man who had once controlled everything, the man who had built the empire that had nearly destroyed him.

He reached the end of the alley, the dilapidated building looming in front of him like a haunted relic. It was the place his father had spent the last years of his life, the headquarters of the Laurent family's operations. The once grand structure was now nothing more than a crumbling shell, its windows broken and boarded up, its walls weathered and worn. But even in its decay, there was something undeniable about it—the remnants of power, of wealth, of influence.

Daniel's jaw tightened as he pushed open the heavy door, the creaking sound reverberating in the empty space. The air inside was stale, filled with the smell of mold and dust. He stepped inside, the dim light casting eerie shadows across the room. The walls, once lined with opulent furniture and priceless art, were now bare—nothing left but the faint outline of what had once been.

There was a strange stillness here, as though the building itself was waiting for something to happen, for something to break the silence that had settled over it like a shroud. Daniel's eyes scanned the room, and for a brief moment, he could almost hear the echoes of the past—the clinking of glasses, the laughter of men and women who had gathered here to celebrate the Laurent empire. But that was all gone

Chapter 77

now. It was just him and the shadows of his father's legacy.

At the far end of the room stood a desk, covered in yellowed papers and dust. It was his father's desk, the one where so many deals had been made, where lives had been altered, where decisions had been made that would haunt Daniel for the rest of his life. But there was something different about this desk—something that drew him in.

His eyes fell on a small wooden box, its surface scratched and worn with age. It sat on the desk, almost as though it had been placed there deliberately, waiting for him. Daniel's heart skipped a beat as he approached it, the air thick with anticipation. He reached out and lifted the box, his fingers trembling as he pried it open.

Inside, nestled carefully within a bed of velvet, was a single object. A diamond. But it wasn't just any diamond—it was the Laurent family's heirloom, the one that had been passed down through generations, the symbol of the family's power and wealth. The very diamond that Daniel's father had promised him would one day be his.

Daniel's breath caught in his throat as he stared at it, the cold, flawless surface reflecting the dim light of the room. It was beautiful, yes. But it was also a reminder of everything that had gone wrong. It was the symbol of the greed, the corruption, the lies that had torn his family apart. It was the diamond beneath the dust—the thing that had been hidden, buried, forgotten—but it had never lost its value. It had always been there, waiting for the moment when it would be reclaimed.

He reached down and picked up the diamond, holding it in his hand. For a moment, he simply stared at it, his mind racing. This was it—the final piece of the puzzle. The last connection to the family legacy, to everything that had shaped him, for better or for worse.

But as he held it, something inside him shifted. The diamond, so perfect, so beautiful, suddenly felt cold and distant in his hand. It was a symbol of the past, yes—but it wasn't the future. The future was the café. The future was Emily. It wasn't the Laurent name, or the legacy that had come with it. The future was something he could shape, something he could build with his own hands.

The diamond didn't define him. He had spent so many years letting it define him, thinking that the weight of his family's name was something he couldn't escape. But now, holding it in his hand, he realized that he didn't need it. He didn't need to be shackled to the past anymore.

With a swift motion, Daniel threw the diamond back into the box, slamming the lid shut. He didn't need the legacy. He didn't need the power, the wealth, the status. What he needed was the life he had built, the one he had worked so hard to create with Emily. He needed the future, not the past.

The sound of the box hitting the desk echoed in the silence, and for the first time in years, Daniel felt a sense of clarity.

Chapter 77

He had finally let go. He had reclaimed his life, his future. He wasn't just Daniel Laurent anymore. He was someone new. Someone stronger. Someone who had the power to shape his own destiny.

As he turned to leave, the weight that had been pressing down on him for so long seemed to lift. He had confronted the past, he had faced the truth, and now, he was free. There was no more running. No more hiding. The café was his, and the future was wide open. There were no more ghosts to haunt him, no more shadows to linger in his mind.

But just as he reached the door, he stopped. A figure stood in the doorway, blocking his exit. It was a man he hadn't seen in years—his uncle, the one who had betrayed him, the one who had been a part of the darkness that had nearly destroyed his family.

"Daniel," his uncle said, his voice smooth, cold, and calculating. "You thought you could just walk away, didn't you? You thought you could take everything for yourself, forget about the family, forget about what we've built. But you're wrong. You're not free. Not yet."

Daniel's heart pounded as he stood there, staring at his uncle, the man who had always been a part of the Laurent empire's corrupt legacy. But now, with the diamond still buried beneath the dust of the past, Daniel was no longer afraid. He was no longer the young man who had been trapped by his father's mistakes. He was someone new, someone stronger.

"You don't control me anymore," Daniel said, his voice steady, his eyes locked on his uncle's. "This is my legacy now. My future. And I won't let anyone take it from me."

His uncle's eyes flickered with something—anger, perhaps—but it quickly faded, replaced by a cold smile. "We'll see, Daniel. We'll see how long that resolve lasts."

But Daniel didn't wait for another word. He turned and walked out of the room, his footsteps echoing in the silence. The final farewell had been made. The past was behind him. The diamond was buried once again, and this time, it would stay buried.

As he stepped out into the cool night air, Daniel knew one thing for certain: the future was his. And no one—no one—could take that away from him. The diamond beneath the dust had been reclaimed, and now, he was free.

Seventy-Eight

Chapter 78

Chapter 78: A Final Threat Averted

The night was unusually quiet for the city, the streets blanketed in a fog that clung to the air, making everything feel distant, muffled. Daniel stood on the balcony of the café, looking out at the darkness that stretched before him. The usual hum of traffic had quieted down, and there was a strange serenity in the air, as if the city itself was holding its breath. The weight that had been on his shoulders for so long seemed lighter now, the final remnants of the battle for his legacy almost behind him. But there was something nagging at him—a feeling in the pit of his stomach that this calm, this peace, wouldn't last.

Daniel's hand gripped the railing tightly, his knuckles white in the dim light. The café was everything now—everything he had fought for, everything he had built from the dust of his father's empire. Emily had been by his side through it all, her unwavering support a steady force, grounding him in the chaos. They had secured the future, or so it seemed. But somewhere in the recesses of his mind, a voice whispered that the past had a way of catching up. And tonight, something told him that the past wasn't done yet.

Behind him, the sound of footsteps echoed in the hall. He didn't need to turn around to know it was Emily. Her presence always brought a sense of calm, and even now, in the midst of his unease, he felt the familiar weight of her gaze on him.

"Everything okay?" Emily asked, her voice gentle, filled with concern. She stood in the doorway, her face partially illuminated by the soft light from inside. The warmth of the café spilled out into the night, a stark contrast to the chill that had settled in the air.

Daniel didn't immediately answer. His eyes remained fixed on the horizon, but the tension in his shoulders was unmistakable. He knew he couldn't keep this feeling to himself—not from Emily. She had always been his confidante, his rock.

"There's something wrong," he said, finally breaking the silence. His voice was tight, uncertain. "I feel like… something's coming. Something we didn't expect."

Emily stepped closer, her fingers brushing his arm in a silent

Chapter 78

gesture of reassurance. "We've made it this far, Daniel," she said softly. "We've fought through worse. If something's coming, we'll face it together. You don't have to carry this alone."

Daniel turned to face her, his gaze searching her eyes for the certainty he needed. He had never doubted her strength, her resilience. But tonight, he couldn't shake the feeling that everything they had worked for was hanging by a thread.

"I don't know if I can protect this," he whispered, his voice tinged with vulnerability. "We've been so focused on rebuilding, on taking back control... but I think we've missed something. Something... or someone."

Emily frowned, her brow furrowing slightly. "What do you mean?"

Before Daniel could respond, the door to the balcony creaked open, and Sophie stepped out, her face pale, her expression tense. Daniel felt his heart skip a beat as he saw the look on her face. There was something urgent in her eyes—something that set his nerves on edge.

"Daniel," Sophie said, her voice low, "we need to talk."

Daniel's stomach dropped, and Emily immediately stepped back, sensing the shift in the atmosphere. They both knew the significance of that tone. Sophie never came to them with bad news unless it was serious.

"Is it about the café?" Daniel asked, his voice already on edge.

Sophie shook her head, her lips pressed into a thin line. "It's about Adrian," she said, her words hanging heavily in the air. "He's not finished."

The mention of Adrian sent a chill down Daniel's spine. Adrian Laurent, the cousin who had been hell-bent on taking back what he believed was rightfully his, had been defeated. His power had been stripped away, his attempts to claim the legacy thwarted. But the mention of his name now, after all the efforts to put an end to his influence, made Daniel's pulse quicken. Adrian had been silent for weeks, and the sense of relief they had been enjoying was palpable. But hearing Sophie's words now, the peace felt like an illusion.

"What do you mean, 'he's not finished'?" Daniel asked, his voice barely above a whisper, his thoughts racing. "We defeated him. We got the papers, the will... everything. There's nothing he can do anymore."

Sophie met his gaze, her eyes flickering with a mix of fear and determination. "I don't think we've seen the last of Adrian. He's been playing a different game all along, and I've just found out about it. We thought it was over, but it's not."

Emily's hand shot out to grab Daniel's arm, her fingers pressing into his skin, trying to keep him grounded. "What

Chapter 78

do you mean? What's he done?"

Sophie glanced around nervously, her voice lowering to a near whisper. "Adrian has a partner," she said. "A silent partner. Someone we didn't know about. Someone who's been helping him behind the scenes. This isn't just about a legal battle anymore. This is something more dangerous."

Daniel's heart began to race, and the once-comforting hum of the café now seemed distant, far away, as if the walls themselves were closing in. "Who's his partner?" he asked urgently, his pulse pounding in his ears.

Sophie hesitated for a moment, looking over her shoulder, as though making sure no one else could overhear. "It's Hector," she whispered.

The name struck Daniel like a physical blow. Hector. The man who had been both an ally and a traitor, a figure whose shadow had loomed over the café from the very beginning. Daniel had never trusted Hector completely, and the realization that Hector had been working with Adrian sent a shockwave of disbelief through him.

"Hector?" Daniel repeated, his voice tinged with disbelief. "But he's been with us. He helped us expose Adrian. He's been part of the team."

Sophie nodded, her face grim. "That's what we thought. But it seems Hector has been playing both sides all along. Adrian didn't disappear on his own—Hector has been funneling resources to him, giving him information, even helping him with the legal battle. They've been building a network in the shadows. And now, with Adrian out of the picture, Hector is moving in for the kill."

Daniel felt his chest tighten, the weight of the revelation pressing down on him. He had trusted Hector. He had believed that, despite their differences, Hector had come around. But now, with this knowledge, everything he had built felt like it was teetering on the edge of collapse.

"How long has this been going on?" Emily asked, her voice shaking with a mix of anger and disbelief.

"Months," Sophie said, her voice filled with regret. "It was only recently that I stumbled upon it. I've been digging through some old financial records, and I found discrepancies. Payments going to Adrian's accounts that didn't make sense. That's when I connected the dots. Hector has been funding Adrian's activities, even from the sidelines."

Daniel's mind raced. He had been so focused on the immediate battles, on securing the future, that he hadn't seen the deeper threat that was still lurking. The one he thought he had already vanquished was now preparing for a final strike. And this time, Hector's involvement made it even more dangerous. Hector knew everything—he knew the café's weaknesses, the people they trusted, the plans they'd made. This wasn't just about money or power anymore; it was personal.

Chapter 78

"What do we do?" Daniel asked, his voice low and steady, the realization of the stakes settling in.

"We stop Hector," Sophie said, her eyes flashing with determination. "We expose him. We get ahead of him before he makes his move. I've already started gathering information. We need to act fast, before he pulls any more strings behind the scenes."

Daniel turned to Emily, his expression hardening. "We've been through too much to let him destroy everything now."

Emily nodded firmly, her hand still gripping his arm, her voice steady with resolve. "We'll take him down. Together. We can't let anyone take this from us. Not now."

Sophie looked between them, her eyes filled with resolve. "We'll need to be quick. We don't know how long we have before Hector makes his move. He's a dangerous man, and he's not going to back down without a fight."

The three of them stood in the cold night air, the weight of the situation settling over them like a dark cloud. Daniel felt the tension coiling in his chest, but there was something else—something he hadn't felt before. A sense of purpose. This wasn't the end. It couldn't be. They had fought too hard to let Hector or Adrian tear it all down now.

"We're not going to let him win," Daniel said, his voice steady, unwavering. "Not this time. We'll expose him. We'll take back control. And we'll make sure the café stays in the hands of the people who truly care about it."

As the night stretched on, they knew the battle was far from over. But for the first time in what felt like forever, Daniel felt the spark of hope flicker in his chest. The final threat might be looming, but he wasn't going to let it take away what he had fought so hard to protect.

Together, they would face it. Together, they would win.

Seventy-Nine

A Life of Purpose

The rain had been falling steadily for hours, each drop tapping against the windows of the café with an eerie persistence. The air was thick with moisture, the sky a dark, ominous blanket that stretched across the city. Inside, the warmth of the café contrasted sharply with the cold, gray world outside, the smell of freshly brewed coffee mingling with the comforting scent of pastries. Yet, despite the familiar comfort of the place, there was an underlying tension in the atmosphere, a sense that something was shifting—something that Daniel couldn't quite place.

He stood by the counter, staring at the swirling patterns in his cup of coffee, his mind elsewhere. Emily had been right about one thing—this battle wasn't just about the café or the legacy he had inherited. It had always been about purpose.

About discovering what truly mattered. And in the wake of all the chaos, the betrayals, and the endless fights to reclaim control of his future, Daniel had begun to understand that this journey, this fight, was never about his family name, or the empire his father had tried to build. It had always been about something deeper. Something more meaningful.

As the rain continued its relentless assault against the glass, Daniel couldn't help but feel the weight of the past settling over him once again. Adrian's machinations, Hector's betrayal—they had all been a part of something larger, something he hadn't been able to see before. But now, in the quiet moments, he saw the truth: they had all been distractions. Distractions from what mattered most. From the life he could create, not for himself, but for others. For the people who had believed in him. For Emily.

The door to the café swung open, and Daniel's attention snapped to the entrance. A familiar face stepped in, wet and windblown, shaking off the rain from her coat. Sophie.

"I thought you might be here," Sophie said with a small, wry smile, brushing a stray lock of hair from her face. She walked toward the counter, her eyes scanning the room as she took a seat on the stool next to Daniel.

"How's the team?" Daniel asked, his voice steady, though he couldn't entirely hide the exhaustion in it.

Sophie sighed, her face softening with concern. "They're good. Everyone's adjusting. But you're right. The rain makes it feel like the whole world is heavy, doesn't it?"

Daniel nodded slowly, taking another sip of his coffee. "Feels like the calm before a storm, doesn't it?"

Sophie leaned in slightly, her voice dropping as she spoke. "You still feeling like there's something left to prove?"

Daniel didn't answer immediately. Instead, he took a deep breath, letting the air fill his lungs, then slowly let it out. "I thought that after we won—after we secured everything—I'd feel different. I thought I'd feel… free, you know?"

Sophie nodded, her expression softening with understanding. "You thought you could just close that door, put the past behind you, and that would be it. But that's not how it works. Not for someone like you."

Daniel's brow furrowed, and he glanced at her, meeting her gaze for the first time with full clarity. "What do you mean, 'someone like me'?"

Sophie didn't hesitate. "Someone who's been carrying the weight of something bigger than themselves for so long. You've always been about the legacy, the café, the fight for what's right. But now… now you're realizing it's not just about winning, Daniel. It's about what you do with the victory. It's about what you build."

Daniel set his cup down, his hands suddenly feeling cold. She was right, of course. He had been so consumed with the battles, with protecting what was his, that he had forgotten to ask the most important question: Why? Why did he fight? What was the purpose behind all of it? Was it just to hold onto a name? A legacy? Or was there something deeper he could build—a life of true purpose?

"I thought I was building a future," Daniel said slowly, the words coming more easily than he had expected. "But what if it's more than that? What if I'm meant to do something more with this—this platform we've created?"

Sophie's eyes met his, and for a moment, the weight of the question hung between them, heavy and real. "You know," Sophie began softly, her voice steady, "a life of purpose isn't just about surviving the storm. It's about finding meaning in the storm itself. What you've built here, this café, it's not just a business. It's a community, a safe space. People come here because they believe in what you're doing. They believe in you. And that's something you can't take for granted."

Daniel swallowed hard, the weight of her words sinking in. "I've spent so much of my life running, hiding, fighting for something I thought would give me peace. But maybe peace isn't something I can have. Maybe peace is something I can give. Something I can build."

The silence stretched between them, the rain tapping a steady rhythm against the windows. Sophie's words echoed in his mind, like the final puzzle piece falling into place. This wasn't just about protecting the café or the legacy anymore.

A Life of Purpose

It was about creating something that could outlast them both. A legacy of his own. Not one born of his father's mistakes, but one he could shape with his own hands.

"I've been thinking about it," Daniel said, his voice steady now, a sense of clarity settling over him. "I can't keep running. I can't keep fighting this battle just to protect something. I need to use it. I need to use the café, the community, the platform we've built. I need to make a real impact. I want to give people something to believe in. Not just coffee or food, but a life of purpose."

Sophie's expression softened into something like pride, her eyes glimmering with quiet satisfaction. "That's the spirit," she said. "You've always had it in you, Daniel. You've just been too focused on the fight to see it. But now, you're starting to understand. This is bigger than you, bigger than all of us. And it's time you let it be."

As Sophie finished her sentence, the door to the café swung open again. This time, it wasn't just the sound of the rain greeting them; it was the unmistakable sound of footsteps—quick, determined steps. Daniel turned around, his gaze immediately fixing on the newcomer.

It was Emily.

She had her coat drawn tightly around her, her cheeks flushed from the cold, but her eyes were alight with something that wasn't just the sharp wind. She was holding a small envelope in her hand, and there was a determined look on her face as she walked toward them.

"Emily, what's going on?" Daniel asked, his concern flaring as she reached the counter.

Emily didn't waste any time. "I've got something we need to discuss," she said, her voice steady but urgent. "It's from the investor group—the international one we've been talking to."

Daniel's heart skipped a beat. He had been so focused on the internal battles, on his own personal struggle, that he had almost forgotten about the investors who had been circling the café, wanting to take it global. They had been part of the future Daniel and Emily had been building, but it had always felt like a distant concept—something that could wait until the café was more firmly established. Now, it was here, knocking on their door.

"What is it?" Sophie asked, her curiosity piqued as Emily handed over the envelope.

Emily opened it with a quiet precision, pulling out a single sheet of paper. She scanned the contents quickly, and then her eyes met Daniel's. The look on her face was unreadable for a moment, and Daniel felt a familiar wave of tension rush over him.

"It's a proposal," Emily said slowly. "They're offering us a partnership. They want to help us scale, yes, but they also have something else in mind. They want us to be the face of a global movement—one focused not just on business, but on social responsibility. They see the potential for us to lead the charge in redefining how companies can operate on a global scale—by putting purpose first."

Daniel's mind raced as the implications of her words began to sink in. This was more than just an offer for financial backing. This was a call to take everything they had built and turn it into something bigger—something that could influence the world on a global scale. The responsibility of it hit him like a tidal wave. But instead of fear, something else stirred inside him—a sense of purpose, of duty. This was the moment he had been waiting for. The chance to truly make a difference.

"Purpose," Daniel whispered, more to himself than to anyone else. "That's what it's always been about. Not just surviving, not just fighting, but building something meaningful."

Emily smiled, the warmth in her gaze softening the intensity of the moment. "You've always known that, Daniel. Now, it's time to act on it."

As Daniel looked around the café—the walls that had once seemed so fragile, the community that had grown from his own desperation and need for redemption—he realized that he had found it. A life of purpose. It wasn't something he could build alone, and it wasn't something that could be forced. But it was something real. Something that had taken shape from the ground up, something that was now ready to reach farther than he had ever imagined.

He stood up, his heart steady now, his resolve unshakable. "Let's do it," he said, his voice full of determination. "Let's take this café, this community, and turn it into a force for good. Let's show the world what it means to lead with purpose."

The storm outside seemed to slow, the rain lessening as if the world itself was taking a breath with him. For the first time in a long time, Daniel felt at peace. The fight wasn't over—it would never be over. But now, he knew that the battle he had been fighting had always been for something greater. Something that mattered.

A life of purpose.

And it was just beginning.

Eighty

The Diamond's Shine

T he café had closed for the night, its familiar warmth now only a memory lingering in the walls. The sounds of clinking cups and idle chatter had long since faded, replaced by the quiet rustling of papers and the rhythmic tapping of Daniel's fingers against the desk. He sat alone in the dimly lit back room, the faint hum of the streetlights outside filtering through the cracks in the window. A storm had rolled in, its thunder echoing across the city, a fitting backdrop to the storm brewing in his mind.

Daniel had thought he understood what it meant to fight for something—what it meant to build something from the ground up, to claw his way out of the shadows of his father's legacy and make a name for himself. But now, as he sat there, staring at the familiar wooden desk that had once been his father's, he realized how little he had truly understood.

The diamond that lay before him gleamed in the soft light of the room. It was the Laurent family heirloom, the symbol of power, wealth, and corruption that had been passed down for generations. Daniel had held it once before, had almost tossed it aside, convinced that it was nothing more than a relic of the past—a burden that had haunted him his entire life. But now, as he stared at it, something shifted within him. The diamond was more than just a symbol of his father's legacy. It was a symbol of everything he had fought for, everything he had rebuilt.

The rain outside beat down harder, its relentless rhythm punctuating the silence that had settled in the room. Daniel's fingers brushed the cold surface of the diamond, and for a moment, he could feel its weight—not in his hand, but in his soul. It was a heavy thing, this legacy. He had thought that by abandoning it, by leaving behind the empire that had once defined him, he could move on, could build something of his own. But now, as he looked at the diamond, he realized that he had never truly escaped it.

It wasn't just about power anymore. It was about responsibility. And tonight, the responsibility he had fought to avoid was now staring him in the face.

As he reached to lift the diamond from its velvet bed, the door to the back room creaked open, breaking his concentration. Emily stepped inside, her presence immediately grounding him. She had been there for him through everything—the battles, the betrayals, the confusion—and tonight, she had that familiar look in her eyes: the look of someone who knew something wasn't quite right.

"Are you still up here?" Emily asked, her voice soft, but there was an edge to it that Daniel immediately recognized. "I thought we were done for the night."

Daniel didn't immediately answer. He simply nodded toward the desk, where the diamond lay. Emily's gaze followed his, her expression shifting when she saw what he was holding.

"The diamond," she said softly, stepping closer. "I thought we put that behind us."

"We did," Daniel replied, his voice steady, though he couldn't keep the uncertainty out of it. "But I think there's more to this than I realized."

Emily hesitated for a moment, her brow furrowing as she took in his words. She had always been able to see the layers in him that others missed, the things he kept hidden. And now, standing before him, she could tell that something was different—something had changed.

"What do you mean?" she asked, her voice gentle, coaxing him to open up.

Daniel sighed, leaning back in the chair, his eyes never leaving the diamond. "When I was younger, I hated this thing," he said, his voice thick with emotion. "I thought it was the source of everything that went wrong in my life—the reason my family fell apart, the reason I couldn't escape my father's shadow. I thought if I could just get rid of it, I could finally be free. But now… now I realize it's not the diamond that was the problem. It's what I thought it represented."

Emily stepped closer, her hand resting gently on his shoulder. "What do you mean, Daniel?"

"The diamond isn't just about my father's legacy," he said, his voice filled with a mixture of realization and regret. "It's about what I've been running from all these years—the idea that I couldn't be something more, that I couldn't carve out my own future. I thought I had to throw away the past, leave it all behind, to make a difference. But that's not it. I can't run from this legacy. I can't run from the things that have shaped me, the things that have made me who I am."

Emily's gaze softened, and she knelt beside him, her hand still resting on his shoulder. "You've never had to run, Daniel," she said quietly. "You've always had the strength to face it. To embrace who you are. This café, the community we've built—everything you've done—it's been about more than just running away. It's about facing the truth and making something real from it."

Daniel met her gaze, the weight of her words settling over him like a warm embrace. He had always known that Emily was different—that she understood him in ways no one else did. But now, as he looked at her, he realized how much she had helped him uncover the truth about himself. She had been his anchor, the steady presence that kept him from drifting into the chaos of his past.

"I've spent so much time trying to outrun my father's mistakes," he admitted, his voice filled with regret. "Trying to prove that I could be different. But I've learned something. It's not about being different. It's about being true to myself. And that means accepting everything—good, bad, everything that came before."

Emily smiled softly, her eyes filled with understanding. "And that's what makes you strong. You've never been about running. You've always been about facing what comes next. Together."

Daniel looked down at the diamond in his hand, the light from the room catching on its facets, making it shine with an intensity he hadn't noticed before. It wasn't just a symbol of his past. It was a symbol of his resilience, of the strength it had taken to build what they had built. The café wasn't just a business. It was a statement. A testament to everything they had overcome, everything they had fought for.

He placed the diamond back in the box, but this time, it didn't feel like a weight. It felt like a piece of history he was no longer afraid of. The past would always be there, but it didn't have to define him. He had chosen a new path—a path of his own making. And that path was one that didn't need to rely on the legacy of the Laurent family. He was forging a new legacy. One built on the values he held dear: honesty, community, purpose.

The sound of the rain intensified outside, the wind howling as it whipped through the trees. But inside the café, there was a sense of peace. A sense of clarity.

"Are you ready?" Emily asked, her voice a soft murmur as she squeezed his shoulder gently.

Daniel turned to face her, his heart steady now, his mind clear. "Yeah," he said, his voice filled with certainty. "I think I am."

Together, they stood in the dim light of the café, the future stretching out before them. The past would always be a part of them, but it no longer had the power to control their lives. They had built something real here—a community, a family, a future. And nothing could take that away.

The diamond's shine was no longer a symbol of the past. It was a symbol of what they had overcome. And as Daniel looked at Emily, he knew that the real treasure wasn't the legacy of his father, but the life they were creating together. A life of purpose.

A life that would shine brighter than any diamond ever could.

Eighty-One

The Promise of Forever

The soft sound of piano music drifted through the café as Daniel stood near the window, gazing out at the city beyond. The storm had finally passed, and the night air felt fresh, crisp, with the promise of change. The world outside was quiet, the streets bathed in the glow of streetlights reflecting off the wet pavement, giving the city a new life. It was the kind of night that made him think that, despite everything they had been through, they had made it. They had finally found peace.

Emily was at the counter, her fingers moving quickly as she prepared the final order of the evening, the rhythmic motions a reflection of the comfort they had found in each other. The café had been closed for hours, but there was something sacred about the moments they spent here, together, in this space they had built. The world seemed to slow down when they were in the café, and everything felt possible.

Daniel's gaze shifted to the empty chair by the table, where they had once sat together after their long days of work, making plans for the future, dreaming of what could be. It wasn't just about the café anymore. It was about everything they had overcome, everything they had rebuilt. He had spent so much time worrying about the past, so focused on protecting the legacy he never wanted, that he hadn't realized what he had already created.

"Almost done," Emily said softly, her voice breaking the quiet, and Daniel turned to find her looking at him, a small smile playing at the corners of her lips. Her eyes were tired, but there was an undeniable warmth in them. She had been by his side through everything—the good, the bad, and everything in between—and now, here they were, standing on the precipice of something new. Something real.

Daniel returned her smile, but his gaze lingered on her face, studying the way the soft light from the café illuminated the contours of her features, the way her eyes seemed to sparkle even when the world around them was dark. He had never imagined a life like this—one filled with love, with purpose, with a future that wasn't defined by the shadow of his past. But here, in this moment, everything felt right. Everything felt like it was falling into place.

"Emily," Daniel said softly, his voice thick with emotion. "I've been thinking a lot about where we're going. About what comes next."

Emily set the cup she was holding down on the counter and walked over to him, her expression soft, but there was something in her eyes that told him she already knew what was coming. She had always been able to see through him, to understand the things he didn't have the words to express.

"I know," she said, her voice steady. "You've been carrying a lot for a long time. And you've been trying to figure out how to move forward, how to let go of the past. But you don't have to carry it anymore, Daniel. We've built something here. Together. And no matter what happens, we'll face it together."

Daniel felt the weight of her words settle over him, and for a moment, the rush of emotions that had been building inside him seemed to calm. The uncertainty, the fear that had haunted him for so long, was finally giving way to something else—a sense of peace. But there was still one thing he needed to say, one thing he needed to do to truly let go of the past and embrace the future.

He reached out for her hand, his fingers closing around hers, and he gently pulled her closer. "I can't imagine my life without you, Emily. You've been my anchor, my strength, and I know I've put you through a lot, but I want you to know that no matter what happens next, I'm with you. I want to be with you. Forever."

Emily's breath caught in her throat, and for a moment,

her eyes filled with something deeper than words could express. Love. Relief. Hope. The emotions were so raw, so powerful, that they filled the space between them like a living, breathing thing. She squeezed his hand, her voice barely above a whisper.

"You don't have to say that, Daniel," she said softly, her voice thick with emotion. "I've always been with you. And I always will be. We've already built something beautiful. Together."

Daniel smiled, a deep, heartfelt smile that seemed to come from a place he hadn't known was possible before. He had always believed that happiness was something to be fought for, something that could be won through hard work and sacrifice. But with Emily, he had learned that happiness was something you built, something you nurtured together. They had created a life out of the broken pieces of the past, and now, as he looked at her, he realized how much they had accomplished.

But there was something else, something more that he needed to do. Something that would solidify the promise he was making—not just to her, but to himself.

He reached into his jacket pocket, his heart pounding in his chest. When he pulled out the small box, Emily's eyes widened, her breath hitching in her throat as she looked at him, a mix of confusion and wonder crossing her face.

"Daniel…" she whispered, her voice trembling slightly.

The Promise of Forever

Daniel opened the box, revealing the simple, elegant ring inside. It wasn't extravagant or flashy. It was perfect—just like everything they had built together. He had spent weeks searching for the right symbol, the right gesture to show her how much she meant to him, how much he was ready to commit to her, to the life they would build together.

"This is for you, Emily," Daniel said, his voice steady, but thick with emotion. "I don't have all the answers. I don't know what the future holds. But I know that I want to spend it with you. I want to build something that will last, something that will stand the test of time. You're my future, Emily. And I want to make a promise—to you, and to me—that we will face whatever comes, side by side."

Tears welled in Emily's eyes as she stared at the ring, and for a moment, the world seemed to stop. Time slowed, the moment stretched out, filled with meaning, filled with love. She had always known that Daniel was the one she was meant to spend her life with, but hearing him say the words—the words that confirmed everything they had fought for, everything they had built together—was something different. It was the culmination of a dream, a dream she hadn't even realized was possible until now.

She nodded, her voice trembling as she spoke. "Yes, Daniel. Yes, I will. I'll be with you. Forever."

Daniel slid the ring onto her finger, the gesture simple, but filled with all the promises of a lifetime. As he did, the storm outside seemed to fade, the world outside shifting into a new rhythm, as if the very air around them had changed. There was no more fear, no more doubt. There was only the future, a future they would build together.

They stood there in the soft glow of the café's dim lights, the rest of the world slipping away. The promise of forever wasn't just in the ring, in the words that had been spoken. It was in the quiet moments they shared, the understanding they had built together, the strength they had found in each other. This was the life they had fought for, the life that had risen from the dust of the past, and now, it was theirs.

For the first time in what felt like forever, Daniel felt the weight of the world lift off his shoulders. The café wasn't just a place—it was their home. It was their foundation, their future. And with Emily by his side, there was nothing they couldn't face.

He pulled her close, his arms wrapping around her as they stood together in the quiet of the café, their hearts beating as one. The promise of forever wasn't just a dream. It was real. And it was theirs.

"We'll do this together," Daniel whispered, his voice filled with certainty. "Whatever comes, we'll face it together."

And in that moment, as they stood there, wrapped in each other's arms, Daniel knew that the future was bright. The promise of forever wasn't just a hope. It was a reality they would create, together.

www.ingramcontent.com/pod-product-compliance
Lightning Source LLC
LaVergne TN
LVHW011925070526
838202LV00054B/4499